# RADICAL NATURE

"*Radical Nature* exposes the biggest con job in the history of human thought—that matter and nature are dead, mindless, unfeeling, and disconnected from ourselves. De Quincey gives us an image that is as hopeful and fulfilling as the old view was empty and depressing. Never have we needed such a view as now."

LARRY DOSSEY, M.D., AUTHOR OF
*HEALING BEYOND THE BODY* AND *REINVENTING MEDICINE*

"*Radical Nature* is a unique book that gets right down to the essence of the challenges facing any science of consciousness. Essential reading for anyone interested in consciousness studies."

PETER RUSSELL, AUTHOR OF
*THE GLOBAL BRAIN* AND *FROM SCIENCE TO GOD*

"Christian de Quincey illuminates a cosmological sense of consciousness with this accessible, pioneering work. His writing sparkles and the ideas sing."

CHARLENE SPRETNAK, AUTHOR OF *STATES OF GRACE*

"*Radical Nature* is a powerful corrective to the prevalent dualisms encoded in our culture and consciousness. De Quincey articulates another way of knowing and appreciating the world that rearranges our universe in quite remarkable ways. These well-researched and thought-provoking explorations are a philosophical road map for bridging the gap between spirit and matter."

SUZI GABLIK, AUTHOR OF *CONVERSATIONS*
*BEFORE THE END OF TIME*

"Christian de Quincey is that rare thing: someone equally at home in analytical philosophy and in the spirit of the New Age. No one knows better how to criticize the materialist position from the inside. I thoroughly enjoyed reading *Radical Nature*. If anything can shake the current scientific complacency about the mindlessness of matter, this will."

NICHOLAS HUMPHREY, PH.D., AUTHOR OF
*A HISTORY OF THE MIND* AND *LEAPS OF FAITH*

"Aboriginal peoples of the world (wherever they're still found intact) know that consciousness goes 'all the way down.' They perceive this as directly and as intuitively as we perceive the humor in a joke. For this reason, it's not really something we can 'discover' any more than we 'discovered' America. Nonetheless, for us latecomers (for whom the concept is a stranger), Christian de Quincey has provided a delightfully accessible foundation for its rediscovery."

DANIEL QUINN, AUTHOR OF *ISHMAEL*

"A brilliant and much-needed book. De Quincey has produced a deep work that is both intellectually satisfying and spiritually reunitive."

JOSEPH PRABHU, PH.D., PROFESSOR OF PHILOSOPHY, CALIFORNIA STATE UNIVERSITY

"*Radical Nature* is a serious, philosophical-scientific treatise that addresses the greatest philosophical issue of all times and throws light on it. The concept of matter as inert and 'dead' was indeed an exception in the long history of intellectual thought, but it came to be equated with self-evident truth in the modern mind. De Quincey shows that this is an aberration—that the universe is far more complex, vital, and 'interesting' than standard materialistic science envisages. It is time to return to the concept that there is consciousness in nature, as de Quincey says, 'all the way down.' The rediscovery of this perennial insight lends both fresh meaning to our individual existence and a fresh impetus to changing our attitude to nature from exploitation to participation."

ERVIN LASZLO, PH.D., AUTHOR OF *WORLDSHIFT 2012* AND *SCIENCE AND THE AKASHIC FIELD*

"A breakthrough in understanding humanity's place in the community of beings. De Quincey brings together a depth of philosophical expertise with a compassionate understanding of our history. He charts a worldview that is fully in accord with the latest scientific discoveries of the role of mind in the cosmos."

CHRIS CLARKE, THEORETICAL PHYSICIST, UNIVERSITY OF SOUTHAMPTON

# RADICAL NATURE

## THE SOUL
## OF MATTER

CHRISTIAN DE QUINCEY, PH.D.

Park Street Press
Rochester, Vermont • Toronto, Canada

Park Street Press
One Park Street
Rochester, Vermont 05767
www.ParkStPress.com

Park Street Press is a division of Inner Traditions International

**Library of Congress Cataloging-in-Publication Data**

De Quincey, Christian.
  Radical nature : the soul of matter / Christian de Quincey.
    p. cm.
  Summary: "An exploration of the consciousness of all matter"—Provided by publisher.
  Includes bibliographical references (p.      ) and index.
  ISBN 978-1-59477-340-2
  1. Panpsychism. I. Title.
  BD560.Q85 2010
  113—dc22

                                                                      2009045753

Printed and bound in the United States by Lake Book Manufacturing, Inc.

10 9 8 7 6 5 4 3 2 1

Text design and layout by Priscilla Baker
This book was typeset in Garamond Premier Pro with Trajan and Gill Sans used as display typefaces

To send correspondence to the author of this book, mail a first-class letter to the author c/o Inner Traditions • Bear and Company, One Park Street, Rochester, VT 05767, and we will forward the communication to the author.

*Every truth passes through three stages before it is recognized. In the first place it is ridiculed. In the second it is opposed. In the third it is regarded as self-evident.*

ARTHUR SCHOPENHAUER

*Nothing [that] is destitute itself of life and reason can generate a being possessed of life and reason; but the world does generate beings possessed of life and reason; the world therefore is not itself destitute of life and reason.*

ZENO THE STOIC
(THIRD CENTURY BCE)

*How needful it is for me to enter into the darkness, and to admit the coincidence of opposites, beyond all the grasp of reason, and there to seek the truth where impossibility meeteth me.*

NICHOLAS OF CUSA
(FIFTEENTH CENTURY)

*All things are full of gods.*

THALES

# CONTENTS

# PART III

## SOLUTION: POSTMODERN PROMISE

# PREFACE

*"If the universe is dead, it tells no stories. And all our vast cosmologies are little more than fantasies, superlative myths we tell ourselves to make some sense that we are here at all. But what if the universe is not dead? What if the universe is itself a story? What could that mean, and how could we fit it into our science and philosophy?"*

In this book I explore the idea that the universe, the entire cosmos of matter and energy, is literally the unfolding of a great metaphysical epic—the grand narrative of nature itself. Nature is adventurous, and matter *feels* to its deepest roots. However, this is not a storybook. It is, rather, a serious philosophical exploration of the metaphysical foundation for all stories—the fact that the universe contains storytellers at all: the fact that consciousness exists.

*Radical Nature* is the first of a trilogy about the nature of reality, about our ways of knowing (*Radical Knowing*), and about exploring the very instrument of knowing itself: consciousness (*Radical Science*). It challenges the dominant myth of matter as essentially "dead stuff" that mysteriously weaves mind and consciousness out of body and brain. This old view splits mind from body, consciousness from matter, and spirit from nature and leaves us trying to make sense of a world where consciousness, soul, and spirit are real—and where matter/energy is, too.

In the following pages I offer a new (and ancient) worldview critically needed for our times—a worldview that restores a sense of the sacred to our lives, a worldview where spirit and consciousness find a natural home in the cosmos. As a philosopher I aim to step beyond the boundaries of the box many of my colleagues believe mark the limits of responsible scholarship. I trust not only in the gift of reason but also in other ways of knowing—particularly the innate wisdom of the body's own feelings. I have set out to tell a new cosmology story aimed at healing the split between mind and body, between consciousness and the physical world.

All previous attempts to overcome this split—in philosophy, science, cosmology, and psychology—have failed to the extent that they have ignored or denied the essential sentience and sacredness of matter. Our culture's desacralization of nature has had profound effects on how we relate to ourselves and the world (our bodies, planet, and cosmic environment). The need for spiritual healing, a deep longing characteristic of our age, will be fulfilled only if we radically alter our understanding of and attitude toward the deep nature of matter.

Once we recognize that matter feels—tingles with interiority—we see that nature and cosmos are themselves intrinsically meaningful, purposeful, and valuable. We learn that the universe is not "dead." *Radical Nature* unfolds the remarkable story of the relationship between matter and mind, a story of philosophy and science in search of a soul.

Philosophy—even when it tackles the deepest problems of metaphysics—does not need to be obscure, difficult, or boring. I was drawn to this discipline because from an early age I felt the poetry of language and ideas. For me philosophy opened up doors to new possibilities and fired my imagination beyond the limits of reason.

I wanted to write a book that, while honoring the rigors of scholarship, does not shy away from the poetics of metaphor—a book that inspires readers to *feel* the power of ideas, a book that takes you beyond dry abstractions to the living heart of pure, honest inquiry. Although I have tried to use the simplest, most evocative language, the reader must be prepared to do some work, too. Getting the most from this book will be a collaborative effort. As we dig deeper into the bedrock of metaphysics and encounter subtleties such as the meaning of consciousness and energy, we may enter passages where we want to slow down, perhaps even stop, to think things through. If you find there are moments when the ideas seem too deep, I encourage you to stop—not only to think and ponder what you have just read but also to allow yourself to *feel* how your body is responding to ideas that may be stretching your mind beyond its accustomed comfort zone.

This is not the way philosophy is usually done. Yet something like this, I believe, needs to happen if we are to break out of the encrusted assumptions and abstractions that weigh philosophy down—and tend to keep the rest of us stuck in a trance of "business-as-usual." In times of crisis, however, a radical alternative is often called for.

*Radical Nature* challenges the dominant paradigm of materialism, tracing the notion of *intrinsically sentient matter* all the way back to the earliest days of Western philosophy and showing that it has survived in an unbroken continuum throughout the centuries. In fact I show that the view of matter as dead is a comparatively short detour—an aberration—in the history of Western thought. Based on a philosophical tradition reaching back millennia, *Radical Nature* is about rediscovering the soul of matter and calls for a radically different understanding of what matter is—if we are ever to come to terms with the mind-body split or develop a true science of consciousness.

This book explores some of our most deep-rooted and cherished notions about the nature of reality and what it means to be a living, sentient being in a vast, perhaps infinite, cosmos. I have tried to present ideas that will inspire you to trust in your own deep intuitions, to move beyond the box of orthodoxy, and see that we live in a world full of feeling and meaning—and that the cosmos is, after all, a magnificent creation brimming with spirit and consciousness.

The second book in the trilogy, *Radical Knowing,* reveals the distortions of modern philosophy and science when they limit knowledge of the world and ourselves to what we can detect through our senses or analyze with reason. Other ways of knowing, such as feeling, intuition, and direct experience of nonsensory realities, are equally valid and need to be encouraged, honored, and developed.

The third book, *Radical Science,* builds on the first two and explores how a true science of consciousness would be possible—by radically altering our understanding of the nature of the world and by expanding our ways of knowing—so that science no longer restricts itself to what can be counted and measured, and opens up to deeper and higher "shafts of wisdom," where dead-bolt mechanism is replaced by the vitality of lived meaning.

But first, we have a problem . . .

INTRODUCTION

# THE PARADOX OF CONSCIOUSNESS

Beyond the world of atoms and stones, stars and galaxies, plants and animals, brains and computers, science is poised to explore a new and ancient world of souls and spirit, the inner universe of the mind. Consciousness, the next great frontier—for science, for philosophy, for our personal and collective well-being—is finally opening up.

This great frontier for science is also the deepest personal paradox for each of us. It is our most familiar reality and yet the most puzzling aspect of our lives. Without it we would know nothing. Yet what consciousness is itself, and how it exists in the world of matter, remains the greatest of all mysteries. How did consciousness come to light up the cosmos, making it possible for creatures like us to know so much about the world and our place in it (and to recognize how much we have yet to learn)? Can we say how our bodies tingle with feelings, how our brains sparkle with thoughts and ideas, and our hearts are moved by meanings and values? Can we explain why we can choose to ask such questions, and pursue our purposes with passion?

These are philosophical questions, questions about the mysterious relationship between mind and body, about how consciousness shows up in a universe of physical things. The story of how these things came to be is the story of science, but it is incomplete—incomplete in a deeply problematic way. What's missing is not a matter of more details in the great cosmological narrative from big bang to human beings. What's missing is what makes the story—*any* story—possible at all. The problem is we have a wonderful

1

cosmology story that fails to include the storyteller—consciousness.

The "hard problem" for science, as philosopher David Chalmers emphasizes, is to account for the fact that conscious experience exists when it seems that the physical universe could get along just as easily without it.[1] It could have turned out that the universe evolved and unfolded in utter silence—*forever* unknown and unfelt, without its story ever being told. But the fact is the universe story is being told, and if there is a story there is also a storyteller.

Expanding the story of the universe to include the storyteller, then, is the next great frontier for science. But to get there, to crack the hard problem, science will need to ask different kinds of questions, and explore other ways of knowing beyond the limits of reason and the spectrum of the senses. Consciousness is not only science's next frontier, its relationship to matter is also philosophy's deepest mystery—a mystery that lies at the heart of the philosophy of mind. This book is an exploration of that mystery and an opening toward that final frontier.

## A Project for Our Times

But why such a book? Why would I invest time and energy into researching and writing about the story of consciousness in the universe, about the mysterious relationship between mind and body? Why should you invest your time reading it?

Why, in short, should we bother with philosophy of mind and exploring the basis for a science of consciousness when there are so many other pressing problems that we, along with philosophers and scientists, could be addressing? Is such a project of any more practical value than the ivory-tower preoccupations of medieval philosophers and theologians trying to decide how many angels could dance on a pinhead? I believe such an inquiry is immensely valuable and sorely needed.

It is critical, it seems to me, that the scientific knowledge that shapes and limits the contours of our social reality—our communal "paradigm"—should be expanded to include and honor nonmeasurable phenomena such as values, meanings, purposes, and feelings. For modern science to do this will require a radical reorientation of its basic metaphysical assumptions about the nature of reality. It will require a thorough reassessment of the epistemology underlying science—of *how we know anything* about the world, particularly consciousness itself.

I am personally and professionally committed to this transformation of science and philosophy, an opening up to a sense of the sacred, and honoring the vast potential of humanity and of the whole living system in which we are embedded—including the domain of consciousness.

Nevertheless, I have been concerned at times about the choice of this project as a professional and academic focus. On the one hand I'm aware there's a certain professional risk involved by taking seriously ideas such as spirit and soul in nature, or feeling and intuition as valid ways of knowing. From the perspective of mainstream philosophy I'm out on a limb with the notion that "matter feels," that consciousness goes all the way down to the most fundamental elements of reality. But I take full responsibility for these ideas, and I'm willing to defend them with all of the philosophical rigor that I can.

On the other hand I am aware that research at the level of metaphysics, of ontology and epistemology, is remote from what matters to most people. I have repeatedly asked myself: "How can this work be of value to the community? Am I selfishly indulging my own passion, while others are 'out in the world' truly being of service?"

From time to time I have volunteered in various capacities—serving the hungry, the old, the infirm. I have known the joy of unconditional service, and received wrinkled smiles, tearful thanks, and gnarled knuckle-gripping handclasps that speak of a communion of souls no verbal language can match. I have shared a little of my presence and my being with people. I have, perhaps, made some small difference. Yet I have seen the persistence of poverty and injustice, of pain and confusion, and the repetitive patterns of ignorance and greed in our society. I have experienced the despair of hopelessness in the face of world hunger, the ingrained sorrow and suffering of the human condition, and global destruction of our ancient and diverse ecosystems. I have asked myself: "What, most of all, needs to be done?" And my soul and cells have answered that I must use my life to help root out the deepest levels of ignorance that got us into this mess. What is the source of the fear and greed that bring us, personally and collectively, repeatedly to the threshold of disaster and extinction?

Until we successfully reexamine the implicit "nuts and bolts" of the philosophical superstructures that condition the *way* we think (more than *what* we think), we will continue to program ourselves to repeat the same kinds of mistakes. A major—perhaps *the* major—element in the conceptual and perceptual matrix that shapes our worldview is our scientific attitude toward consciousness and its relationship to the world of matter. For, from this view, we look out on a world devoid of any real intrinsic value, of any inherent purpose, meaning, or feeling.

Science has exorcised the ghost from the machine and left us with a desacralized and despirited world. And it has done this because its fundamental beliefs about the nature of the world (its ontology), and what we can know about the world (its epistemology), and how we can know the world (its methodology) are based on a set of assumptions grounded in the metaphysics of matter-in-blind-motion, of reductionistic mechanism and materialism. This is what must change. Without such a profound metaphysical shift, all the good works in the world will never amount to anything more than well-intentioned bandaids.

While doing research for this book I came across a remarkable collection of essays by philosopher and psychologist Steven M. Rosen, *Science, Paradox, and the Moebius Principle,* and I realized why a commitment to digging out the metaphysical roots of our scientific practice is relevant to the community at large. One word made the difference for me, a word that Rosen himself coined: "epistemotherapy."[2] He was writing about the need for Western science and philosophy to get beyond the split between psyche and physis—between mind and matter—so decisively established by René Descartes nearly four hundred years ago. Ever since, Western philosophy has struggled with the mind-body problem, with the intractable difficulty of explaining how unextended mind could possibly ever interact with spatially extended matter. The solution proposed within materialistic science was that we can't—and we don't need to—explain this because "mind" is just a fiction, a ghostly epiphenomenon of the material brain.

Out went all subjective, nonquantifiable, unmeasurable, unpredictable, and uncontrollable mental phenomena, including values, meanings, and purposes. Feelings were "reduced" to electrochemical interactions in the brain, nervous and hormonal systems. The world became one giant machine, without any intrinsic feeling, without any real meaning or purpose. Its only value was its potential for exploitation by science and technology to serve the functions of industry, commerce, and government. In such a world, guided by such motivations, it should be no surprise if our collective actions—as nations, as governments, as businesses, even as individuals— turn out to be pathological. They are pathological because they take no account of the profound interdependence of living systems, because they take no account of consciousness or experience inherent in nature.

This pathology is Descartes's split writ large—between ego (his *cogito*) and the rest of the natural world. For Descartes, only human beings had a soul, only humans were conscious and had feelings. Given this attitude and the scientific motivation for control, the way was open for unbridled experimentation, including vivisection. Animals could not feel any pain, said Descartes, because they were no more than biological machines. By extension, plants, rocks, rivers, oceans, and atmospheres certainly could feel no pain, could suffer no dis-ease. Science, and its stepchild, technology, could—and did, and does—carry out Francis Bacon's dictum of "putting nature to the rack," excavating and exploiting the environment in the name of research and social progress. Descartes's ego-writ-large is the collective ego of nations, governments, and corporations. All values, meanings, goals, and purposes are created by and lie within these collective egos. Nature's only value is how it can serve them; it has no inherent sacredness or meaning.

The underlying pathology, therefore, is metaphysical: a split between matter and mind. This fragmentation runs right through our science, our medicine, our education, our social and legal systems, our interpersonal relationships, and our relationships with the rest of the natural world. It even conditions our relationships with our own selves, splitting body from mind. It is deeply ingrained in the way we think, and in what and how we know anything. It is truly "epistemopathology"—or "epistemopathy," as psychologist Sigmund Koch called it.[3] An effective response, as Rosen so rightly observed, is "epistemotherapy"—a reintegration of the collective ego with the Self of the physical world, of psyche and physis.

So, I see this work in the spirit of epistemotherapy, a commitment to doing what I can to raise awareness within the collective consciousness that both psyche and physis matter. Whether or not my contribution makes a significant difference, I am convinced that our task as individuals and as collectives is to transcend the artificial Cartesian split between mind and body, and to reintegrate the subjective and the objective, the psychic and the physical, the qualitative and quantitative, meaning and mechanism, order and chaos, unity and multiplicity at all levels of our being-in-the-world. Without this deep "metatherapy," I believe all our other individual and social forms of therapy and change will always, in the end, be overrun by the tremendous force of the status quo. The radical epistemology of consciousness that I had been working on at the Institute of Noetic Sciences with Willis Harman before his death is a first, small step toward this healing.[4*]

## A Postmodern Paradigm of Paradox

In this book, we will encounter, again and again, a number of interrelated themes centered on a common issue: in philosophy it shows up as the "mind-body problem"; in science we see it as the "fact/value" dichotomy; in psychology and psychotherapy we deal with it as the pathology of existential schism between self and other; in society, if we pay attention, we recognize it in the alienation of humanity from the rest of nature. What all of these share, one way or another, is a common assumption of a metaphysical split between consciousness and matter. Once that separation has been introduced, once consciousness has been "removed" from matter, we are either left with a mystery of how these two domains could ever interact, or we are left exclusively with a material world without feelings, without meaning, without consciousness.

In its efforts to understand and control the world of matter, science has achieved a large measure of success by the very simple, though

---

*"Noetic" derives from a Greek word for which there is no single English equivalent. It means "having to do with intelligence, wisdom, mind, soul, spirit, insight, gnosis." Perhaps a useful way to think of noetic sciences is that they refer to explorations of the nature of consciousness, particularly of the nonrational, intuitive aspects of consciousness, and how consciousness relates to the body, ecosystem, and larger cosmos, including its spiritual dimensions.

immensely consequential, device of completely ignoring consciousness and subjective experience. By focusing exclusively on matter or physical energy, science has presented us with a world without mind. Among the recurring themes we meet as a result of this move is the stark paradox of *subjectivity* in an otherwise objective world. How can this be?

As long as we remain within the current dominant paradigm of science—of universal materialism and mechanism—the puzzle of subjectivity will continue to confound us, and we will continue to be troubled by our failed efforts to find value and meaning in the complex dynamics of chaos and emergent order of insentient atoms in the void. The paradoxes will continue to show up in philosophy, in science, in society, and in our personal lives. If we don't know how to face the paradoxes they will, sooner or later, manifest as intellectual, institutional, psychological or other systemic pathologies.

The way forward, according to the thesis presented here, is for a profound shift in our cultural paradigm. At the heart of this shift is the need for a new relationship with paradox itself. Instead of trying to remove it, our task will be to move into it and to know it in a new way.

The postmodern "paradox paradigm" proposed here asserts the primacy of extrarational experience. Although we need reason to recognize the pitfalls of Cartesian dualism and to begin healing the schism between mind and body, when we reach the limits of reason—when it finally pushes us into paradox—we must reach beyond it to some other way of knowing.

Part of the paradox of consciousness, then, is this: Our science and philosophy are based on some combination of empiricism and rationalism. We use our senses to locate and define the data of the world—its "given" ingredients; we use reason to analyze the data, and to form inferences, hypotheses, theories and models about the nature of the world beyond what is revealed by our senses. Empiricism gives us the details, rationalism fills in the blanks. To be comprehensive and adequate to the whole cosmos, empirical-rationalistic science would have to account (at least in principle) for all that exists within it.

But here we have a twofold problem: First, empiricism works only because at the end of the chain of events through which our senses pick up information about the world there is an *experience* of the data; second, reason works only because at the end of the chain of events through which the logical relations between propositions or statements are known there is an *experience* of the abstract relations. In other words, both empiricism and rationalism—the very essence of science—depend, inevitably, on the existence of an *experiencer,* of *consciousness.* But nowhere among the data of the senses, nor even among the abstractions of logical relationships, will we ever locate the concrete reality of consciousness *as an experience.* Here's the paradox: Science and philosophy exist only because of consciousness, yet consciousness is precisely what cannot be found *anywhere* within modern science or philosophy. We have a story without a storyteller.

One of the greatest physicists of our time, Erwin Schrödinger, recognized this impasse:

> Mind has erected the objective outside world of the natural philosopher out of its own stuff. Mind could not cope with this gigantic task otherwise than by the simplifying device of excluding itself—withdrawing from its conceptual creation.[5]

How, then, could we ever meaningfully talk of philosophy of mind or of developing a true science of consciousness? This book proposes that an adequate answer to this question will involve a radical transformation of our current epistemology—beyond the recursive limitations of empiricism and rationalism—and adoption of a radically different fundamental ontology.

Epistemologically, we must engage the paradox. "Paradox" means, literally, "beyond" (*para*) "opinion" or "belief" (*doxa*). Paradox, then, takes us into that "space" that is *beyond belief*—into experience itself. Ontologically, it invites us into the ambiguity of being—an ambiguity of neither this-or-that nor this-and-that, neither either/or nor both/and, but all of these together.

# PART I

# CRISIS

## OUR MODERN
## COSMOLOGY STORY

# A PLACE FOR MEANING

*That man is the product of causes which had no prevision of the end they were achieving; that his origin, his growth, his hopes and fears, his loves and beliefs, are but the outcome of accidental collocations of atoms; that no fire, no heroism, no intensity of thought and feeling, can preserve an individual life beyond the grave; that all the labors of the ages, all the devotion, all the inspiration, all the noonday brightness of human genius, are destined to extinction in the vast death of the solar system, and the whole temple of man's achievement must inevitably be buried beneath the debris of a universe in ruins—all these things, if not quite beyond dispute, are yet so nearly certain, that no philosophy which rejects them can hope to stand.*

BERTRAND RUSSELL, *A FREE MAN'S WORSHIP*

This may be the most terrifying story ever told—nevertheless, it is the one we are born into.

It expresses the terrible poetry of a meaningless universe, rolling along entropic channels of chance, blind and without purpose, sometimes accidentally throwing up the magnificence and beauty of natural and human creations, but inevitably destined to pull all our glories asunder and leave no trace, no indication that we ever lived, that our lonely planet once bristled and buzzed with colorful life and reached out to the stars. It is all for nothing.

Such is the plot and substance of modern science boiled down to its bare essentials, a legacy from the founders of the modern worldview—Bacon, Galileo, Descartes, Hobbes, Locke, Newton, Laplace, and Darwin.

Somewhere in our nested system of beliefs that story lurks, ready to rob our visions and our dreams, our loves and our passions of any meaning, of any validity beyond the scripted directions of a blind, unconscious, purposeless plot maker. If something in our experience stirs and reacts to this with disbelief, even with a question, it is surely worth paying attention to because the possibility that that story is wrong or incomplete has far-reaching consequences.

What if that sweeping physicalist vision leaves something out? What if there is something other than an "accidental collocation of atoms" at work in the universe? What if, for instance, the experience or consciousness that contemplated the world and discovered the atoms was itself real?* What if the ability of "collocated atoms" to purposefully turn around and direct their gaze to reflect on themselves was more than "accidental"? What if consciousness participates in the way the world works? What if consciousness can dance with the atoms and give them form and direction? What if the atoms themselves choreograph their own dance? What then?

In this book, I will explore an alternative story—one where the atoms do choreograph their own dance—a worldview that tells us consciousness matters and that matter is conscious.

## Deserts of Meaning

Today the branch of knowledge most explicitly concerned with exploring the nature of consciousness and its relation to the physical world is philosophy of mind.

It is a discipline whose time has come. Although it has a relatively short

---

*"Real" in the sense of existing *sui generis* as an actual causal agent, neither emerging from, nor an epiphenomenon of, physical systems such as nervous tissue or brains.

history, it has a long past. As a distinct branch of study, philosophy of mind dates back only to the 1950s, following the "ghost in the machine" debates initiated by Gilbert Ryle's *The Concept of Mind*. However, the question of the relationship between mind and body dates back at least two millennia, with versions of the debate in Plato and Aristotle, and strains of it running through the early and late medieval period in the philosophies of Plotinus (204–269), St. Augustine (354–430), and Thomas Aquinas (1225–1274). The central problems in philosophy of mind gained currency in the seventeenth and eighteenth centuries, mainly due to the writings of René Descartes, John Locke, George Berkeley, Gottfried Leibniz, David Hume, and Immanuel Kant. Today the field is one of the fastest growing areas in philosophy.

Yet despite all the attention in recent years, philosophy of mind is sometimes perceived (along with much else in philosophy) as a discipline without a cause, or at least without much, if any, recognized practical relevance to society or science. Furthermore, following Ryle, much of the work done in philosophy of mind has been aimed toward either reducing consciousness to brain events, or even eliminating the notion altogether as a linguistic fiction, a hangover from outmoded folk psychology. Part of the reason for this was the combined influences of the rising academic popularity of logical positivism and linguistic analysis and a deepening respect within philosophy for the empirical data of the physical sciences.

In the onrush of these movements, the branch of philosophy known as metaphysics—and along with it the subspecialties of ontology and epistemology—was considered to be practically a waste of time (and funding), tending to be shunted into academic backwaters. Metaphysics was seen to be about as relevant to the practical needs of science and society as, for instance, theology or cosmology. How could theoretical investigations into the nature of reality (ontology) and the nature of knowledge (epistemology)—central issues in the philosophy of mind—ever contribute to the advance of science and technology or throw any light on baseline social issues such as human relations, economics, or politics?

It turns out—as I hope to show in this book—that these issues are critically important to the development of both science and society. The time for philosophy of mind is *now* for a number of reasons. Perhaps most important of these is that each year it is becoming clearer that our society's profound reliance on the authority of scientific knowledge and its applications in technology is inadequate to resolving the growing crises we face as communities and as individuals. Besides environmental problems of global proportions, our science and technology appear helpless in the face of burgeoning population problems, with attendant international crises of poverty and hunger. Our societies are stressed with internal pressures of social, racial, and economic unrest, and with external pressures fueled by excesses of governmental, military, and corporate policies that impact across national boundaries creating economic and biological havoc and, in extreme situations, wastelands and deserts.

These deserts are not only environmental, such as the destruction of the planet's dwindling rainforests and marshlands; there are also existential deserts—deserts of the spirit, of the soul, and of the mind. Deserts of *meaning*. It is precisely this aspect of the global crisis that calls out for a rigorous and inspired philosophy of mind. We begin the twenty-first century living in a technological society based on science, and we live with a science based on a materialistic paradigm. We live, in other words, in a world lacking any grounding in meaning, in values, in purposes or goals. With few exceptions, the goals and "purposes" that do exist within our social institutions have no metaphysical foundation. They emerge, for the most part, as expressions of an economic philosophy based on a materialistic metaphysics *that denies any foundation to goals, purposes, and values—* other than biologically driven preferences or the relativity of social power plays. Our religious and artistic traditions have attempted to fill the gap, but increasingly succumb to a social preference for scientific knowledge as the final authority on how we should govern our lives.

But it is precisely the wisdom of meaning, of value, of experience, that our societies need to balance the knowledge of physical science and the obsessive push for technological progress. In short, we critically need a *science of mind* to match our science of matter. But in order to develop a science of consciousness we need first to examine the unexplored metaphysical assumptions upon which our contemporary science is based. We need to investigate our ontological and epistemological assumptions about the nature of reality and the nature of our knowledge. We need to reexamine our basic narrative premise to see what alternative story (or stories) science might tell.

What is needed now, perhaps more than ever, is to find a way to restore a sense of the sacred to science and to the world—to embody mind and to "enmind" matter. But to do this we will need to develop a true science of consciousness, and for that we will need philosophy of mind to guide us in reexamining our hidden ontological and epistemological assumptions. We will need, in fact, a radical approach to studying consciousness—complemented by a transformative approach to philosophy of mind, where the researcher is profoundly changed in the process.

In this book I will look at the mystery of consciousness, at why mind should appear so alien in our scientific view of the world. I will also examine the motivations for undertaking any such scientific investigation at all. Why do we want knowledge about matter, about mind, and about their relationship? How do our motivations shape the questions we ask, and what we do with the answers we get?

The origins of the mind-body problem and philosophy of mind are critical to our understanding of the pathological schism of the mind-body split. Traditionally, questions central to philosophy of mind have been approached with the assumption that the rational, cognitive, categorizing human mind could untangle the mind-body knot. This book proposes a different approach: The paradoxes are confronted head on, not as a knot to be untied, but as an experiential phenomenon to be embraced as it presents itself—through a shift in the being of the explorer.

We should use our intellectual faculties as best we can to distinguish between *artificial* paradoxes and mysteries created by our own minds (such as the mind-body problem) and *natural* mysteries (such as the origin of the universe, the origin of consciousness, and perhaps the origin of life).[1] Nevertheless, there comes a point where rational understanding fails to take us any further. We may untangle much, even all, of the accumulated confusion surrounding the paradoxes of mind, but when we touch the dynamic heart of natural paradox itself, we must let go of rationality and logic and switch to a different mode of *being with* the phenomenon. At that point, the philosophy of paradox turns as much on *feelings*—on emotions, intuitions, and felt sense—as on the pivots of language and rational analysis. We must commit ourselves to peeling away the logical tangles, squeezing the most out of our rational, cognitive, and verbal faculties. But in the end, when we come to that point where intellect can take us no further, we must bow in silence before the mystery—and participate with it on its own ineffable terms.

Back and forth, we must switch between intellect and intuition, between rational, objective knowledge and embodied paradox. Achieving such a synthesis involves a shift to *"participatory* epistemology"—a way of knowing that takes us into the heart of mystery and invites the paradox of consciousness into our very being.

With such an opening, we are ready for a breakthrough, ready to step into a new way of knowing, ready to hear a new story of the cosmos.

# 2

Breakthrough

---

# A NEW COSMOLOGY STORY

This is a story about how we came to tell ourselves that the world has no meaning—and what we need to do to put the missing meaning back. It is a story of the relationship between matter and mind, a story of philosophy and science in search of a soul.

We need a new cosmology story, an ecological account of the world in which we humans find our fit, our place, our home. It will be a *"cosmoecology"*—a story that gives a rational account (logos) of the grand order (cosmos) in which we feel at home (ecos). We need the new story because the current dominant cosmology, based on modernist science, has left us alienated in the universe, without a sense of being at home. It has failed to integrate "cosmos" with "ecos"; it has failed to arrive at *cosmoecos.*

In the modern story we have been left to drift through a material cosmos without meaning—adrift in a cold, unfeeling universe without purpose or direction. We are left unanchored in the vast immensities of space and time, knocked about by the mechanical pushes and pulls of random "collocations of atoms" rushing blindly and mindlessly through the void. And without a home in the grand scheme, our personal lives are drained of any deep meaning.

I argue that the loss of personal and cosmoecological meaning is an inevitable consequence of a metaphysical paradigm that posits mechanical matter as ultimately real. By "mechanical," I mean matter that is moved about entirely by external forces—for example, the colliding and ricocheting of atoms like so many billiard balls, or even the invisible fields of force pushing and pulling matter through its gyrations. In a purely mechanical universe, all motion of matter is caused from without, there is no possibility of *self-motion,* and therefore no possibility of aim or purpose.

Following the Cartesian mind-body split in the seventeenth century, our philosophy and science in the nineteenth and twentieth centuries lopped off one half of the spirit-matter dualism, exorcised the ghost from the machine, and left us a despirited reality of pure matter. But it is an empty matter—cold and dead, without any self-agency, without any intrinsic purpose, value, or meaning. Yet, as beings born of the "stuff" of the cosmos, we need not only material sustenance, we also need meaning. We thrive on meaning and need a new cosmology story that provides it. To put the new story in context, it will help to remind ourselves of the main elements of the "old story" and to highlight its inadequacies.

## Limitations of the Old Story

The "old story" central to Western philosophy and cosmology, which has shaped the story of science for nearly four hundred years, is based on an assumption of ontological dualism—a separation of mind and body.* In the

---

*"Ontological dualism" refers to a fundamental split in the nature of reality itself. Although we can trace the history of this idea back to the early Greek philosophers, especially Plato, in modern times the notion was firmly established in Western thought by the seventeenth-century French philosopher René Descartes. In essence, the idea is that there are two fundamentally different kinds of reality—in this case, (1) matter or physical reality of things extended in space (e.g., atoms, tables, mountains, animal bodies), and (2) mind or spiritual reality of things without any extension in space (e.g., thoughts, feelings, desires, beliefs, souls). Somehow, these two utterly different kinds of reality happen to interact—one can cause effects in the other. The perennial riddle for philosophy is *how?* How could something as ghostly as a thought, a mind, or a soul impact anything as solid as a human body?

fourth century BCE, Plato separated the cosmos into the ontological realms of transcendent Forms and mundane matter.* Only the Forms were perfect, and material bodies were merely imperfect "representations" or "reflections" of transcendent Ideal Forms. For example, every actual table is merely an imperfect reflection of the perfect Form of "tableness." No table could exist unless its matter took on the essence of "tableness." Mundane forms derived their reality only by participating in the transcendent Forms. Plato never adequately explained how the immanent, mundane, imperfect material forms could "participate" in the transcendent Forms.

Aristotle, Plato's most famous pupil, attempted to soften his master's extreme ontological dualism by bringing the forms down to Earth. He changed the abstract Platonic Forms into concrete, earthly forms. For Aristotle, forms were not disembodied, transcendent Ideas, but were immanent in matter. By coupling matter (*hyle*) and form (*morphe*) together in his ontology of *hylomorphism,* Aristotle developed a metaphysics of "ensouled matter" and "embodied soul."†

Despite Aristotle's attempt to rectify Plato's ontological transcendent-immanent split, this dualism continued to influence the development of Western thought through the pagan Neoplatonists, such as Plotinus, and his Christian followers, such as St. Augustine. Augustine continued the Platonic (and Neoplatonic) dualism of spirit and matter in his dichotomy of the "City of God," where human consciousness was directed at the heavenly sphere, and "City of Man," where the human appetites were directed at worldly and fleshly concerns.

---

*According to Plato there were two kinds of world: (1) the ideal world of Forms and (2) the earthly world of matter. The world of Forms (also called "Ideas" or "archetypes") exists beyond the world of matter. It is eternal, unchanging, pure, and perfect. It is transcendent. By contrast, the world of matter is impermanent, subject to change, impure, and imperfect. It is immanent. The perfect reality of the Forms shows up as imperfect copies or reflections in the shapes and changing forms of the material world. Ultimate reality, according to Plato, resides in the transcendent domain of pure Forms—which means that the entire world of material forms is ultimately illusory or second-rate. Plato, thus, includes matter in his ontology (his accounting of reality) but gives it at best only a derivative and imperfect status.

†Nevertheless, Aristotle retained a dualism of a perfect superlunar realm governed by perfect circular motions and an imperfect sublunar realm of rectilinear motions. And Aristotle's God, or Prime Mover, remained utterly transcendent.

Platonic-Augustinian dualism was further entrenched in the Western mind in the seventeenth century with Descartes's substance dualism* of (transcendent) mind and (immanent) matter. According to Descartes, on the one hand, *res cogitans*—mind/spirit (disembodied Platonic Forms)— were wholly immaterial, without extension, occupying no space; whereas on the other, *res extensa*—matter/body (embodied nature)—were defined as having extension in space. Only mind had sentience. Matter (nature) had no feelings, no intrinsic value, purpose, or meaning. The problem with Descartes's mind-body dualism, as even he himself was aware, was that the connection, interaction, or mode of influence between mind and body remained a mystery—seemingly requiring a miraculous supernatural intervention by God via the human soul, located in the pineal gland.

A fundamental idea of the Cartesian ontology was that only minds or souls had sentience (could feel), whereas matter was "dumb," without intrinsic sentience. Descartes, thus, defined matter as insentient substance and set in place the mind-body dualism that was to determine the direction for so much of Western philosophy and science during the subsequent three hundred years.

Following Descartes, Isaac Newton (1642–1727) focused his science almost exclusively on only one side of the Cartesian split—on (dead) matter in motion. Applying rigorous mathematics, Newton developed the fundamental laws of motion that were to become the foundation for the science of classical mechanics that dominated physics for centuries. Except for gravity, all interaction in the cosmos was to be explained via exchange of physical forces, by "push/pull" contiguous contact (all set in motion by a remote God). In Newtonian mechanics, therefore, bodies could influence each other only by local contact. Separated by "dead" empty space,

---

*For Descartes, both matter and mind were "substances." He inherited this term from the medieval scholastics who defined a "substance" as something that could exist, or subsist, wholly independently of anything else. Thus, the domain of matter could roll along on its own course without any necessary relation to mind—and vice versa. Both domains subsisted independently of each other. Neither needed anything else in order to exist. Of course, as a Christian, Descartes pointed out that the only true "substance" is God. Only God needs nothing else in order to exist, whereas both matter and mind depend, ultimately, on God for their existence. Minds and material things, therefore, were created substances.

bodies were sealed up in individual, self-contained clumps of matter.

Newtonian mechanics leads to strict causality and determinism, immortalized by Laplace's famous image of the universe as a gigantic clockwork. Within the Newtonian universe, all events that ever happened anywhere at any time were wholly determined by prior mechanical causes. All causality, therefore, was to be explained in terms of an unbroken chain of mechanical causes and effects. The present was wholly determined by the past, and the future likewise would be merely an extension of this same deterministic chain of events. There was no room for a nonmaterial, nonmechanical mind to step in and influence the causal chain. In such a universe, there could be no room for true creativity. Anything "novel" was merely the rearrangement of already existing pieces of matter. Everything in the world could be reduced to the mechanical workings of its smallest parts. Complete knowledge of the workings of the parts would yield complete certainty about future events. The promise of Newtonian science, therefore, was the possibility of complete causal explanations of wholly deterministic events, giving us complete certainty. And, once science uncovered all the various mechanical laws, it could fulfill Francis Bacon's early promise of giving us control and mastery over nature.

Following the scientific revolution in the seventeenth century, the rise of positivist science and philosophy in the twentieth century completed the mechanistic project begun by Newton. According to positivism, the only positively certain knowledge we could have is whatever could be revealed by the scientific method—and this implied knowledge gained by observation and measurement using the five senses. If you couldn't see it and measure it, it wasn't real. Since science couldn't see or measure mind, the positivists dispensed with the "ghost in the machine"[1] and declared that only matter was real. The universe, therefore, consisted wholly of insentient matter in motion—mere atoms in the void—until nervous systems and brains evolved.

Another great landmark in the development of the old story—the paradigm of mechanism and materialism—was Charles Darwin's theory of evolution first published in 1859. Darwin said that all the varieties of animal and plant species populating the Earth were the result of chance variations subjected to a process of natural selection.

Combining Newtonian mechanism-materialism with Darwinian evolution, neo-Darwinians argued that all life forms were the sole result of chance mutations and the blind selection of a dumb and blind natural "watchmaker."[2]

New species emerged in evolution through random genetic mutations—spontaneous reshuffling of molecules in the genes—and these novelties survived if they happened to improve the host organism's ability to produce offspring. "Survival of the fittest" meant the survival of those offspring with genes for producing further offspring well adapted to a particular ecological niche. It was all a matter of chance and necessity—the randomness of mutations channeled by the determinism of mechanism in the interplay between organism and environment.[3] There was no room for purpose in nature. All progress, all evolution, was due merely to the injection of novelty through mutations, selected according to the necessities of survival in a particular niche.

Taking their cue, then, from Newtonian science (where the cosmos was viewed as a clockwork) and neo-Darwinian evolution (where consciousness was viewed as a by-product of chance events in mechanical nature), scientists presented us with a view of the world as a giant mechanism, composed of "dead" matter. Consciousness, when it finally arrived late in the game, was merely an epiphenomenon,* an ineffective by-product of matter that had evolved to the complexity of nervous systems and brains.

---

*Two key words in the materialist view of evolution of consciousness are "epiphenomenon" and "emergence." They are often closely related, but need not be. In all versions of materialist evolution, consciousness is considered an "emergent" property—it "arises" out of the complexity of dead matter. "Emergent consciousness" is epiphenomenal if, having emerged from the brain, it can produce no effect back on the brain. It is powerless, ineffective—like the rattle of a steam train. The causal path is exclusively upward, from brain to mind. But some theorists who accept the view that mind emerges from matter deny that it is epiphenomenal. They argue (apparently from the plain fact of their own everyday experience) that the mind very clearly *does* act back on the body through the brain. They accept "downward causation" from mind to brain. In this view, consciousness, though emergent, is nevertheless causal (though always dependent on the matter of the brain from which it emerged—this is called the "supervenience" of mind on brain).

# Breakdown of the Old Story

In the early decades of the twentieth century, hot on the heels of positivism, key details of the old story began to break down. Gaps or anomalies in the mechanistic worldview appeared with the advent of the "new sciences"—relativity, quantum, and complexity theories.

## RELATIVITY THEORY

*Matter is energy.* The universe is made up of events. One of the cornerstone assumptions of the old story of matter was that it consisted of things, solid little objects called atoms. The colliding and bumping around of these solid little things created the forces that we know as mechanism—linear, predictable, clockwork-like interactions between pieces of matter. Einstein's Theory of Relativity radically challenged the simplistic, mechanistic view of matter.

In the Special Theory of Relativity Einstein showed, using his most famous equation $E = mc^2$, that matter itself is a form of energy, not solid "stuff." The solid, immutable foundation of matter gave way to a fluid, transformative energetic process. Matter-energy came to be viewed as consisting of "events," not things. Einstein abolished also the absolute space and time characteristic of Newton's universe. Instead, he proposed a *space-time matrix*—a continuous field of matter-energy in incessant transformation. The universe was now seen as a web of space-time *events*—not composed of isolated things with empty space between.

The familiar world of rocks and other solid objects, such as houses, tables, and chairs, turned out not to be composed of solid little bits of matter interacting mechanistically, but of whirling dances and fluxes of energy exchanges. What we perceive as solidity is, in fact, merely the stability of energetic patterns that endure for some time. When the patterns of energy break down—for example, when molecular bonds break apart—the structures that we perceive as matter lose their former stability and solidity. In biological organisms, we recognize this breakdown of matter as death and decay.

*No possibility of action-at-a-distance.* General Relativity showed that Newtonian gravity, with its mysterious action-at-a-distance, was an illusion.

Instead of a "force" acting across the void of empty space, Einstein's gravity was explained as warps, or tensions, in the space-time matrix. There was no empty space for the so-called force of gravity to act across. Gravity was a geometric property of space-time itself. In the universe of relativity, events are "local," defined and confined by the speed of light. There is no possibility of action-at-a-distance (i.e., influences exceeding the speed of light).

The shift from things to events as the fundamental nature of the material world forced physicists to question the old notions of mechanism. Einstein's relativity served as a correction to errors and inadequacies in Newton's classical mechanics, thus accelerating the breakdown of the old paradigm. Nevertheless, ironically, relativity's abolition of Newton's mysterious action-at-a-distance blocked a key element in the radical shift required for a truly postmodern paradigm—as we shall see.

Although relativity shook up the old paradigm, it is still in some ways an extension of the old worldview. In place of Newtonian mechanistic matter, relativity theory introduced geometric patterns of energy. But these more abstract relativistic patterns were still objectivist, causal, predictable, and local—just as much as Newtonian mechanism and materialism. Despite his profound insights into the relationships between matter, energy, light, space, and time, Einstein's universe had no need for sentience, subjectivity, or consciousness. "Observers" in relativity theory could be mindless robots or zombies. In this sense, relativity was still determinist and mechanist.

## QUANTUM THEORY

Quantum theory, by contrast, has proved to be the most decisive challenge to the old story. It pulled the screws out of the cosmic clockwork by showing that subatomic physical events are *not causal:* Quantum events are inherently uncertain and unpredictable. Physical nature, it turned out, defies either/or logic: Quantum entities are both waves and particles, or "wavicles." Quantum events are *nonlocal*—unhindered by distance. Furthermore, quantum events also involve the choice or consciousness of the observer (i.e., events that are considered "objective" are in some way influenced by the observer's subjectivity). A number of key notions establish quantum theory as a paradigm-breaker par excellence:

*Energy comes in quanta.* Whereas relativity theory presents a view of the universe as a continuous matrix of space-time, quantum theory paradoxically describes a physical world of matter-energy that is *not* continuous. The central concept in quantum theory is that of the quantum itself, described as a packet of energy or action. Energy or action, then, is *quantized*—that is, energy comes in discrete "bundles" of indivisible packets called "quanta"—with *nothing in between*. In a quantum universe, the world is full of "gaps." But these are strange "gaps": They form the quantum void, an infinite sea of quantum potential, of probability waves, which *when observed* collapse to form the world of actualities.

Here, the old story is challenged on two fronts: Mechanism cannot be the whole story if there are quantum gaps in the world—because mechanism requires continuity and contact between adjoining objects to transmit the energy of their collisions. Furthermore, if quantum events happen only when *observed,* the supposed objectivity of science that goes hand-in-hand with mechanism comes into question. Clearly, if the subjectivity or consciousness of an observer is somehow responsible for "collapsing" quantum probabilities into an actual event, objectivity is compromised at a fundamental level.

*Events, not "things."* Although quantum theory contradicts relativity theory, describing gaps rather than a continuum, they both agree that *events,* not things, lie at the core of physical reality. Since the quantum is a "packet" of *action* (strictly speaking, Planck's quantum equation refers to action rather than energy), events or processes are now understood to be the fundamental nature of physical reality. The cosmos is a verb, not a noun. The universe is "quantuming" or *"cosmosing."*

If, as both quantum and relativity theory tell us, events, processes, or durations lie at the heart of reality, then reality cannot be wholly objective, cannot be wholly mechanistic—cannot be made up of "dead" matter (despite the foundational assumption of materialism common to both relativity and quantum theory). For, as we will see in chapter 7, "Resolution: Whitehead's Postmodern Cosmology," the notion of time, of duration, of process is intimately related to subjective experience. Subjectivity and sentience, not mere mechanism, appear to be fundamental in the emerging story.

*Noncausal.* Quantum events are *not* causal. They are inherently unpredictable. The exact instant when an electron jumps orbit, or when a radioactive particle is emitted from an atom, is entirely random, entirely uncaused. To say that an event is "entirely uncaused" amounts, logically, to saying that it is "self-caused"; and this, as philosopher Arthur Young argued, is tantamount to saying that the event *chooses,* that is, exhibits consciousness.[4]

This logical and observational identity of randomness and choice is a critical implication of quantum physics. Young's point is this: If some entity, say an electron or a photon, is exercising true self-action, free will, or choice in how it will move, its behavior will be undetermined (by any prior causes) and will be unpredictable. *To an observer,* its behavior will appear utterly random, uncaused. That's exactly what is observed in the behavior of quantum particles. The observer will not be able to detect *any* difference between choice-driven action and purely random behavior. But to the quantum entity making the choice, there would be a world of difference. The quantum event would be *self-caused,* not uncaused. It is uncaused only in the sense that no causes external to itself influence its behavior.

This notion of "quantum choice" is further supported philosophically by examining the logic of emergence. If, as we know to be certainly true, consciousness and the ability to make choices exist in our own case, then we can generalize and say that consciousness and choice exist at the macro-level. Now, we know, too, from biology, chemistry, and physics, that macro-level entities are composed of hierarchies of lower-level microentities. If these lower-level entities were utterly devoid of choice (as mechanism assumes), how could we account for the emergence of choice *anywhere* in the hierarchy? How could entities lacking all capability for self-agency, free will, or choice ever give rise to entities that did have this capability? The only way we can coherently explain the existence of choice at our macro level is to assume that it must go "all the way down" to the lowest-level micro entities.* Choice—the exercise of free will and self-agency—must exist to some degree at the micro level if it exists at the

---

*See chapters 8, "Panexperientialism: Consciousness All the Way Down?" and 9, "Past Matter, Present Mind."

macro level. Otherwise, the emergence of choice from the utter absence of choice would require a miracle.*

*Indeterminacy.* The unpredictability of quantum events, their randomness, is not merely an artifact of imprecise human measurement—the indeterminacy is *intrinsic* to the quantum events themselves. This is ontological, not merely epistemological, uncertainty. In the quantum wonderland, therefore, causal determinism gives way to uncertainty built into the structure of reality itself. This feature of the quantum domain has been expressed in Heisenberg's famous Uncertainty Principle.

*Complementarity.* Not only are quantum events uncaused and indeterminate, they defy the conventions of ordinary, classical, Aristotelian logic. Because of quantum indeterminacy, it is impossible to measure the position and the momentum of, say, an electron. We can know only one feature, not the other. A similar situation occurs in a number of other so-called conjugate pairs, for example, wave-particle duality. But this "duality" differs radically from Cartesian dualism with its ontologically incompatible pairing of self-subsisting body and mind, or object and subject. Quantum dualities are not discrete opposites, they are *complementarities*—meaning that although they are mutually exclusive, they are also mutually necessary. The nature of quantum events is nondual complementarity, requiring a new logic different from either/or. For example, quantum events are *both*

---

*"Miracles" are a measure or indication of our ignorance. When we don't understand how something could happen, but want to insist that it did happen nevertheless, we invoke the non-explanation of "miracle." This is not to say real miracles can never occur. It just means that if they do, they are beyond our ken. Miracles lie beyond the pale of knowledge. As far as epistemology is concerned, the great problem with miracles is this: By what criteria do we decide when to invoke their occurrence? What are the rules of evidence by which we decide when and where to insert a "miracle" into our explanations, revealing a breakdown in our sequence of reasoning? If miracles are evidence of our ignorance, what prevents us from invoking a miracle every time we are at a loss to explain something? (Science replaced magic as a method of knowledge and action because it did not accept gaps in explanation—in contrast, superstition invoked spirits and miracles whenever something happened beyond the reach of the knowledge of the time.) If we allow miracles to pepper our explanations, then what's to stop any of us resorting to "and then a miracle occurred" every time we fail to understand anything? Why bother with seeking any explanations at all? Why not just say "it's all a miracle" and leave it at that?

waves *and* particles. Quanta are paradoxical: spread out over space (waves) and infinitesimal point-events (particles).[5]

*Quantum participation.* The ideal of mechanistic physics is objectivity—the acquisition of pure knowledge unadulterated by the point of view of the observing subject. We could call it "plate-glass" science, where the object of knowledge is supposed to be shielded from the observer who is outside looking on. One of the most challenging—and to scientists committed to objectivity, most disturbing—revelations from quantum science is that no such plate-glass separation between object and subject exists. The observer is not—and cannot—be separated from the object being investigated. The so-called observer is actually a *participator,* an integral part of the quantum system.

The essence of the revelation is this: The quantum domain consists wholly of possibilities or probabilities "existing" together in a kind of suspended animation. In quantum physics, these probabilities are described as a matrix of wave functions—mathematical *waves of probability.* The remarkable thing is that any particular probability becomes an actuality *only when observed.* In quantum-speak, this is called the "collapse of the wave function"—one particular actuality is "collapsed" out of many superimposed probability waves. For the actual world of material objects to exist, then, it is necessary for an observer to step into the quantum system and observe it.

It's as if the only way the realm of quantum possibilities can become actual, manifest reality is for an observer to reach in with his or her consciousness and *choose* one of the probabilities; this probability then becomes an actual physical entity, such as an electron or a photon. In short, by *participating* in the quantum system, the "observer" helps create reality by collapsing the quantum wave function. In some as yet unexplained way, a quantum observer—and that means an observer's *consciousness*—participates in the creation of physical reality. It is more like "looking-glass" science, where manifest reality reflects the intentions and choices of sentient participators. *The entire material world arises out of collapsed quantum events and therefore is partly created by some participating consciousness.*

*Quantum nonlocality.* From the viewpoint of the classical paradigm, by far the most notorious and dramatically challenging aspect of quantum mechanics is the experimental evidence for the phenomenon called *nonlocality*. According to the old view, supported by relativity, no two things or events could ever communicate or interact if separated by a distance so great that they could not touch or exchange a signal. Yet following predictions based on quantum theory, experiments show that quantum events, separated by superluminal distances (distances that would require communication greater than the speed of light), do *respond* to one another.

The most famous evidence for quantum nonlocality comes from the set of experiments conducted by the French physicist Alain Aspect,[6] later confirmed by other physicists. He demonstrated that when two quantum objects (say photons) are separated in space so that no signal could possibly pass between them during the interval of the experiment, nevertheless by changing a property on one photon the other was observed to undergo a complementary change—*as if it somehow knew what had happened to the first photon.*

Quantum events, therefore, defy the presumed impossibility of action-at-a-distance. That is, either quantum events *can* exceed the speed of light (which, per relativity, is impossible), or quantum events are *nonlocal*. That is, they are correlated in such a way as to behave as though they were a unity—even when apparently separated by superluminal distances. In other words, quantum events are *interconnected* at some deep level of reality. In David Bohm's terminology: At the implicate quantum level, reality is an undivided whole.[7] Everything is connected to everything else. Quantum nonlocality has been repeatedly confirmed experimentally.

## COMPLEXITY THEORY

*Order out of chaos.* Finally, the trio of the "new sciences" is completed with the advent of complexity and chaos theories. Although not identical, both chaos theory and complexity theory belong to the same "family"—and are first cousins to systems theory. All recognize the fundamental interrelatedness and interdependency between the various parts of a whole system. The notion of independent, isolated, or isolatable, parts—a cornerstone in mechanism—is seen to be unrealistic. The implications for all kinds of systems—including ecological, economic, social, political, and climatic—are profound.

Because of interdependence, nature is recognized to be a highly complex, interlocking network of nested systems. Relationships between "parts" are dynamic, ever-changing, because they involve complex networks of feedback and feedforward loops. It becomes difficult, if not meaningless, to identify or isolate individual causes. In dynamic systems, effects feed back into their causes and so alter the causal pathways in nonlinear ways. Such nonlinear evolution means it is impossible to accurately predict the behavior of complex systems (e.g., weather, economies, social groups). The best that can be hoped for is the identification of large-scale patterns. But because of their complexity and nonlinearity the evolution of the patterns is uncontrollable.

Any attempt to control a complex system by introducing an overriding cause will fail because the cause immediately produces nonlinear effects that reverberate throughout the system and affect the performance of the cause itself. As examples, note failed attempts by well-intentioned people to intervene in environmental, economic, or social dynamics. The problem is we are part of the system, and therefore we are part of the very changes and evolution of the system we are attempting to control. The bottom line in complex systems is that no part can control the whole— because *every* part contributes to the changes of the whole and therefore of the parts themselves.

So, given the complexity of nature, and given the insights from complexity theory, the dream of mechanism—the dream of complete prediction and control of nature for the benefit of humanity—must be given up. *We are part of the system,* and ultimately always at its mercy. Instead of control, the sciences of complexity and systems dynamics are telling us—just as quantum physics tells us—we can only *participate.* We always participate, and participation counts. Every individual, every part, makes a difference. These kinds of systems insights have been central to Eastern philosophies, such as Taoism and Buddhism, for millennia.

What chaos and complexity theories have given us are mathematical tools for analyzing and understanding complex systems. From chaos theory we know, for example, that even a simple initial system—a system with just a few parts and a few simple rules—will soon give rise to chaos and deep complexity if feedback iterations are part of what can happen in the system. Computer-generated fractals are one example of this. With just a few simple algorithms (instructions), the computer screen fills with unpredictable, yet patterned, complex swirls of shapes and colors. Fractals vividly show us that not only can chaos and complexity arise from simplicity and order, but the reverse can happen too: Order arises out of chaos.

Complexity theory shows that order spontaneously arises from chaos in systems *far from equilibrium.* When a system becomes highly complex it can also become highly unstable: It is on the edge of chaos. But this high instability can also be a source of new patterns, of new order, of creativity.

Getting order or creativity out of chaos or disorder was unthinkable in mechanism—except by pure chance. According to the old view, standard thermodynamics tells us that all systems when left to themselves spontaneously and naturally decay into greater disorder, or thermodynamic equilibrium. Energy dissipates into entropy—degraded energy in an unusable form. Yet, as Nobel laureate Ilya Prigogine has shown, certain systems—namely, those *far from thermodynamic equilibrium* on the edge of chaos—do not decay into disorder. On the contrary, they spontaneously create new patterns of order and organization by *dissipating entropy,* not energy, from the structures within the system. Prigogine called these sources of new order "dissipative structures."[8]

From the sciences of complexity and chaos, then, we learn that matter, or the structure of reality itself, has the inherent capacity to generate order from "fractional dimensions," or fractals, within chaos. We live in a world that is continuously dancing between chaos and creativity, a world where order is continuously breaking down into chaos, and from chaos new order spontaneously arises. The material world itself, then, has the capacity to generate its own new order. Matter is in some sense creative. We have come a long way from Newtonian mechanism and Russell's blind "collocation of atoms."

The new sciences—particularly of quanta and complexity—show that many fundamental elements of the old paradigm can no longer be assumed to be universal "truths." With the new sciences, severe limitations of the old story are highlighted. The old ideals of mechanism, reductionism, causal-determinism, and objectivity have been undermined. But most of all, the assumption of universal *physicality* (that the world ultimately wholly consists of matter or physical energy) is called into question.

The old cosmology story leaves no room for consciousness as a causal reality. Consciousness is merely an epiphenomenon "squirted out" by matter, as philosopher John Searle so vividly observed.[9] But worse: Matter *by itself* is inherently nonconscious and insentient—therefore all material bodies are without purpose or intrinsic meaning.[10] The cosmos is "dead," with only chance pockets of life and consciousness. Nothing in such a cosmos could have any intrinsic value—it would be nothing *for itself.* Only an entity with consciousness, with subjectivity—a subject—can feel what it is like to be uniquely that entity, to experience its own existential value. Whereas objects can have only external value projected onto them, a subject does not need valuation from external valuers because it has it for itself.

## Anomalies That Challenge the Old Story

Up to this point I have examined how the new sciences seriously undermine the old story. Even in the absence of the data from relativity, quantum, and complexity sciences, the old worldview of materialism, mechanism, physical causality, objectivity, and reductionism is profoundly challenged by three significant anomalies: the causality of consciousness, sentient bodies, and nonlocal (psi) phenomena. If our science and philosophy are not to remain inadequate and incomplete descriptions of the cosmos, they must be able to account for these anomalies.

### CONSCIOUSNESS IS CAUSAL

Physicalism, the assumption that reality is ultimately composed of only physical energy, leaves no room for consciousness as a causal reality. Within such a metaphysic, the agency of consciousness is a fiction. Only physical interactions can produce measurable effects in the world. Standard philosophy and science attempt to explain away consciousness as an epiphenomenon—an emergent by-product of evolutionary processes. In other words, matter produces mind. Yet each of us daily experiences the causal efficacy of our own consciousness. And in science, quantum experiments show that the consciousness of the observer (at least in some interpretations of quantum theory) causes the collapse of the wave function.

## BODIES FEEL

According to the old story, matter—even living bodies—cannot feel. Only minds can feel, and the matter of the body merely responds mechanically. The ability to feel and to have experiences (in short, *subjectivity*) is assumed to be merely a consequence of the complexity of matter that is otherwise *insentient*. By itself, then, matter is inherently nonconscious and nonexperiential. And without the capacity to feel and to evaluate, matter is purposeless, meaningless, and without any intrinsic value. Nature has no meaning. All life, consciousness, and meaning are merely chance pockets of order in an otherwise dead and insentient universe. Yet, as each of us experiences daily, we navigate our way through the world as bodies that most certainly do feel.

How can a science of "dead" matter ever account for the *fact* of consciousness? To say that consciousness or sentience emerged from matter that was wholly insentient to begin with—as scientists such as Richard Dawkins[11] and philosophers such as Daniel Dennett[12] claim—requires a miracle. Philosophers such as Thomas Nagel,[13] Colin McGinn,[14] Galen Strawson,[15] and David Griffin[16] have pointed out that nothing ontologically new and different in kind, such as subjectivity, could possibly emerge from something wholly objective (such as "dead" matter) that had not the slightest trace of subjectivity or sentience to begin with.[17] If the brain is made of insentient, nonconscious matter—such as neurons, molecules, atoms, electrons, and protons—then getting consciousness out of it would be more of a miracle than getting wine from water. As Colin McGinn said: "Somehow, we feel, the water of the physical brain is turned into the wine of consciousness, but we draw a total blank on the nature of this conversion. . . . The mind-body problem is the problem of understanding how this miracle is wrought."[18]

If our bodies *feel,* and we know they do, then unless we assume a miracle of emergence, the matter of our bodies must be able to feel, too—all the way down.

## COMMUNICATION AT-A-DISTANCE

According to mechanism and materialism, not only are bodies made of "dead stuff," each body is isolated in space and can exchange signals or energy only through contact or via a common physical medium. If bodies are isolated, as mechanism says, they could not respond to each other nonlocally, at a distance. And this is precisely the position of materialism. According to this worldview, phenomena such as empathy, telepathy, clairvoyance, and psychokinesis are impossible. Yet the literature of parapsychology manifestly contradicts this.[19]

Unfortunately, the standard scientific response to such anomalous data is that they must be either mistaken, due to poor experimental protocols, or the product of skillful fraud. Such out-of-hand dismissals are typically made by skeptics who "know" beforehand that psi phenomena are impossible. Given this kind of dogmatic bias, no amount of rigorous data would ever be sufficient to persuade the skeptic. But precisely because of prolonged hostile skepticism, responsible psi researchers go out of their way to ensure their experiments meet the highest scientific standards. Even so, the anomalous data still persist, pointing to flaws, not in their experimental designs, but in the scientific worldview that rejects them.

Besides these anomalies, the mechanistic denial of nonlocal effects, of action-at-a-distance, leads to some interesting, if unappealing, implications for our relationship with the universe—far beyond the laboratory:

*Cosmic events cannot affect terrestrial bodies.* Where distances are great, the speed of light prevents communication, or mutual influencing, between bodies within their respective lifespans. Thus, a human body living on Earth today cannot be "in touch" with cosmic forces or dynamics that originate beyond, say, eighty light-years away *during that human's life.* Cosmologically, eighty light-years is an insignificant distance. Therefore, most of the universe is off limits—available only as a historic event captured in the light rays (and other radiation) streaming from ancient celestial bodies, many of which may no longer even exist. Simultaneity and *participatory sharing* of presence is, therefore, impossible between great stretches of the cosmos. We are confined (or condemned) to relativistically isolated "light-cone" event horizons and incommunicado "bubble" universes.

*Terrestrial isolation.* Not only does this mean that the contemporary Earth is isolated from most of the cosmos, but even here on Earth, bodies are assumed to be isolated within their separate "skin-encapsulated" selves. They are presumed to be capable of being "in touch" only if physically proximate, or by exchanging physical signals, such as sounds or gestures (aided, where appropriate, by electronic encoding). Since matter is assumed to be intrinsically insentient and inert (moved only by physical contact), there could be no medium through which one body might *feel* the presence of another body at a distance.

## The Curious Paradox of the Modernist Story

Given this dominant worldview, we are born into a curious paradox: On the one hand, we are rooted in a "corpsed" materialism, a universe of dead matter; yet, on the other hand, this very notion has been achieved by the analytic constructions of a rational *disembodied mind*—the very "ghost" we are told does not exist. *How can that which has no real existence construct the story in which its own existence is denied?* Only by the artificial device of pulling the subject (self, soul, consciousness) out of the picture has modernist philosophy and science been able to construct the worldview of objective material reality. In order to attain the ideal of objectivity, the rational ego, bequeathed to us by the Enlightenment, had to extract itself from the corporeal world—to separate subject from object.

Yet, and this is the heart of the paradox (as quantum physicist Erwin Schrödinger noted in his wonderful essay "Mind and Matter"), having made that move, having consciously extracted mind from the world picture, modernist philosophy and science promptly forgot that it had done so and then, examining the despirited world picture, declared that it could not locate mind or spirit anywhere in it. Mind was outside looking on.[20] This was the early modernist position of dualism.

Then, in late modernism, when dualism gave way to materialism, mind was not even outside the physical world; it had no real existence of its own. Consciousness (spirit, soul) was declared nonexistent, a mere convenient fiction, brewed up in the electrochemical soup of the wholly material and objective human brain and nervous system.²¹ There is no mind, no consciousness, no soul, no spirit, no subjectivity of any kind according to this extreme worldview called "eliminative materialism." What we take to be consciousness, with all its subjective qualities such as sensations of color, of pleasure, of pain, of beliefs and desires and intentions, are mere "folk figments, " the naive concoctions of scientifically unsophisticated and ignorant people. These figments we call "minds" are really nothing more than highly complex productions of otherwise very ordinary objective *physical* events and processes in the brain. It's all a play of physical objects, pure objectivity. It just *seems* as though subjectivity is going on. But, in response to such eliminativism, we should ask: Who or what is doing the "seeming"? How can anything "seem" to be either what it is or what it is not to a purely physical object, which by definition and declaration has no point of view?

We are, thus, left dangling in the paradox of corpsed matter and incorporeal mind—the first dead, insentient, and without the possibility of meaning or creativity, the second a ghost, a mere figment or phantasm "squirted" out by chance arrangements of the first. *Yet it was precisely this subjective "fiction" that had somehow managed to construct the objective world picture in the first place.*

Of course, this is a deeply unsatisfactory state of affairs. It fails philosophically to make any sense—how, if all there is is "dead" matter, did consciousness come to be? To put it another way, how could subjectivity ever arise from wholly objective matter? *How could something that lacks all mind and imagination perform the miracle of imagining itself to have a mind?* The dominant story fails us because a world without subjectivity is not only a world devoid of any intrinsic meaning, it is a world that could never know itself. Yet this world *is* known by creatures within it. According to extreme materialism, this simply couldn't happen.

Concerned, even alarmed, at the profound consequences—philosophical, social, psychological, ecological, and spiritual—of the dominant story, a long line of critics have taken modernism to task in recent years, including feminists, ecofeminists, and ecological postmodernists.²² Strong themes common to many of these scholars include critiques of disembodied rationalism, a determined advocacy of a body-centered approach to philosophy, and an ecologically oriented call for an "embodied, embedded" philosophy.[23]

Clearly, from the feminist, ecofeminist, and ecophilosophical critiques, traditional Western philosophy requires a radical overhaul. However, even though many of these voices have raised challenging questions about ontology and epistemology, and even though some have proposed insightful and scholarly alternatives, I believe philosophy needs to go even deeper than the standard feminist and ecological critiques—valid, useful, important though these may be. Such critiques have been motivated by laudable ethical and pragmatic concerns to do with the distribution of power.

Building on this, the pressing task of philosophy is to get at the underlying, prevailing metaphysical "building-block" formative assumptions of the modern worldview. A move in this direction is there in feminism and ecologism, when its scholars talk of, for instance, feminist ontology, or embodied ontology and epistemology.[24] But, I think, the ontological critiques do not go deep enough; they do not yet get at the core assumptions. They do not dig into the ontological bedrock of Western philosophy to expose our paradigmatic and limiting assumptions about the nature of matter and mind. Without a radical revision of modernist ontology along the lines suggested by Whitehead, I believe none of the other attempts is likely to succeed.

In this book, I outline the direction for a "deep ontology," a profound shift in our assumptions about the nature of reality, that needs to happen before we can begin to tell ourselves a new, and meaningful, "cosmoecology story"—a story that includes the intimate relationship between matter and consciousness.

# 3

Narratives

---

# REDISCOVERING THE SOUL
# OF MATTER

If the universe is "dead," it tells no stories. And all our vast cosmologies are little more than fantasies, superlative myths we tell ourselves to make some sense that we are here at all. But what if the universe is itself a story? What could that mean, and how could we fit it into our science and philosophy?

The universe is either already "dead" or it is meaningful.* If it is "dead" in this sense of being wholly mechanical, without any intrinsic capacity for self-motion and feeling, then all instances of life and consciousness in the universe are ultimately insignificant evolutionary by-products. If this is true, then the universe would be essentially meaningless, it would be "absurd," just as the existentialists Sartre and Camus

---

*By "dead," I don't mean that the universe was once alive and is now expired. I'm not even referring to the cosmological prediction of entropic "heat death of the universe," when all available physical energy is used up, and all pockets of negentropic life will have disappeared forever. I mean "dead" in a more figurative sense where the "stuff" of the universe, its matter/energy, is wholly without sentience. Either the matter of the universe is itself intrinsically sentient, or it is without meaning. By "meaningful," I'm referring to a universe in which its raw ingredient (we may call it "matter," "energy," "ether," "void," "force field," or "quantum potential," it makes little difference to the argument) has the intrinsic capacity to *refer* to something (other entities or other parts of itself), it has the capacity to be *about* something, to signify, or point to something. In short, it has an intrinsic capacity for *intentionality*. By "meaningful," then, I am saying that if the matter of the universe is not "dead" mechanical stuff, it would have a capacity for creating significance and would itself be intrinsically significant.

said. All meaning would be contingent, created by minds that themselves arose by chance from the blind mechanical collisions of atoms in the void. When the brains that produced the minds died, all the meaning that they created would vanish with them. There would be no longer even pockets of meaning in an otherwise meaningless universe. The universe would just simply *be*. It would be *for* nothing.

A universe that is *for* nothing is not *about* anything; it is a universe without a story. Stories are the unfolding of meaning: They represent changes of states where the later states require reference back to their antecedents to complete their own being. More simply, stories require *memory* of what has happened, *experience* of what is happening, and *anticipation* of what is to come. All this requires consciousness.

Stories reveal how things came to be the way they are. They tell of beginnings, and of middles, and, if they don't always have endings, they point, and leave the way open. Stories are suggestive, rather than certain. They are lures or invitations to action. Stories enact the process of creation, whereby actualities emerge from a pool of potential. They make explicit, through becoming, the implicit fecundity of being.

If the universe is "dead," it tells no stories. The implication of this is that if the universe is not "dead," if it is not simply a huge mechanical system running according to a handful of laws at work in a vast ocean of chaos, then it is in some sense "alive." A more accurate term would be "sentient"—an inherent capacity for feeling or experience. In other words, to make explicit the main argument of this book: The matter of the universe, its raw "stuff" or ingredients, has within itself the essence of what we call "consciousness." There is something about matter itself, some quality or property, some intrinsic principle, that moves matter from within, an automotive urge toward self-organization, evolution, and complexity. In short, matter feels and moves itself. It doesn't require external forces pushing and pulling it.

This is a radically different view of matter and the natural world.

Evolution, then, is not so much a story of a struggle between conflicting external forces impinging on matter and shaping it according to vagaries of environmental conditions. It is more a story of matter feeling its way forward toward ever-increasing complexity and higher levels of order and organization. Matter is adventurous. And in some very real sense, the story of this evolution is a story that matter tells to itself. It is a story in which matter communicates the details of its earlier, less organized stages, to its later more organized stages, so that each stage is *meaningful*—is full of meaning, full of reference to its antecedent conditions. Matter is full of information about its past, about its evolutionary and holistic past—about its own structure and dynamics, about its *process*. Cells contain information about molecules, molecules contain information about atoms, atoms about quantum particles and fields. And the matter of brains contains information about all of these; and so the human mind can reflect on the history of matter and tell to itself the story of biological and cosmological evolution.

## The Intrinsic Narrative of Matter

Stories work because they create meaning. Human knowledge about the cosmos and our place in it is basically a story we tell ourselves. It is based on a narrative about how the world came to be the way it is. When telling children about the world, we call it a "story," but when telling ourselves and each other about the world we prefer to use more important-sounding terms such as "cosmology," "ontology," "metaphysics," "paradigm" or, if we are a little less self-important, "mythology." But they are all stories just the same. We are usually clear, however, that our ontological and cosmological stories are not the world, they are *about* the world. They are the ways we have of telling ourselves about the world, of representing it to ourselves as an unfolding narrative. But, we are sure, our stories are not the world itself. There is the world, and then, separately, there are our stories.

And because our stories are separate from—only "about"—the world, they do not impact the world in any significant sense. The stories, after all, are only in our minds, while the world is "out there," existing independently in the reality of physical space. Of course, this view of separate mind and physical nature is just as much a part of the story we tell ourselves—it is implicit in our modern Western ontology (the story of the nature of being) and cosmology (the story of the universe).

In this book, I question that "commonsense" worldview, inherited from the founders of modern philosophy and science. I propose, instead, a different story: a story that echoes the profound cosmological insights of an unsung sixteenth-century genius, Giordano Bruno (1548–1600).* Bruno's cosmology was so radical, such a profound challenge to the supernaturally ordained authority of the late medieval Church, that they burned him alive rather than risk having his heretical ideas about "intelligent matter" and an infinite, acentric universe corrupt other scholars and spread throughout Christendom. Had Bruno lived, his radical view of the nature and relationship of matter and mind may well have established a very different philosophical foundation for the development of modern science. Instead, we got Descartes and his dualism of separate spiritual soul and mechanical matter.

Bruno, however, was not the first to present a theory of intelligent matter, and he has had successors. The "new" postmodern solution to the mind-body problem has a very long lineage in Western thought. In fact, modern materialism can be shown to be a relatively recent and short-lived aberration. Besides Bruno, the long lineage of radical naturalism, or panpsychism, can be shown to pass through Goethe, Leibniz, Paracelsus, and the Neoplatonists, all the way back to the beginnings of Western philosophy, in the thought of Presocratic philosophers, and even beyond to the shamanic-inspired cults of Orpheus, trailing off into the mythologies of pre-Indo-European neolithic and paleolithic cultures.† For instance, the "new story" I propose to tell has antecedents in the writings of early Greek philosophers such as Anaximander (ca. 610–547 BCE) and Aristotle (384–322 BCE) and in our own century in the work of philosophers such as Alfred North Whitehead, Charles Hartshorne, and David Ray Griffin. A thoroughgoing and profound panpsychist metaphysics—a new cosmology—was worked out by Whitehead in *Process and Reality.*

But I am proposing not just a different story about the cosmos. I'm proposing a story in which the narrative itself tells us that our cosmologies and ontologies do, very significantly, impact the world. It is a story that says our stories matter. In fact, it is a story that tells us our *matter stories.*

Briefly, what I mean by this rather strange phrase is that there is

---

*Unsung, that is, in the Anglo-American world as a philosopher/scientist until the recent publication of *The Acentric Labyrinth: Giordano Bruno's Prelude to Contemporary Cosmology,* by Ramon G. Mendoza.

†See chapter 6, "Panpsychism: A Long Lineage of Mind-in-Matter."

something about the nature of matter itself—including the matter of our bodies—that is inherently the "stuff" of stories. Matter, we might say, has an intrinsic narrative. This view is radically at odds with the dominant modernist paradigm that conceives of matter as essentially, purely and simply, mechanical. According to this paradigm, only minds create stories, only minds possess meaning, only minds feel and pulse with purpose— and that all such mental activity is no more than an incidental by-product of the mechanical evolution of matter.

I argue here that our cosmological and ontological stories certainly do make a difference in and to the world of nature. I argue, as many postmodern and critical theory philosophers do, that at the base of every ontology, cosmology, metaphysical system, and mythology is a *narrative premise*—a set of assumptions about the nature of reality that dramatically shapes the way we know and interact with the world.

The narrative premise of insentient matter lies at the foundation of our modern Western cosmology and cosmogony, of a world created in a primordial big-bang, spewing forth a blazing plasma-radiation that, after eons of cosmic evolution, cooled and condensed into a universe of galaxies and stars. Nowhere in all of this was there anything resembling mind, or feeling, or point of view. The entire universe evolved according to a combination of blind chance events shaped by blind mechanical laws, utterly undirected, unknown, and unfelt. Life and consciousness eventually appeared much, much later—roughly 12 billion years later—only when conditions on a lump of rock and water circling one of the stars (and perhaps elsewhere) permitted the evolutionary processes to shape dead matter into sufficiently complex forms, such as cells, nervous systems, and brains.* Mind, in the dominant version of this cosmology (modern science), is merely an emergent evolutionary by-product of inert matter—an epiphenomenon.

Our metaphysical assumptions shape the questions we ask, the methodologies we use, the kinds of data we acquire, as well as interpretations of the data on which we evaluate and decide how to act. They, therefore, shape how we relate to the world and have concrete, practical effects. The

---

*Any living biological forms, according to this view, are merely the chance results of "accidental collocations of atoms" that are themselves dead—without any trace of life or consciousness.

foundational assumption, upon which all the others rest, is what we take to be the fundamental nature of the world—our ontology. Do we assume the world to be ultimately made of matter or physical energy (materialism), of mind or spirit (idealism), or of both mind and matter (dualism)? None of these views is satisfactory philosophically, nor adequate to account for the empirical data.

It might be helpful at this stage to make explicit the basic narrative premises (italicized below) of each worldview, and say why I think all are problematic as coherent cosmology stories.

**Dualism:** *Both matter and mind are real, but they are different substances and exist separately.* Dualists claim that consciousness exists independently and separately from matter—that it is a *completely* different kind of "stuff." But if this were the case, we would be left with the unyielding problem of explaining how two mutually alien substances could ever interact. There is no conceivable way that *unextended,* ghostlike mind could ever exert an influence or cause an effect on solid, weighty, extended matter. This, of course, was Descartes's problem, and one that has never been solved. Dualism requires the intervention of a miracle.

**Materialism:** *Only matter or physical energy is ultimately real.* If (as is currently the case) science is anchored in materialism, the problem is to explain how "something" that has no mass, occupies no space, *and has subjectivity* could ever evolve or emerge from something that was massive, spatial, and *wholly* objective to begin with. To achieve this feat—of getting mind from matter, subjectivity from objectivity—would also require a miracle (the kind of miracle philosopher Colin McGinn meant by "turning the water of the physical brain into the wine of consciousness")—an inexplicable ontological jump.

How could sentience and subjectivity *ever* emerge from wholly insentient and objective matter? The standard answer is "complexity." But if you *begin* with purely objective matter, *without the slightest trace of mind or subjectivity,* then no amount or degree of complexity will yield mind or consciousness. It is inconceivable that objectivity could ever give rise to subjectivity or "interiority," that "dead" matter could ever produce matter or minds that *feel.* If the universe is "dead" to start with, it stays dead.

Whereas dualism has been discredited by modern philosophical critiques, materialism has so far managed to evade a similar fate by generating a thick theoretical cloud cover that obscures the profound problems involved in the notion of mind emerging from matter. Materialism defends the paradoxical position that everything real is natural, physical, and objective—including mind, which is undeniably subjective. But in a world made up wholly of objective physical stuff the appearance of subjective mind could not happen naturally. Such emergence would require an inexplicable ontological jump—a miracle. In a purely physical world, the appearance of mind would be a supernatural event.

## The Dream of Idealism

**Idealism:** *Only mind, consciousness, or spirit is ultimately real.* A third major cosmological alternative to scientific materialism and ontological dualism is found in many Eastern religious traditions and as a kind of undercurrent running through the history of Western thought. It is a school of metaphysics known, variously, as "idealism" or the "perennial philosophy." This ontology is hardly given serious attention these days in Western philosophy or science, yet it provides a way to overcome the deep problems with materialism and dualism.

Here, the narrative premise flips materialism upside down and claims that consciousness is primary and universal and that matter is either (a) merely an illusion or (b) an emanation from spirit. According to absolute idealism, the nature of ultimate reality is spirit or pure consciousness, and the world of matter is an illusion, a sort of cosmic dream, what the Hindu tradition calls *maya.*

However, though less problematic philosophically, maya idealism nevertheless poses a major problem pragmatically. We just don't live as though matter is an illusion, and we wouldn't survive very long in the world if we treated all material objects (such as cars on the highway or poisonous substances) as unreal "dream stuff." Interacting with material bodies produces very significant consequences.

Another version, emanationist idealism, is based on what I have identified as a "continuum ontology."[1] Here, the basic narrative premise is that the cosmos is structured according to a hierarchy of ontological levels, from matter, body, mind, soul, to spirit. It is an evolutionary hierarchy where higher levels emerge from and embrace their preceding levels, where matter is a sort of "condensed" physical manifestation or involution of spirit.

Emanationist-idealism is problematic because it runs the risk of reducing spirit to physics: If matter emanates from spirit, *and is real,* then ultimately spirit itself must be, at least partly, intrinsically physical in some way—otherwise, it would amount to a miracle of producing something physical (real matter) from wholly nonphysical being. Believing in such a miracle is no more justified than believing in the materialist's miracle of producing consciousness from matter.

The problem with idealism is logically less severe than with either dualism or materialism, but nonetheless needs to be addressed: If all is spirit, and matter is ultimately illusion or manifestation of spirit, how do we account for the universal, commonsense, and pragmatic supposition of realism—that the world is real in its own right (and not just a concoction of some Cosmic Mind or plurality of lesser minds)? Absolute idealism denies the reality of matter; its aim is transcendent—intended to take us away from living as embodied beings in the world. (Plotinus, a mystical philosopher from the third-century CE, said that matter is closest to "non-being" because it is furthest from spirit.)

All of these cosmologies—dualism, materialism, idealism—at some point need to offer an account of the presence in the world of mind and matter, and of their interrelationship and modes of interaction. As we've just seen, there are profound difficulties with all three. Each of the three major worldviews requires us to accept some form of supernatural intervention into the world of nature.

Thus, if we want to acknowledge that we are embodied conscious beings, embedded in a real embodied world, we need an alternative ontology and cosmology.

## The Fourth Alternative

For decades the key focus of my work in philosophy of mind has been an exploration of this mind-body problem and of various solutions offered from different schools of dualism, materialism, and idealism. The fourth alternative I offer, *radical naturalism,** takes a radically different view of the mind-body relationship. Drawing on ideas from process philosophy—particularly the work of A. N. Whitehead and Henri Bergson—I argue that the major difficulty in the mind-body problem is not so much accounting for the nature of mind or even its interaction with matter (although these remain problematic). The solution to the mind-body problem, I propose, involves a radical revisioning of our understanding of the nature of physical reality. In short, it is not mind that is the problem but rather our limited conception of *matter.*

We need a different starting point for our cosmology story. We need a new narrative premise, a revised ontology, if we are to successfully give an account of the world as it is, a world that contains both objective material bodies and subjective experience/consciousness in intimate relationship.

Radical naturalism (also known variously as "panpsychism" and "panexperientialism") avoids the difficulties of the other three. Like every other ontology, radical naturalism also begins with its own fundamental assumption (or assertion): *"It is inconceivable that sentience (subjectivity, consciousness) could ever emerge or evolve from wholly insentient (objective, physical) matter."* Expressed positively: If consciousness exists now, it must

---

*By "radical naturalism" I mean a view of nature and matter radically different from the standard view in physics and Western philosophy; I mean intrinsically *sentient* nature and matter. The term is appropriate because "radical" comes from the Latin *radix,* meaning "root," the foundation or source of something. Etymologically, "radical" is related to "radial," which means branching out in all directions from a common center or root, and to "radiant," which means, variously, filled with light, shining, sending out rays of light, emanating from a source, manifesting well-being, wholeness, pleasure, or love. "Radical nature," therefore, implies nature that is sentient to its roots, composed of matter that *feels* something of the nature of wholeness and love all the way down to its ontological roots, and that radiates, or moves itself, from the depths of its own being. Teilhard de Chardin suggested something similar in his concept of "radial energy," which he proposed was the *interior* source of universal attraction and love between all elements of the cosmos, pulling them toward increased complexity (contrasted with "tangential energy," the energy physicists work with, pulling in the direction of entropy). When scientists or philosophers say that the only kind of matter or energy that exists is wholly insentient physical stuff, I refer to that ontology as "absolute materialism."

always have existed in some form. Similarly, if matter exists and is real now, it must always have existed in some form.

I will argue here that the assumption of consciousness and matter as coextensive and coeternal is the most adequate "postmodern" solution to the question of consciousness in the physical world. Where materialism, idealism, and dualism fall short as adequate ontologies for a science of consciousness, radical naturalism provides a coherent foundation. The central tenet of radical naturalism is that *matter is intrinsically sentient—*it is both subjective and objective. Radical naturalism confronts head-on the essential paradox of consciousness: We exist as embodied subjects—as *subjective objects* or feeling matter. We know consciousness only as embodied beings, yet we know it not as body or matter. It is simultaneously our most intimate reality and our deepest mystery.

In this alternative view, matter and consciousness are not separate "substances" but co-eternal, mutually complementary, realities. *Matter and psyche always go together—*all the way down. In Whitehead's ontology, the basic ingredients of the world, whether atoms or quanta, are essentially "experiential events," "moments of experience." Matter-energy, then, is the form that reality takes in response to the in-forming activity of psyche or consciousness. And this in-forming is intrinsic to matter; it is matter's own *interiority—*its self-shaping dynamics. Some neo-Confucianist Chinese philosophers recognized this complementarity in medieval times in their concepts of *ch'i* (matter-energy) and *li* (organizing principle). In recent years much "new paradigm" literature has focused on the borrowed concept of *ch'i,* but its authors have typically ignored the other essential half: the *li* that is necessarily interior to *ch'i.* Radical naturalism aims to restore the balance by focusing on the intrinsic self-organizing dynamic (*li*) of matter (*ch'i*).*

Radical naturalism provides a foundation for a new science of consciousness and matter—or consciousness-within-matter—and a way out of the philosophical, scientific, and psychological impasse familiar to us as the Cartesian "mind-body split." The underlying motivation for the thesis of radical naturalism is to explore how an assumption of intrinsi-

---

*See chapter 10, "Stories Matter, Matter Stories."

cally sentient matter would restore a sense of sacredness to the human body, the body of the Earth, and the cosmic body of the universe—by recognizing that consciousness, or spirit, is intimately and always the interior dynamic of matter throughout its long evolutionary journey. In the following chapters, I will look at some of the cosmological implications of radical naturalism.

But before we can continue our exploration of radical naturalism, we need to be clear about what we mean by key words such as "consciousness," "energy," and "matter." In the next chapter, I tackle this issue head-on by asking, "Is consciousness a form of energy?"

# PART II

# OPTIONS

## CLASHING WORLDVIEWS

# 4

Meanings

# LANGUAGE, ENERGY, AND CONSCIOUSNESS

New Age holistic-spiritual metaphysicians and materialist-reductionists make strange bedfellows. Nevertheless, when it comes to talking about consciousness, both turn to concepts and images derived from physics. Materialists claim that consciousness is ultimately "nothing but" a form of matter-energy; New Agers often talk of consciousness or spirit in terms of "vibrations," "waves," "fields," and so on, as though it were a form of subtle energy.

At least the materialists are consistent. Since, according to them, everything is physical, it makes sense to talk of consciousness in terms of energy. But the New Agers, it seems, are muddled and confused. They want it both ways: On the one hand, they claim that ultimate reality is spirit or consciousness (meaning distinct from matter), yet on the other hand they want to describe consciousness in the language of physics—using "energy talk."[1] The problem with both materialists and New Agers is that they are trapped in the "strange attractor" of conceiving the world in terms of spatial-kinesthetic (i.e., mechanical) metaphors. To advance in our understanding of mind and how it relates to matter, I propose that consciousness talk needs to shift from using mechanistic metaphors to meaning metaphors and from "space talk" to "time talk," derived from our direct experience of consciousness itself.

# A Bias in Our Language

"We are hanging in language. We are suspended in language in such a way that we cannot say what is up and what is down," Niels Bohr lamented in the 1920s when confronted with the paradoxes, absurdities, and seeming impossibilities encountered in the then newly discovered quantum domain. The problem, he insisted, was not the quantum wonderland itself, but our language, our ways of thinking and talking about it. His colleague Werner Heisenberg went a step further and proclaimed that events in the quantum wonderland are not only unspeakable, they are *unimaginable.*

The same situation confronts us today when we try to talk about consciousness and how it relates to matter-energy. Go fishing for consciousness using the net of language and it always, inevitably, slips through the holes in our net.

Recognizing the limits of language—and of *imagination*—in talk about consciousness opens up a crucially important issue for philosophy of mind and for a science of consciousness. I believe the "energy question"—and the language we use—is central to any significant advance we may make into understanding consciousness and how it relates to the physical world.

A major challenge facing philosophers and scientists of consciousness (and anybody else who wishes to talk about it) is finding appropriate concepts, words, and metaphors. So much of our language is derived from our two most dominant senses: vision and touch. Vision feeds language with spatial metaphors, whereas touch—or rather, kinesthetics—feeds language with muscular push-pull metaphors. The visuo-muscular senses dominate our perception and interaction with the world, and consequently metaphors derived from these senses dominate our ways of conceiving and talking about the world. It is no accident that spatial and mechanical descriptions and explanations predominate in physics—the paradigm science (and our culture's paradigm for all knowledge). Given our evolutionary heritage, with its selective bias toward vision and kinesthetics, we live predominantly in a spatial push-pull world—the world of classical mechanics, a "billiard-ball" universe of moving, colliding, and recoiling massive bodies. Ours is a world of matter in motion, of things in space acted on by physical forces.

It should not be surprising, then, that when we come to talk about consciousness our grooves of thinking channel us toward physics talk— expressed today as "energy talk." Forces are *felt*—experienced in the body—and we are tempted to think that the *experience* of force is identical to the energy exchanges between bodies described by physics. But this is to confuse *the feeler's feeling* (the subject) with what is *felt* (the object).

The "language problem" is at least as old as Descartes's mind-body dualism. When the French philosopher made his famous distinction between mind and matter, he found himself "suspended in the language" of physics. He could find no better way to define mind than negatively in the terminology of physics. He defined matter as that which *occupies space—res extensa*, "extended things." He defined the mental world as *res cogitans*, "thinking things"—and thinking things differ from physical things in that they do *not occupy space*. The problem was how could material, physical things interact with nonphysical things? What conceivably could be the nature of their point of contact—material or mental? Centuries later, Freud, too, resorted to physics-energy talk when describing the "mechanisms" and dynamics of the psyche—for example, his concept of the libido. Today the same tendency to use energy talk is rife in much New Age dialogue about consciousness, soul, and spirit.

Because of our reliance on the senses of vision and kinesthetics, we have an evolutionary predisposition, it seems, to talk in the language of physics or mechanics. Yet all such talk seems to miss something essential when we come to speak of phenomena in the domain of the mind—for example, emotions, desires, beliefs, pains, and other *felt* qualities of consciousness. The inappropriate clunkiness of mechanistic metaphors borrowed from classical physics seems obvious enough. The mind just isn't at all like matter or machines, as Descartes was keenly aware.

But then came Einstein's relativity, followed by the quantum revolution. First, Einstein's $E = mc^2$ showed that matter was a form of energy, and so, with the advent of quantum theory, the material world began to dissolve into unimaginable, paradoxical bundles of energy or action. Matter itself was now understood to be ghostly swirls of energy and began to take on qualities formerly associated with mind. A great physicist, Sir James Jeans, even declared that, "The universe begins to look more and more like a great thought." Quantum events were so tiny, so undetermined, so *un-mechanical* in the classical sense, they seemed just the sort of thing that could respond to the influence of the mind.

The quantum-consciousness connection was boosted further by the need (at least in one interpretation of quantum theory) to include the observer (and his or her consciousness) in any complete description of the collapse of the quantum wave function (which describes the event where actual reality emerges from the domain of quantum possibilities). According to this view, the quantum system *must* include the consciousness of the observer for the "collapse" from possibilities to actuality to take place.

Together with ghostly energy fields from relativity, the quantum-consciousness connection triggered the imaginations of pop-science writers and dabblers in New Age pseudo-science: Shelves of books invoke the mysteries of the quantum as the latest explanation for age-old questions about consciousness. Quantum theory, many believe, has finally opened the way for science to explore and talk about the mind.

But the excitement was—and is—premature. It involves a linguistic and conceptual sleight-of-hand. Whereas the clunky classical mechanical language of matter was obviously at best *metaphorical* when applied to consciousness, it now seemed more reasonable to use the language of energy *literally*—particularly if cloaked in the "spooky" garb of quantum physics. But this shift from "metaphorical matter" to "literal energy" was unwarranted, unfounded, and deceptive.

## The Challenge of Subjectivity

Dissolving matter into energy makes neither of them any less *physical*. And the mark of the physical, as Descartes had pointed out, is that it is extended in space. Despite the insuperable problems with his dualism, Descartes's key insight remains valid: What distinguishes mind from matter is precisely that it *does not occupy space*. And this distinction holds just as fast between mind and energy—even so-called subtle energy (hypothetical "subtle energy" bodies are described as having extension and other spatial attributes such as waves, vibrations, and frequencies). Energy, even in the form of infinitesimal quanta or "subtle vibrations," still occupies space. And any theory of energy as a field clearly makes it spatial. Notions of "quantum consciousness," "field consciousness," or "vibrations," "ripples," or "waves" of consciousness, therefore, are little more than vacuous jargon because they continue to fail to address the very distinction that Descartes formulated nearly four hundred years ago.

But that's not even the most troublesome deficiency of energy talk. Even supposing physicists were able to show that quanta of energy did not occupy space; suppose the behavior of quanta was so bizarre that they could do all sorts of "un-physical" things, such as transcend space and time; even if it could be shown that quanta were not "physical" in Descartes's sense . . . even supposing all of this, any proposed identity between energy and consciousness would still be invalid.

Energy talk fails to account for what is fundamentally most characteristic about consciousness, namely its *subjectivity*. No matter how fine-grained or "subtle" energy could become, as an objective phenomenon it could *never* account for the fact of subjectivity—the "what-it-feels-like-from-within-experience." Ontologically, subjectivity just cannot emerge from wholly objective reality. (As a card-carrying panpsychist, I want to wear a T-shirt or use a bumper-sticker that says, NO ONTOLOGICAL FREE LUNCHES!) Unless energy, at its ontologically most fundamental level, *already* came with some form of protoconsciousness, protoexperience, or protosubjectivity, consciousness, experience, or subjectivity would *never* emerge or evolve in the universe.

## Metaphors of Meaning

Although our language is biased toward physics-energy talk, full of mechanistic metaphors, this is clearly not the whole story. The vernacular of the marketplace, as well as the language of science, is also rich with non-mechanistic metaphors, metaphors that flow directly from experience itself. Ironically, not only do we apply these consciousness metaphors to the mind and mental events, but we apply them also to the world of matter in our attempts to understand its deeper complexities and dynamics. For example, systems theory and evolutionary biology—even at the reductionist level of molecular genetics—are replete with words such as "codes," "information," "meaning," "self-organizing," and "function," which is code for the p-word: purpose.

So we are not limited to mechanistic metaphors when describing either the world of matter or the world of mind. But—and this is the important point—because of our bias toward visuo-muscular images, we tend to forget that metaphors of the mind are *sui generis,* and, because of our scientific and philosophical bias in favor of mechanism, we often attempt *to reduce metaphors of the mind to metaphors of matter.*

My proposal for consciousness talk is this: Recognize the limitations of mechanistic metaphors, and the inappropriateness of literal energy talk, when discussing consciousness. Instead, acknowledge the richness and appropriateness of metaphors of meaning when talking about the mind. Drop mechanistic metaphors (energy talk) and take up meaning metaphors (consciousness talk) when talking about consciousness.

Let's look at this more closely.

## Why Consciousness is Not Energy

If you tune into someone's "vibrations," are you picking up some form of energy they are emitting—perhaps something we might call "psychic energy"?

It may be tempting to think so—to think of consciousness as a form of energy. But is it? What might be going on when we say we feel someone's vibrations?

Well, one possibility is that their brain or their body could be sending out waves of energy—something, perhaps, like electricity. If so, it must be far more subtle than any form of energy known to modern science, because no physical instrument yet devised has detected any such energy.

But even if the vibrations were subtle energy waves they would still be *physical,* because they pass through space. Anything that moves through space must be *located* somewhere in space. And anything that is located in space can be measured. That's what "physical" means: It occupies space. It is objective. It can be measured.

But no one has ever measured consciousness. No one has ever been able to pinpoint it in space. If they had, questions such as these would make sense: "How big is consciousness (or any of its contents, such as a thought, a feeling, or a desire) . . . is it an inch, a foot, a mile, a light-year?" or "Where exactly is consciousness?" But such questions baffle us.

Even though it is absurd to talk about the "size" of consciousness, some people may not think it so strange to say that consciousness (and its contents) is located somewhere in the brain. But where? No one has ever succeeded in finding any part of the brain (large or small) where consciousness is. Yes, it certainly seems to be associated, or *correlated,* with the brain—but it is not *in* the brain (not in the way your brain is inside your skull). Consciousness has a completely different kind of interiority.

So if consciousness has no size and has no location, what does it mean to say it is in space? And if it is not in space, what does it mean to say it is a form of energy?

Maybe, then, consciousness is a form of *non*physical energy? If that is the case, how are consciousness and energy related? We have three options:

1. **Consciousness is a physical form of energy** (even if it is very, very subtle energy). If we say that consciousness is a form of energy that is physical, then we are reducing consciousness (and spirit) to physics. And few of us, unless we are materialists, want to do that.

2. **Consciousness is a nonphysical form of energy.** If we say that consciousness is a form of energy that is not physical, then we need to say in what way psychic energy differs from physical energy. If we cannot explain what we mean by "psychic energy" and how it differs from physical energy, then we should ask ourselves why use the term "energy" at all?

3. **Consciousness isn't any form of energy.** Our third alternative is to say that consciousness is not a form of energy at all—either physical or nonphysical. Unlike energy, which is some kind of "stuff" that spreads out in space, consciousness isn't made of stuff and is not located in space. If this is true, then consciousness would not only be different from energy, it would be *nonlocated.*

This is not to imply that consciousness has nothing to do with energy. In fact, according to panpsychism or radical naturalism, consciousness and energy always go together. They cannot ever be separated. But this is not to say they are not distinct. They are distinct—energy is energy, consciousness is consciousness—but they are inseparable (like two sides of a coin or, better, like the shape and substance of a tennis ball. You can't separate the shape from the substance of the ball, but shape and substance are definitely distinct).

So, for example, some spiritual traditions talk of kundalini experience, where a meditator may feel a rush of energy up the chakra system . . . but to say that such energy flow is consciousness is to mistake the object (energy flow) for the subject, for what perceives (consciousness) the object. Note the two importantly distinct words in the phrase "feel the rush of energy . . . " On the one hand there is the "feeling" or a "knowing," on the other, there is what is being felt or experienced (the energy). Even our way of talking about it reveals that we detect a distinction between feeling (consciousness) and what we feel (energy). Yes, the two go together, but they are not the same. Unity, or unification, or holism does not equal identity. To say that one aspect of reality (consciousness) cannot be separated from another aspect of reality (matter-energy) is not to say both aspects of reality (consciousness and matter-energy) are identical.

Simply stated: *Consciousness knows. Energy flows.*

Consciousness is the "witness" that experiences the flow of energy, but it is not the flow of energy. We could say consciousness is the *felt interiority* of energy/matter. To grasp this experientially you might take a moment to pay attention to what's going on in your own body right now. The physical matter of your body—including the flow of whatever energies are pulsing through you—is the "stuff" of your organism. But there is also a part of you that is aware of, or feels, the pumping of your blood (and other energy streams). That aspect of you that feels the matter-energy in your body is your consciousness.

We could express it this way: "Consciousness is the process of matter-energy informing itself." Consciousness is the ability that matter-energy has to feel, to know, and to direct itself. The universe could be (and probably is) full of energy flows, vortices, and vibrations, but without consciousness all this activity would be completely unfelt and unknown. Only because there is consciousness can the flow of energy be felt, known, and purposefully directed.

While I'm on the topic, I want to clarify another important, increasingly common misunderstanding about the nature of consciousness based on ideas imported from physics.

## Consciousness: Nonlocal or Nonlocated?

If consciousness does not occupy space, are we justified in calling it "nonlocal"? Certainly we may say it is "nonspatial," but this is not quite the same as saying it is "nonlocal" in the sense used in quantum physics. In quantum physics nonlocality refers to a measurement of correlated behavior of two quantum events separated in space in such a way that there is no possibility of a light signal passing between them (in a given time). Therefore there cannot be any energetic causal connection between them, even though the behavior of one event is experimentally demonstrated to be clearly associated with the behavior of the other.

"Nonlocality" in quantum physics refers to an effect *separated in space* from a correlated event that seems to act as cause. But since such correlations cannot be accounted for by any exchange of energy or information, the coupling of the "effect" with the "cause" confronts us with the conundrum of "action-at-a-distance." How can something "here" affect another thing over "there" if there is no possible medium connecting them? Physicists call this phenomenon "nonlocality" because the effect takes place in a region of space energetically and informationally separated from the apparent cause.

The effect is nonlocal in the sense that it occurs beyond the space-time cone of the apparent cause. If all effects and their related causes must be located within the same space-time cone (i.e., they occur in the same "local" space-time region), then by extension, any effect that occurs beyond the space-time cone of its purported cause must be "nonlocal." Of course, both the "effect" and the "cause" are "local" to their own respective space-time regions. Both are located in space—but in energetically *isolated* regions of space. Thus, "nonlocal" means isolated regions of space-time. It does not mean "nonspatial."

This is very different from the kind of "nonlocality" we attribute phenomenologically to consciousness. Consciousness does not occur in any region of space-time isolated from any other space-time region. It is not merely nonlocal in the physical sense, it is *nonlocated*—it is not located anywhere in space at all. It is nonspatial.

However, if we still choose to talk of "nonlocal" (rather than "nonlocated") consciousness or intelligence, it would be inconsistent to then speak of consciousness permeating space and time as a field. How can something that is either nonlocal or nonspatial permeate anything? It is not that consciousness permeates space like a field, but, as just noted, it is simply *not located anywhere in space at all.* This is why the metaphor of "field" is misleading when applied to mind or consciousness.

Yet it is experimentally true (according to a series of intriguing experiments described by psi researcher Dean Radin in *The Conscious Universe*) that consciousness associated with matter located at one region of space appears to affect matter located at some distant location in space and that consciousness associated with groups of people spread out in space appears to affect the behavior of matter some distance away. This certainly looks like "consciousness spread out in space" or "field consciousness." But actually all the data reveal is that the (inferred) state of mind of a group of people in one (or multiple) location(s) is correlated with the behavior of distant or "nonlocal" matter (in this case, random number generators). It is a leap of faith or imagination to assume that the nonlocal effect is "caused" by consciousness rippling through space like undulations in a field.

That there is an effect at-a-distance is clearly suggested by the data; and since similar effects are accounted for in physics by, for example, electromagnetic or gravitational fields, we may be tempted to assume that the at-a-distance effects correlated between consciousness at one (or multiple) location(s) and some physically unconnected, distant location must also be a "field." But this would imply that consciousness spreads itself out in space—which is incompatible with phenomenological and empirical data. Perhaps the most we can do is use "field" as a metaphor and talk of "fieldlike" effects of consciousness—but not of literal "consciousness fields."

My own guess is that if there is any relationship at all between *non-local* quantum events and *nonlocated* consciousness events, and between the notion of "quantum field potential" and "field consciousness," it has far more to do with the nature of time and probabilities than with space. So-called quantum fields are not actually fields in any spatial sense. They are abstract mathematical descriptions of matrices of probabilities (of tendencies for certain events to occur). It is only the *representations* of such probabilities that take on the characteristics of fields. Probabilistic events, as tendencies of events to occur, are temporal—perhaps even psychological. In the end, statements of probability are statements about psychological expectations.

As a temporal, and not a spatial, phenomenon, consciousness may, perhaps, in some highly mysterious way, affect the probabilities of some physical events. The key phrase, as far as theory and explanation go, is the throwaway "in some highly mysterious way"—how this mind-matter interaction *could* occur is at the heart of the perennial mind-body problem in philosophy. All we have are anomalous data; we have no coherent theory to account for them—unless, following A. N. Whitehead, we take the radical step of shifting from "space-talk" to "time-talk," recognizing that both the ontological nature of and relationship between consciousness and matter grow out of *process* rather than substance.*

But if consciousness is not an energy field, what is it? In the rest of this chapter, I will examine more closely different uses and meanings of consciousness. I will also look at what consciousness is not—such as "matter," "energy," and "information." By becoming familiar with the meanings of these words, we should come to a clearer and more coherent understanding of the kinds of pitfalls and dead-ends we are likely to meet in our excursions into philosophy of mind and toward a science of consciousness.

---

*I return to this point later in chapter 9, "Past Matter, Present Mind."

I'll begin with "consciousness." Since it is *the* key concept in this study, I will devote more attention to it than to the other terms and approach understanding it from a variety of perspectives.

## Consciousness

Consciousness is notoriously difficult to define. It is paradoxically our deepest mystery and our most intimate reality. Debates in philosophy and psychology frequently run aground in confusion because participants use the word "consciousness" with different meanings.

In my experience the most common misunderstanding arises from a basic confusion between *philosophical* and *psychological* uses of the term. I find it helpful, therefore, to distinguish between two basic meanings:

**Philosophical Consciousness.** Philosophically, consciousness is a *state* or *quality of being* with a capacity for *sentience* and *subjectivity*. It is contrasted with being "nonconscious," a state of affairs wholly without sentience or subjectivity. For example, a person (awake or asleep), a dog, or a worm would exemplify consciousness in this sense; a rock, a cloud, or a computer would not. Philosophical consciousness is about the *context* of consciousness; it is about the *mode of being* that makes possible any and all contents of consciousness.

**Psychological Consciousness.** Psychologically, consciousness is a *state of awareness* characterized by being awake or alert and is contrasted with the "unconscious," a state of being asleep, or with psychic contents below the threshold of conscious-awake awareness. For example, a person engaged in conceptual cognition would be conscious in this sense; a person in a coma, or a worm, would be examples of being unconscious. Psychological consciousness is about the *contents* of consciousness and about the *mode of access* (conscious or unconscious) to these contents.

Looked at this way, it is clear that the philosophical meaning is more fundamental—for without consciousness as a state of being (i.e., an ontological reality) there could be no psychological states or contents. Even the psychological unconscious has something psychic or mental going on. To be unconscious is still to be sentient (worms and sleeping people still feel), whereas to be nonconscious is not (rocks and computers do not feel).*

This initial distinction between the psychological and philosophical meanings of consciousness is important. But no matter how fine we make our distinctions, consciousness may inevitably and finally resist definition because of its self-recursive nature: We need consciousness to define consciousness. Such a move runs all the logical and semantic risks of infinite regress in Gödelian loops and tangled hierarchies. When we try to define consciousness we become like one of those figures walking on a paradoxical Escher stairway: While it seems we are always going down, we end up back where we began.

There is another aspect to this difficulty: By definition, "definition" means to delimit, outline, circumscribe, put a boundary around, and to "fix"—as in photographic development. In other words, to define something is to freeze it in a moment, to suck it out of time, to abstract it.

We may aim to be precise in our definitions, but in the process we lose the dynamic, organic character of language and thinking. As David Bohm pointed out, there is a world of difference between "thinking" and "thought." Thoughts, concepts, and words are the dregs of experience. They are the abstracted skeletons of the living, concrete experiences that express themselves in consciousness. To define consciousness, then, is to single out a certain aspect of it, to wrap it up in a symbol, and close out

_____

*I'm aware that some people will want to challenge the idea that rocks (or computers, or even thermostats, beer cans, tables, chairs, cigarettes, and so forth) are not conscious. My purpose here is not to declare which bodies of matter do or do not *in fact* possess consciousness, but to make use of what are generally taken to be paradigm cases of nonconsciousness in order to emphasize an ontological point. Most (though certainly not all) people I know regard rocks as inert, insentient, nonconscious lumps of matter. *If* that is indeed the case, then rocks serve as a paradigm case of nonconscious matter as distinct from organisms that do possess consciousness.

Whether or not *in actual fact* rocks (computers, etc.) do have consciousness is a *scientific* question, to be decided if and when science ever develops to the stage of actually detecting evidence for the presence of consciousness. The *philosophical* issue remains unchanged whether or not rocks (or computers or any other entity) are conscious: Consciousness in the philosophical, ontological sense is contrasted with whatever does not have even the slightest trace of interiority, sentience, subjectivity, experience, or consciousness. For the sake of argument, I've used rocks.

the multiplicity of meanings that inhere in the direct experience of the phenomenon itself.

Yet without some clarity and agreement in terminology—especially in the field of philosophy of mind—we run a great risk of thinking and talking past each other.* The word "consciousness" is used in many different ways in philosophy, in science, in psychology, in spirituality, and in common discourse. No one usage is necessarily right or better than another, though within a particular model a particular definition of "consciousness" may help give the model clarity and consistency.

For the purposes of this book I will adopt a broad meaning of consciousness based on the following:

## CHARACTERISTICS OF CONSCIOUSNESS

When trying to decide whether or not some entity has consciousness, what kinds of evidence should we look for? In other words, what kinds of attributes characterize consciousness and distinguish it from nonconscious entities? If some creature has consciousness it will be capable of the following (a nonconscious entity will lack all of these):

1. **sentience/feeling** (capacity to experience)
2. **subjectivity** (capacity for experienced interiority; for having a unique and privileged point of view)
3. **knowledge** (capacity for knowing anything)
4. **intentionality** (ability to point at, or be about something else)
5. **choice** (capacity to create "first cause"; to move itself internally)
6. **self-agency** (capacity to orient and/or move itself externally)
7. **purpose** (capacity to aim at a goal)
8. **meaning** (capacity to be intrinsically "for-itself")
9. **value** (capacity for intrinsic worth)

To be a creature with consciousness means to be a creature that possesses any or all of these characteristics. Notice that none of these characteristics is amenable to mechanistic reduction, measurement, or objective

---

*See, for example, chapter 8, "Panexperientialism."

description. Consciousness, therefore, is a phenomenon beyond discourse in terms of "energy."

Consciousness encompasses all experience—all sentience, all feeling, subjectivity, all interiority—the "within" of things, as Teilhard de Chardin poetically expressed it;[2] the "whatitfeelslike from within," as Thomas Nagel put it. It is whatever endows an entity, being, or thing with the ability to "prehend," to take into itself, the essence of what it experiences.[3]

Consciousness, in this sense, is primitive, primordial, and cosmic; it is the dynamic substratum of all mental or psychic phenomena. As it includes both conscious and unconscious awareness, it is explicitly distinct from either "the conscious" or "the unconscious" as used in Freudian and Jungian, and many other, psychologies.

As used here consciousness is evolutionary and may (and does) evolve from more primitive to higher states of consciousness. Although different qualities or states of (psychological) consciousness may evolve or emerge as nervous systems and brains evolve, (philosophical) consciousness, as such, is not an emergent phenomenon. It is ontologically prior to the material and biological complexity of nervous systems and brains.

Whenever we speak or write about "consciousness," therefore, it helps if we are clear about what we mean: Do we mean the *state* of awareness contrasted with being unconscious (psychological meaning), or do we mean the *fact* of awareness contrasted with the complete absence of any mental activity whatsoever (philosophical meaning)?

## A THING OR A PROCESS?

The difficulties in defining consciousness have been recognized by philosophers for a long time. For Descartes, in the seventeenth century, as we have seen, consciousness was a *thing*—a thinking substance. In contrast, when William James (1842–1910) asked in an essay, "Does consciousness exist?" he concluded that it didn't. He didn't mean that it was just a fiction or illusion—as behaviorists and eliminativists were to claim later on—but that it didn't exist as a *thing*. For James, consciousness was not a noun; it was more like a verb. In fact, James defined consciousness in different ways depending on whether he was wearing his philosopher's or his psychologist's hat. Perhaps his most famous metaphor is what he called the "stream of thought." For James, consciousness was a *process*.

If great philosophers like Descartes and James could not agree on a definition of consciousness, there's probably little chance that we would do any better. But even if we can't come up with a definition, we can still get clearer on what we mean—at least to establish that we are more or less talking about the same "thing" (or process, or whatever).

In *Cultivating Consciousness,* Ramakrishna Rao examined a variety of ways the word "consciousness" is used in philosophy and psychology, and he cited the great American philosopher John Dewey to the effect that consciousness "can neither be defined nor described." How, then, can we usefully employ the term, and how can we decide among the many different ways the word is used?

As Rao pointed out, consciousness is perhaps the most fitting description of the human condition, and it would be a shame if we didn't understand what consciousness is.[4] Yet, in a way, we all know what consciousness is—it is the one thing we know directly in our subjective experience. But it is a phenomenon we find difficult to deal with intellectually. It may be useful, therefore, to spend time exploring some of the varieties of ways "consciousness" and allied terms are used.

Rao immediately draws attention to one of the paradoxes inherent in how we use the word "consciousness" in the West. For instance, besides meaning many different things, it also includes its own negation. He explains: Following Freud, we are now familiar with the psychodynamic model that includes the nonconscious, the preconscious, and the unconscious. According to Freud and his successors, we must include these aspects of the psyche as part of our understanding of mental life. (Clearly, as an aspect of the psyche, the Freudian "nonconscious" cannot be equated with wholly insentient, wholly nonsubjective, and nonexperiential ontological nonconsciousness. Freudian "nonconscious," as we will see, refers to a form of psychic apprehension so dim, so beyond the fringe of awareness, it hardly even qualifies as awareness—nevertheless, as an aspect of the psyche, it must involve some trace, even if minimal, of ontological consciousness, sentience, or subjectivity.)

## FRINGE AND FOCUS AWARENESS

Philosopher Thomas Natsoulas identified seven distinct meanings for "consciousness" given in the *Oxford English Dictionary*—all of which defined consciousness by reference to *awareness*. Perhaps, then, awareness may be what lies behind the multitude of different meanings of consciousness?

However, awareness is itself an ambiguous concept. For example, right now as I write I'm aware that I'm sitting in front of my computer. I'm also aware that there are frogs croaking in the fog outside. But before I wrote that last sentence, I wasn't *consciously aware* of the frogs or of anything else going on outside. It is only now, especially because they have *stopped* croaking, that I am focusing my awareness on them.

I have here distinguished between the *focus* of my conscious attention and the periphery of my attention. If I so choose, I can shift or expand the focus of my attention to include what was a moment ago on the periphery. Events on the periphery of my attention are accessible to my consciousness even when they are subliminal. In other words, there is a *fringe* as well as *focus* to my consciousness.

Furthermore, something may have happened in my vicinity without my conscious awareness, and if someone later pointed it out I would still be unable to recall it. It was not an event that entered either my (recallable) fringe or focus awareness. Yet that same person could point out that at the time of the event (say, for instance, somebody had mentioned my name) a shift in my behavior or body posture might have indicated that I had indeed somehow detected the event. Such "awareness" is beyond my ability to recall, report, or recognize even if I want to. It is not something I can choose to attend to. Although detected somewhere in my system, it remains beyond conscious awareness.

In other words, *if consciousness is awareness, awareness can be "conscious" or "unconscious"*—some scholars even talk of *"nonconscious awareness."* See how easy it is to get into difficulties with this terminology? Part of the problem, as I've tried to show, is that there are two basic ways of talking about consciousness: philosophically and psychologically. In this book I focus on the philosophical meaning—that is, "context consciousness"—*consciousness as a quality of being.* By this I mean: any entity, any actuality, any region of reality that includes *sentience,* *subjectivity,* and *self-agency*—three key characteristics of consciousness. Sentience refers to an ability to *feel* anything; to be aware of, however dimly, anything either within or beyond the locus of sentience.* Subjectivity refers to having a first-person point of view—a perspective from which anything "seems like" something, a *phenomenon.* And self-agency

---

*The phrase "locus of sentience"—and similar phrases such as "center of experience," "center of feeling," and "node of subjectivity"—reveal one of the hard knots in philosophy of mind: What is the relationship between consciousness and space? For if, following Descartes, we assume that consciousness is defined as something that does not occupy space, how, then, can we meaningfully talk of a "locus," "center," or "node" of sentience, subjectivity, or experience? How can a mind without spatial extension have or be a center? How can it be a locus without being *located?* The dilemma deepens if we say we use "locus" or "center" metaphorically—that consciousness (sentience, experience, or subjectivity) doesn't *really* have a locus in any spatial sense. For then, how do we distinguish between feelings in different subjects? Clearly, the pain I feel is located where my organism is, not over there where you are. We are never confused about each other's pains (or any other qualia).

So it certainly *seems* as though consciousness can have a location. But this would mean it is in space, and this in turn would mean it has extension—in other words, it would be *physical.* But how can consciousness—characterized by sentience, subjectivity, and self-agency—be physical? How can something physical possess sentience, subjectivity, and self-agency?

The alternative seems to be Cartesian dualism: Separate realities, one of which is spatial (physical) and another that is extra-spatial (mental). But this raises the hoary problem of interaction: How can something nonspatial (mind) interact with something extended in space (matter)?

The solution proposed in this book is that Descartes was wrong to *separate* mind and matter, when in fact they are inseparable. According to the position developed here, while it is true to say that consciousness is nonspatial, and therefore nonlocated, it is *always* associated with some body (some form of energy or matter) that *is* located in space. And because of this inseparable association between mind and body, we can meaningfully talk of particular instances of consciousness (the subject that is me, for instance) associated with a particular body or organism in a particular region of space.

A "locus" of sentience or subjectivity, therefore, refers to an occasion of experience associated with a particular organism. The organism, the body, is located in space, while its experience or consciousness is not. An analogy would be the relationship between numbers and things. For instance, we could point to two cows over there in the field, knowing that the number two itself is not located in the field. Numbers are nonspatial, yet they may be coupled with things in space (in fact, that's precisely what measurement is). The central issue is, of course, just what is the nature of the "coupling," the "association," between consciousness and matter, between mind and body? As we will see later, this relationship has more to do with time than with space.

refers to an ability to *choose,* to move or direct the self in a chosen direction.

All three characteristics of consciousness—sentience, subjectivity, and self-agency—are deeply interrelated and mutually implicated. For instance, ontologically, the presence of feeling anywhere in the world implies a subject who is the locus or center of the feeling. Sentience *requires* subjectivity. There are no disembodied, generalized feelings just floating around out there without ownership. Sentience always *belongs* to some subject. Similarly, to be a subject implies being a center of sentience. To be a locus for a point of view means the subject must be able to feel, or "prehend," whatever seems or shows up for it as a phenomenon. And, as we will see in chapter 9, "Past Matter, Present Mind," being a subject, being a center of sentience, involves a creative act of choice—an ability to select among an indefinite number of options streaming in from the past that will become constitutive of the self in the present moment.

It is this last aspect of consciousness—its creative self-agency—that underlies, I believe, the impulse to describe consciousness as a form of energy. For to be a self-mover, to initiate *tele*-motion—that is, directed, purposeful motion as distinct from determined mechanical locomotion—means an ability to move through space as *first-cause.* Self-agency, the source of free will, means making a creative choice between available options. When the options involve choosing between directions or locations in space, self-agency necessarily involves moving a *body*—for only bodies (that is, regions of matter or energy) are located in and can move through space.

But it is not the mind or consciousness that is moving through space. It is the body, the matter-energy. Consciousness is the *act,* or creative choice, that impels or directs the body in its motions. The subject creatively selects (feels or prehends) those objects from its immediate past that constitute the self in the present. But the self (as a mind-body unity) is not wholly constituted by the objective matter-energy it has selected to form its body. Always, and necessarily, the self includes—*in the moment*— a creative "spark" or "quantum," the source of its freedom and originality. *This* is its consciousness.

I will return to the relationship between consciousness, self-agency, and time in later chapters. I'd like now to look at the other side of the coin, and discuss the meanings of physical concepts such as "matter" and "energy," as well as some other key ideas related to consciousness.

## Matter

Next to "consciousness," perhaps the most difficult term to define is "matter." Just as we tend to assume we know what consciousness is—because we know what it is to be conscious—we tend to assume that we know what matter is because we inhabit a material body, and are in daily contact with multiple forms of matter. However, to know what it is to be conscious does not mean we know what consciousness is (see above: being conscious is just a special case of consciousness). What consciousness is beyond our own conscious awareness—what its nature is apart from its contents—remains a mystery to us (some mystics excepted, perhaps).

Similarly, just because we are familiar with numerous instances or forms of matter does not mean we know what its intrinsic nature is—apart from its appearances. The mystery of matter has intrigued and challenged philosophers from Aristotle to Kant, and today in science it is shrouded behind the impenetrable veil of the quantum uncertainty principle. Matter, under the gaze of physicists, has dissolved into ghostly swirling packets of energy and fields of force, of "no-things," with immense regions of nothingness in between. Both matter and mind, then, are fundamentally mysterious in themselves, so it should be no surprise that their interaction is a complete puzzle.

Both David Ray Griffin and Steven Rosen have pointed out that the critical question in the mind-body problem is not, as is usually thought, so much the nature of mind—it is *matter* that is problematical. We don't know what matter is any more than we know what mind is; though we tend to think we do. The problem, as we might expect by now, lies with Descartes's definition. He defined mind negatively in terms of matter as that which does not occupy space; and he defined matter negatively in terms of mind as that which is insentient. In other words, not only could nonspatial mind never communicate with spatial matter, the entire natural world of matter was forever alienated from sentient mind. By itself, matter was dead, capable of nothing but random mechanical movements.

Our modern conception of matter inherits this notion of inert substance. By itself matter has no intrinsic motion; it requires external forces, such as the collision of particles or the action of fields. Yet, following Einstein, we now know that matter is essentially energetic. But we are still asked to think of this dynamism as extrinsic, as something that happens to matter-energy through external forces.

Matter is the stuff of our bodies and of the world around us. We live in it, eat it, breathe it, reproduce it, shape it, sell it, and even die in it. We cannot step outside it. If everything is made of matter, you might think by now we would know what it is. But we still haven't a clue. Some of the great minds of history could not agree on what matter is:

**Democritus:** Atoms in the void.

**Plato:** Imperfect reflection of perfect Forms.

**Aristotle:** Pure potentiality. That which changes.

**Plotinus:** Nearest to nonbeing, furthest from spirit.

**Augustine:** Formless substrate. No existence by itself.

**Aquinas:** Prime substrate. Unknowable by sense or reason.

**Descartes:** Extension in space.

**Locke:** Mysterious source of sensory qualities. ("We know not what.")

**Berkeley:** Something that doesn't exist.

**Hume:** Don't know.

**Kant:** Can't know.

**Whitehead:** Moments of experience.

**Einstein:** A form of energy.

**Bohr, de Broglie, Heisenberg, Schrödinger:** Uncertain quantum waves.

**Eddington:** Mostly ghostly empty space.

**Bohm:** Forms of explicate order.

## Energy

Energy, too, is a slippery creature. Try to pin it down and it disappears like the Cheshire cat. It remains elusive whenever we attempt to define it as a thing or substance. The best science can do is offer a functional, operational definition: Energy is "the capacity for doing work." Energy, then, is a capacity, a potential for producing activity, for applying a force. But what is it that carries the capacity or potential? And how can something as abstract as a "capacity" or "potential" (something that, by definition, does not yet fully exist) occupy space (remember, according to Descartes, anything physical—matter or energy—occupies space)?

But what is it? Einstein said $E = mc^2$—energy is equal to the mass of an object multiplied by the velocity of light squared. So is energy equal to mass in some way? And since mass is defined by the curvature of space-time, energy may be as nebulous as warps or kinks in the matrix of space-time . . . whatever that means. But even so, how does energy get its dynamic character?

As we trace the lineage of matter-energy back in the directions of its origins, as far as our knowledge and imagination permit us, we find it dissolving into the very fabric of the universe—from elementary particles through quanta of energy vibrations to hazy tensions in the warps of space-time. But at this level the term "energy" vaporizes into a purely abstract mathematical concept that has no relation to our experience.

Forced to give a definition, we may say energy is what is exchanged between atoms in their interactions, and the patterns of these exchanges are manifested in the structure of matter. Does that help? Not really. We are left with a vague, intuitive understanding of energy as a kind of homogeneous, primordial flux in which all that has shape in the world is just a series of fleeting vortices. The primordial flux is coextensive with the universe—the physical universe is the total amount of energy. In this view energy cannot be divided up into neat little pieces with nothing in between.

As the flux converges here and there into vortices of concentrated packets—energy quanta—it must diffuse elsewhere. Nothing can happen anywhere in this total energy matrix without it affecting the whole. The universe, it seems, is a cosmic quantum (within the universe as a whole, energy cannot be created or destroyed). From a thermodynamic systems perspective, energy may be defined as the flow of information or order from regions of high concentration to regions of low concentration.

All the "bits and pieces" of the universe, from galaxies down to elementary particles, up to living beings, are systems of vortices—concentrated packets of energy—all interrelated and interdependent. Every "particle" in the universe is a thread in the cosmic tapestry—each one woven by all the others. If we attempt to pull out a thread for close examination, we find the rest of the tapestry beginning to fray, and the pattern as a whole becomes incoherent. The universe must be considered as a whole, otherwise it loses meaning.

Ultimately, energy is an abstraction, a concept we introduce to account for the universe's capacity to do work, to account for the fact that anything at all ever happens. But how can the world of solid, material stuff—of tables and chairs, of mountains and cities—be ultimately made up of an abstract concept?

It is very difficult, then, to be clear what anybody means by the term "energy." It is similar to the word "force" in that it seems to explain something, but actually only disguises a deeper mystery. For the purposes of this book, I will use the physicists' definition—vague though it is—where energy refers to some physical quantity. It is something that can be measured, even though neither we, nor the scientists, really know what it is that is being measured. And since energy is a physical quantity, we should not assume that it is appropriate to use the term when talking about the nature or dynamics of consciousness.

Recognizing an ontological distinction between objective matter-energy and subjective consciousness, yet also recognizing the obvious fact of their intimate relationship and interaction, Whitehead knew that no ontological dualism could ever account for their difference-cum-interaction. For any subject-object or mind-body interaction to be possible, they must share an ontological commonality. *Something* about the nature of matter must be ontologically similar to the nature of mind. Whitehead proposed that both the objective mechanics of matter-energy and the subjective dynamics of consciousness derive from a deeper, ultimate ontological nature that he identified as *creativity*. Ultimately, it is the inherent creativity of the universe that gives rise to what we call "energy" and "consciousness." As we will see in chapter 9, "Past Matter, Present Mind," their ontological difference is accounted for in terms of *process*—a temporal, rather than a spatial or substantial, difference.

# Information

"Information" comes from the Latin *informare,* which means to give form. In the sense that information gives form, order, or organization to the contents of our minds, we call it knowledge. For hundreds of years, information in common usage has been almost equivalent to "knowledge." When we gain more information about something we effectively reduce our uncertainty and become more knowledgeable about it. And since "knowledge is power," governments, corporations, and individuals are willing to spend immense amounts on access to and acquisition of more and more information—hence the explosive information revolution and information industry. But if we attempt to define information as knowledge we slip into an infinite self-referential loop, and we fail to clarify our understanding of either. The common dictionary definition won't get us very far.

Just as we saw for energy, "information" is a concept without a fixed semantic abode. Nevertheless, many contemporary philosophers and scientists attempt to get around the problem of energy in relation to mind by talking instead of "information." In some cases, energy and information are equated as different expressions of the same phenomenon. In others, they are treated as a kind of dualism—where energy and information belong to different categories.

One example of this is the use of the term information in computer or communications theory. For instance, on the one hand a computer consists of matter/energy (the hardware), whereas on the other it consists of information in the form of programs (the software). Some computer scientists and cognitive scientists interested in the mind-body problem claim that the interaction puzzle can be solved by using the analogy of how a computer program (information) interacts with the material hardware, the computer's hardwired circuits. Some go even further and claim that the software-hardware explanation is more than analogy. They say that the mind *is* the information content of programs running on the hardware of the brain.

Although on the surface the software-hardware theory may appear to provide an explanation of the mind-body problem, there is a deep misconception underlying this view. And the misconception is based on a confused use of the term "information."

As a scientific term information comes from communications theory and has no clear meaning in any of the other sciences. In communications theory, information is an engineering term—analyzed as bits (or **b**inary dig**its**). And as an engineering term, *meaning* is precisely what binary digits do not contain.[5] When physicists, chemists, biologists, neuroscientists, and psychologists adopt "information" as an explanatory term, they often do so based on a confusion of categories and a misunderstanding of its function in communications theory.

In communications theory the mathematical definition of information is a measure of something (such as the accuracy or probability of transmitting signals or symbols through a communications channel). It may have nothing to do with knowledge or meaning inherent in the content of the symbols. Warren Weaver, one of the founders of communications theory, wrote: "The word *information,* in this theory, is used in a special sense that must not be confused with its ordinary usage. In particular, *information* must not be confused with *meaning*."[6*]

It is important to keep in mind that in science the word "information" has a mathematical definition and is a measure of *physical* processes that have nothing to do with meaning. In common usage we usually understand "information" to mean a transfer of knowledge or meaning between people or things. To repeat: This is precisely *not* the scientific definition of the term.

In this book, when using the word information, I am not referring to the engineering concept. I mean something much less precise, something much more akin to its etymological roots—"to give form." In order to get a clear understanding of information, it seems we may need to go back to its roots and develop a better understanding of the dynamics of form. How does form imprint itself on such diverse phe-

---

*In the Shannon-Weaver formula, information (called *H)* is a measuring device, and to equate this with information as it is usually understood (either in the other sciences or in common speech) is to confuse the measuring device with what is measured. As Paul Young pointed out in *The Nature of Information,* "A formula that measures the amount of apples in a barrel obviously is not the same as the apples" (1987, p. 8).

nomena as language, ideas, sounds, images, matter, and energy? What is the *process* of in-forming that gives shape to our world of *psyche* and *physis?* Only when we can answer such questions, it seems, will we be able to come to an understanding of information, not simply as an objective measure but something that includes intrinsic meaning.

## Meaning

Meaning has two kinds of meaning. One, the kind of meaning philosophers focus on: the meaning of words—linguistic or symbolic meaning. The other is the kind of meaning that matters most to many of us: for example, the meaning of life. This second kind of meaning is more the domain of the sage than the philosopher (though, of course, they are not mutually exclusive).

*Symbolic or Linguistic Meaning.* Philosophers search for meaning in language—they explore what words mean, and how words and ideas can refer to other words and ideas or represent things in the world. For instance, the word "ball" is a sound or image that refers to a spherical object. The word "ball" itself, however, is not spherical. Words, therefore, can be very different from the things they mean. Words are *symbols;* they point to, or signify, something else. Language, philosophers are fond of reminding us, is a symbolic system.

The philosopher's kind of meaning, then, is linguistic or symbolic. Philosophers are experts in answering questions such as "What do *words* mean?"—that is, bridging the gap between the word and what it refers to or symbolizes. This is a very useful gift to master when we want to make ourselves clearly understood, especially about difficult, abstract ideas and concepts.

*Experienced or Existential Meaning.* Sages and mystics search for a different, deeper kind of meaning. They explore whether life and the universe have meaning. For them meaning is not a question of which words refer to which things, but what meaning or meanings do individual lives and the whole cosmos have *in themselves.* This kind of meaning is *intrinsic*—it is part of the nature of a thing in itself. It is direct meaning, not merely symbolic, and is *experienced* as something worthwhile in itself—it is closely related to experiences of purpose and value.

Both kinds of meaning, however, do have something in common: They both refer to what is beyond themselves. In the case of language, words have meaning because they refer to things beyond the words themselves. In the case of a person's life, the life itself gets its meaning within the larger context of the world or cosmos as a whole. Our life—as it is actually, concretely lived and experienced (not just as an abstract word, idea, image, or symbol)—gets its meaning from participating as part of a greater whole, whether in time or space, or beyond. Thus, although it may be true to say that your life has *intrinsic* meaning—that is, it is meaningful in and of itself—such meaning gets its richness from its interconnectedness and interdependence with the whole. For instance, if we feel disconnected from the whole (whether life as a whole, the universe as a whole, or existence as a whole) we feel that our life has lost its meaning. The more we feel connected with the whole, the more we experience life to be rich with meaning and possibilities.

The first kind of meaning, then, is philosophical, where meaning depends on *symbolic* connections grasped by reason. The second kind of meaning is psychological, mystical, or spiritual, where meaning depends on *experienced* connections revealed through intuition or mystical insight. This is not to say that philosophers never concern themselves with the deeper kind of meaning—many of them do, especially those who follow in the tradition of Socrates and Plato. But when writing or talking about the deeper kind of meaning, they recognize the great value of paying attention to the "lighter," or symbolic, kind of meaning. It is one thing to *experience* meaning, it is something else to *talk* about it. When we feel moved to talk or write about our experience, it helps greatly to make use of the philosopher's gift of reason.

Meaning, of course, is closely related to mind, to consciousness. It is difficult to imagine how there could ever be any meaning in a purely material, wholly objective universe. What meaning would such "meaning" have? In a universe without consciousness, without an experiencing psyche, all there could be would be blind *physis,* the random-deterministic dance of "atoms in the void." Nothing would be significant.

In materialistic science, meaning is reduced to mechanism, to explanations of causal physical relations. When a particular model or theory is said to correspond with empirical data, with how phenomena in nature are observed to interact (i.e., with measurement), we say we have scientific explanation. But such a definition of meaning as causal explanation leaves something out of what we normally mean by meaning, something that has to do with significance, something that resonates in some way with our experience of self.

Meaning involves intentionality in the above sense of directed awareness. It is awareness that refers to something beyond itself with which it participates in some way. When one thing means some other thing, at least part of its being is about that thing. Meaning, therefore, implies connection with not-self through some form of awareness or knowledge. It represents or signifies—projecting itself into the "other" or introjecting the "other" into itself.

As a useful working definition of meaning we might pursue the following line: Meaning is about significant relationship between the experiencing self and the event or item being experienced. It is about communication and information flow. As a locus of being or experience, the self as bodymind is in constant communication with its environment, constantly exchanging energy and information in multiple forms—food, air, water, light, sound, smells, radiation, ideas, emotions, concepts, and so on. We are constantly sharing messages with the world around us, picking them up in our bodymind, processing or metabolizing them, and expressing some residue back out. We call this process "life."

The significance of this exchange of messages—this discourse with our environment—depends on the quality of relationship between self and not-self. In short, it depends on the fit between self and its environment. If the bodymind self cannot receive, process, or feedback information or energy with its environment, it experiences a "misfit," and its survival is at stake. If the misfit is sufficiently acute or chronic, the individual will die.

The significance, or meaning, of the messages, then, is ultimately a matter of the organism's survival. Meaning is the experienced fit between self and its environment. As the self opens up to respond to more environment—whether physical, mental, or spiritual—the experience of self expands and more of what was not-self is incorporated.

Ultimately, when the sense of self expands to encompass the entire realm of being, as mystics tell us, the distinction between individual self and the cosmic Self, or Cosmic I, disappears. The entire cosmos, then, resonates with meaning.

How do we get there? How do we shift the dominant worldview that shapes our culture and civilization from meaningless "collocations of atoms" to meaningful patterns of experience? How do we restore a sense of the sacred to nature? We must begin by examining our philosophy and science, by digging deep into our culture's metaphysical heritage to unearth foundational assumptions about the nature of consciousness. Not only must we ask unanswered questions, we must probe even deeper and expose those assumptions that keep our modern world alienated from the rhythms, vitality, and intelligence of nature. Only then can we move into its mystery with appropriate humility and participate creatively with harmony, balance, and wisdom.

In this spirit we will now explore the three core problems in philosophy of mind: other minds, mind-body relation, and free will.

# 5

Knots

# THE PROBLEMS OF CONSCIOUSNESS

For hundreds of years we have lived in a world without soul, a world made of matter and energy that lacks feeling and self-motion, a world without purpose or deep meaning. This, at least, is the complicated tale told to us by modern philosophy and science. A story without a storyteller.*

It is a story that separates psyche from physis and prevents human consciousness from participating intimately with nature. Our alienation runs deep: We experience a gulf between self and other, between humanity and the rest of nature, between our niche on this lonely planet and our place in the great cosmos. We are afflicted by a pathology of the soul—a split within ourselves, within our relationships, and within the world of matter and spirit.

The defining problem of our times is a human creation. It flows from a particular worldview we have taken on and is shaped by the dominant story we tell ourselves. At its core it is a problem rooted in our metaphysics, in our assumptions about the ultimate nature of the world, and about how we can know the world. In short, our pathology grows from our ontology and epistemology—from our stories about the nature of reality

---

*Strictly speaking, it is a story without a *place* for a storyteller. Obviously, there is a storyteller—in fact billions of us—but our culture's dominant story, our materialist worldview and big bang cosmology, cannot account for the fact that anything like a storyteller, a conscious, feeling, observing, meaning-seeking being, could ever exist.

and our ways of knowing. These stories seep into our lives, a corrosive force seeking out the cracks and fissures in our beliefs, splitting us apart from ourselves and from nature.

We need to tell ourselves a new story, a healing story that replaces split and schism with holism and integration. To do this, I believe, we will need to trace the roots of the split back to its origins and see where we took a wrong turn. We've already seen that the origins of the mind-matter split lie in the nearly four-hundred-year-old ontological separation of psyche and physis, established as the basis for modern philosophy and science by René Descartes. This "Cartesian schism" underlies the core issues in philosophy of mind and sets the terms of the debates about developing a science of consciousness.

I have approached philosophy of mind from three perspectives: motivations, origins, and meanings. The motivation for this book is "epistemotherapy"[1]—a search for a way to heal the split between knower and known, and to develop a worldview that includes the storyteller. I am seeking, therefore, a profound shift in epistemology, in our ways of knowing; and such an epistemology will involve acknowledging a radically different ontology—a radical shift in our assumptions about the fundamental nature of the world—an ontology that will, in fact, result in resacralizing science and nature.

The central problems in philosophy of mind are epistemological, ontological, semantic, causal, and methodological. Although different philosophers, and different philosophical traditions, emphasize different issues, most would agree on the following problems as central to any comprehensive approach to philosophy of mind:

- *Ontological problem*—also known as the "mind-body problem": What is the ultimate nature of reality and the status of mind and matter within that reality? How are mind and body related? How can they interact?
- *Epistemological problem*—also known as the "problem of other minds": How can we know that other minds exist? And the "problem of self-consciousness": How can consciousness know itself?

- *Semantic problem*—also known as the "problem of meaning": Where do our common-sense terms for mental phenomena get their meaning? How can we decide what would be an adequate definition of the terms we use?

- *Causality problem*—also known as the "nomothetic" problem and the "problem of free will": How can freedom of action and choice exist in a world governed by universal laws, in a world of mechanistic determinism?

- *Methodological problem*—the problem of perspective: objectivity, subjectivity, or intersubjectivity? Can mind be studied objectively? Can science include subjectivity? In pursuing a science of consciousness, should we use first-person introspection or meditation (idealism, phenomenology, or spiritual discipline) or third-person measurement of observable behavior and manipulation of artificial analogs (physicalism, cognitive science, and artificial intelligence)? Is *intersubjectivity* a valid third perspective?

In this chapter I will outline the three core problems in philosophy of mind that have a direct bearing on attempts to develop a science of consciousness. How we approach solving these philosophical problems also relates directly to how we may heal the deeper schisms and alienations that fracture our relationship to others, nature, and the cosmos.

The three key issues in the philosophy of mind are: (1) the problem of other minds, (2) the mind-body problem, and (3) the problem of free will. The first is essentially a problem of epistemology: How can we know that some other being is a center of consciousness? The second is a problem of ontology: What is the nature of mind and matter and their relationship? The third involves a combination of the first two, and specifically addresses causality: Is consciousness causal? That is to say, does free will or volition exist or is everything ultimately determined by physical causes?

Becoming familiar with these problems, and understanding the kinds of issues they raise, will provide a valuable foundation for explorations into philosophy of mind and the chapters ahead.

# The Problem of Other Minds

The only experiences you can ever have are your own.* Experience is a private affair, the exclusive privilege of your unique point of view. Nobody else can have direct access to the feelings, sensations, perceptions, ideas, thoughts, volitions, desires, fears, hopes, wishes, and all the other phenomena that flow through your experience. The only way anyone could have knowledge of what it is like to be you, living your life as you experience it from within your own subjective domain, is if you tell them, or if they observe your behavior.

But you may deceive people by what you say, and they may misobserve or misinterpret how you behave. Even if you speak your mind truthfully, and even if others are skilled observers of behavior, there is still no way that others can be certain that what you say or how you behave is an accurate and reliable reflection or representation of your experience. And even if these were accurate, others could have access only to their own private experience of how your speech or behavior affects them. There is no way for another person to know whether their experience really matches yours.

## THE PROBLEM OF "MATCHING QUALIA"

This is the problem of "matching qualia." *Qualia* (singular *quale*) is a philosophical term that refers to those inner, private qualities of experi-

---

*Until I make a case for an alternative worldview in later chapters, here I'm assuming the modern Western notion of subjectivity inherited from Descartes—where each individual subject (ego, "I") is a self-contained entity, a spiritual substance, or soul, absolutely distinct and separate from all other subjects. Without such a private and privileged subject at the center of our sense of self-identity, it seems we would not be able to retain our individuality—and along with it our experience of self-agency, freedom, and responsibility. But this is only one meaning of "subjectivity." In book two, *Radical Knowing*, I explicitly question the Cartesian assumption, identify different meanings of subjectivity, and explore the possibility and implications of individual centers of subjectivity arising from a more fundamental intersubjective reality.

Thus, given the Cartesian assumption of isolated, individual subjects, the problem of other minds has been a long-standing puzzle in Western philosophy. In this chapter I outline the nature of the problem, and in *Radical Knowing*, I discuss how a process-based ontology together with an intersubjective epistemology may provide a solution to this seemingly intractable knot.

ence populating our consciousness. They cannot be measured or observed because they have no objective, public reality. Qualia are subjective—the private privilege of their unique possessors. We know about them directly only in ourselves and can only infer them in other people by observing how their behavior (including speech) matches ours. But we cannot match the qualia themselves.

Take taste, for example: How can you know if your taste of chocolate is the same as mine? (Or whether your sensation of red is not my sensation of blue?) Now, it is true that we both can tell the difference between chocolate and vanilla. But how do you know that *my experience* of chocolate is not *your experience* of vanilla? It's possible that our "wiring" is reversed, and we'd never know the difference.

Even if we both receive exactly the same stimulus and process it exactly the same way, we have no way of knowing that those identical stimuli are *experienced* identically by each of us. You can correlate the stimuli only with *your* experience (and I with mine). In my case the stimuli may be correlated with an entirely different kind of experience.

For all you know, the experience you associate with the taste of chocolate is experienced by me as an auditory symphony. (This is not as absurd as it may sound. The phenomenon of synesthesia is well documented in neuropsychology, where certain individuals can "taste shapes" or "hear colors."[2]) But since every time I put chocolate in my mouth I experience a symphony, I call *that* "the taste of chocolate." Since "the taste of chocolate" is precisely how you describe the correlation of the stimulus of brown cocoa-derived candy with what goes on in your experience, we both *assume* or *infer* that we are talking about the same experience. *And there is no way we can compare experiences to find out if our assumption is true or false.*

This is what is meant by the statement "experiences are private": We never have access to each other's experiences. As noted above, all we can know are each other's reports and other behavioral responses. In other words, experiences are *subjective:* They are private and inaccessible to anyone but ourselves. In philosophical terminology: Experiences are *privileged* epistemically (only I have the privilege of knowing my own experiences). By contrast, both the originating stimuli and the resultant behaviors are *objective*—they are open to public scrutiny. They are objectively observable.

Just because two people may *behave* the same way when affected by the same stimulus (say grimacing and salivating when lemon juice is placed on their tongues) does not guarantee that their *experiences* are the same. (For instance, maybe to me lemon tastes sweet, and my reaction to sweetness is to scrunch up my face and drool.) In short, not only may correlations between stimuli and experiences be different between people, but equally correlations between behavior and experiences may also be different. Neither commonality of stimuli nor replication of behavior are necessarily correlated with common experiences. In fact, taken to extremes, it may be the case that *none of my experiences ever matches yours and that none of our experiences ever matches those of anyone else.* We may each of us live in an experientially unique world, *and we have no way of knowing whether we do or not.* Yet, of course, for the most part we assume we don't live in experientially isolated universes. I assume that when you say or show that you feel pain, for instance, it is the same or similar to what pain feels like to me. That is the basis for my gestures and feelings of compassion and empathy. But these are, ultimately, based on an assumption that our experiences are alike.

Empathy and compassion, of course, *could* still be legitimate cognitive-emotional responses even if our experiences were utterly different. I don't need to know that your toothache feels the same as my toothache for me to wish you didn't have one. The fact that you say or show that you are "in pain" is sufficient. But, here again, I would be relying on perception of your *objective* behavior (speech such as "ouch!" or gestures such as pressing your jaw with your hand). I would still not have access to your experience of pain (and, therefore, it is always possible that you are lying or that I am misinterpreting your behavior). The point is I have no way of *knowing* that you are in pain in the way that you can know your pain. Your pain (and any other experience) is epistemically privileged and private. I can only take your pain on faith.

This is part of "the problem of other minds." But it gets worse.

## THE "ZOMBIE" PROBLEM

Not only can we not know that others' experiences—whether qualia such as red, bitter, harmonious, beautiful, fearful, exciting, desirous, or mournful—are experienced in the same or even similar ways by any two people; but the problem of other minds is also that we cannot know if anybody else (besides ourselves) *even has a mind.*

For all you know, I and everybody else in the world is like a zombie or a sophisticated robot. We may all be excellently adapted to produce all the behaviors that you correlate with experience or consciousness. We may be, as Thomas Nagel put it, "just elaborate biological machines . . . [and] have *no inner experiences whatever.*" How would you ever know the difference? Is there any test you could contrive to establish that anybody else in the world had experiences? Since any test that would involve observation of behavior could reveal only *objective* correlates (which you may associate with *your* experience of consciousness), no such test could establish the presence of *subjectivity* in any other creature.*

Just because certain behavior is correlated with subjective experience *in your case* does not logically establish a similar or identical correlation in any other case. It may simply be that the correlation is factual only in one

---

*As long as we can never test for the presence of consciousness in others (even humans), how can we ever develop a science of consciousness that could resolve, for instance, whether dogs or dolphins—never mind cells or molecules—have consciousness? How, in other words, can we ever resolve the question of whether consciousness does go all the way down and, if not, then how far down? How can science help us identify the "cut-off" line in evolution below which there is no trace of consciousness? Where can we place the "consciousness cut"?

This is indeed a problem for science and philosophy—but only as long as we hold to some deeply entrenched metaphysical assumptions about the nature of reality (ontology) and about how we can know that reality (epistemology). In this case, as long as we assume an ontology of *substance* (that the world is made of "stuff") and an epistemology of sensory empiricism (that all knowledge of the world must come through the senses in the form of physical signals), then the philosophical problem of other minds and the scientific problem of the consciousness cut will remain.

Part of the purpose of this book is to question these assumptions and to propose alternatives (a *process* ontology and an epistemology of *presence*) that tell a different story about the fundamental nature of reality and our ways of knowing it. With such a shift in assumptions, the other minds problem in philosophy and the consciousness cut problem in science can be resolved. Part 3 of this book focuses on an alternative ontology that lays the groundwork for an alternative epistemology of consciousness explored in *Radical Knowing*. A key theme of this thesis is that in studying consciousness—both in philosophy and in science—we need to cultivate other ways of knowing beyond reason and sensory empiricism.

instance—namely in your case. In every other case the inference of such a correlation may be unfounded in fact. Just because people *appear* to be sentient beings does not mean they are *in fact* sentient. The appearance may be all there is; there may be nothing else behind the façade. Only in one case do appearance and fact converge: When it appears to me that I experience something (say, pain) it is a *fact* that I experience that something. If I hop in pain having stepped on a thorn, I am in no doubt that my "painful" behavior, my *appearance* of pain, is rooted solidly in the *fact* of real, experienced pain.

The problem of other minds, therefore, has two related components: (1) the problem of "matching qualia" and (2) the "zombie problem," the problem of other minds *per se*. There is also a third aspect to the problem, the flipside to the issue of whether any other creature in the universe is sentient besides me (or you in your case—assuming, of course, that you are sentient and conscious). Instead of asking, "How can I know if any other being is sentient?" the third question asks, "How can I know if there is any other creature *without* consciousness or sentience?"

## THE CONSCIOUSNESS CUT

In other words, if experience or consciousness is privileged, a private affair known only to its possessor, what test could I devise to find out if some other creature was insentient? It may be the case, after all, that *every* individual being in the world possesses subjectivity. What grounds do I have to doubt this? How far down the evolutionary ladder does consciousness extend? Where is the "consciousness cut"?

According to Nagel:

> Ordinarily we believe that other human beings are conscious, and almost everyone believes that other mammals and birds are conscious too. But people differ over whether fish are conscious, or insects, worms, and jellyfish. They are still more doubtful about whether one-celled animals like amoebae and paramecia have conscious experiences, even though such creatures react conspicuously to stimuli of various kinds. Most people believe that plants aren't conscious; and almost no one believes that rocks are conscious, or kleenex, or automobiles, or mountain lakes,

or cigarettes. And to take another biological example, most of us would say, if we thought about it, that the individual cells of which our bodies are composed do not have any conscious experiences.[3]

This question of how far down the evolutionary scale consciousness goes is central in this book. I raise the question here in the context of epistemology: How can we *know* if any other creature is sentient? But later in the book I will approach the question from an ontological perspective: Is sentience integral to the *being* of other creatures? The two questions— epistemological and ontological—are closely related, of course, but they are nevertheless two different kinds of question. One is about how we can gain *knowledge* of other minds, the second is about whether other creatures have minds as essential ingredients of their being.

## CAN COMPUTERS BE CONSCIOUS?

Earlier I introduced the question of how we could know whether other people were really sentient beings or whether they just appeared to be so. How could we tell the difference between a zombie or a robot and a real sentient person, with real subjective feelings? Perhaps all other people are in reality empty of all consciousness and experience—just like robots or computers are.

But now let's flip the question again. *How do we know that zombies, robots, or computers are* not *sentient—or at least* could *be sentient?* More simply, to raise an issue hot in philosophy of mind, particularly in the fields of cognitive science and artificial intelligence (AI): Can a computer be conscious? If we have such great difficulty establishing whether other people are sentient, why would it be any easier to know whether a computer is sentient or not? If a genius electronics engineer builds an advanced, sophisticated computer—with massive parallel processing, neural nets, complete with quantum mechanical gate arrays, and so on—and claims that his machine is conscious, what grounds would we have for doubting his claim (or, conversely, for accepting it)?

How could we be sure? How could we ever confirm or refute such a claim? If consciousness, by definition, is subjective we could never get "inside" the computer to see whether it had the kind of consciousness that organisms have, or indeed any kind of consciousness at all. Opponents of the "computers-can-be-conscious" idea say that the best machines can do is *simulate* consciousness (in other words, produce behavior of some sort that mimics the behavior of beings that are sentient), but that there is no *experience* of consciousness or subjectivity, no *feelings,* in the computer. On the other hand, supporters, such as Marvin Minsky or Daniel Dennett, of the "computers-can-be-conscious" school insist that consciousness is not a matter of experiential subjectivity but is, instead, a matter of *functional relations* between components of a highly organized system—whether these are based on silicon chips or carbon-organic neurons. Supporters of AI functionalism say that *any* system of sufficient complexity is by definition conscious.

However, since the functional relations are observable, they are objective. If this were the full story, AI consciousness would therefore lack true subjectivity, all the private *feel* and privileged point of view that conscious-sentient creatures like us possess. If computer consciousness is objective, it ends up being a strange kind of consciousness—in fact, it would be nothing like what we know and experience as consciousness because it would lack the very qualities that define what we know as consciousness: namely, subjective qualia.

But here's the rub, as far as the problem of other minds is concerned: Even if the kind of consciousness claimed by AI researchers for computers—objective consciousness—could be demonstrated (no easy task), *that would still not mean we (or they) could legitimately claim that the computers possessed subjective consciousness.* The problem is—since subjective experience is private and privileged—how could we ever know? Computers (like zombies, robots, or amoebae) may or may not be conscious and we could never tell for sure.

## The Mind-Body Problem

The second of the trio of key issues in philosophy of mind is the so-called mind-body problem—and this takes us right to the heart of ontology, the fundamental nature of being or reality itself. Here, we shift from "How can we *know?*" to "What *is?*" Clearly, of course, to answer the second question, we need an answer to the first.

For most philosophers and cognitive scientists, the mind-body problem translates into the "mind-brain" problem—how can the brain and mind interact, or how can the brain cause consciousness, and can consciousness act back on the brain? For some philosophers, notably metaphysicians, the mind-body problem translates into a wider issue of the grander ontological relationship between matter in general and consciousness in general.

Here I will focus on the narrower issue of the mind-brain relation. Later I will return to the wider issue of the cosmological relationship between consciousness and matter.

Nagel begins discussion of the mind-body question with an assertion: "Everybody knows that what happens in consciousness depends on what happens to the body. If you stub your toe it hurts."[4] Well, yes, everybody, we may assume, is aware of this intimate relationship between consciousness and the body. At some time in our life we have all experienced some injury or illness, for example, and experienced how this bodily disturbance changed the quality of our consciousness.

But is it true to say that *everything* that happens in the mind must first also happen in the body? What about a mathematical computation, or a wish, or an image of a loved one, or a dream? What bodily events happened in association with these subjective events? Most scientists and philosophers would say that such mental events are accompanied by changes in the brain. Nagel, in fact, goes on to say: "The evidence shows that for anything to happen in your mind or consciousness, something has to happen in your brain."[5]

Clearly the assumption here is that either consciousness is produced by the brain (materialism) or that consciousness is coupled with brain events but has its own independent existence (dualism). (I will look at a third option, "double-aspectism," below.) What this view overlooks or denies is that consciousness may be associated with more primitive evolutionary structures, such as cells. If we assume that consciousness depends on activity in the brain or must always be associated with brain events, then we should be aware that we are ruling out the option of extra-cerebral consciousness or experience, such as whole-body consciousness or cellular consciousness.

It may turn out that the assumed necessary connection between mind and brain is correct, but until such a connection is demonstrated, and all other cases ruled out, we should declare our starting assumption and be prepared to justify it. At the very least, we should be prepared to recognize that any assumption may be wrong or incomplete.

Without confirming evidence that consciousness or experience can occur *only* in connection with a brain, we should remain open to the possibility that consciousness may exist in the absence of a brain. It may be possible, for instance, that creatures such as a worm or a jellyfish, or even a single cell, could be conscious, not to mention molecules, atoms, and elementary particles.

But leaving aside the larger mind-body and consciousness-matter issues for the moment, let's look at the mind-brain relation. The central question for philosophy of mind in this context is this: "Is your mind something different from your brain, though connected to it, or *is* it your brain?" In other words, is consciousness *identical* to brain events (as identity materialists claim) or is it something *additional* to the brain? Is it something different that emerges from the brain (as emergent materialists claim) or is it something that can exist quite independently of the brain but interacts with it or runs parallel with it (as dualists claim)?

## MATERIALISTS AND MIND-BRAIN IDENTITY

Identity materialists would claim, for example, that your taste of chocolate can be explained as *nothing but* physiological activity occurring in the brain. For them, mind *equals* brain. Now, from experimental evidence it is clear that when someone tastes chocolate (or has any other sensation) changes do occur in the brain. But the key question is whether such brain activity is the full story. Is there something else going on besides the physiological and chemical events in and between your taste buds and your brain's neurons and their synapses? Can your actual *tasting* of chocolate be adequately explained by such physical (that is, objective and potentially public) processes?

If the taste were truly objective, then it would be possible (at least in theory) for a scientist or surgeon to take off the top of your skull, lick your brain and taste chocolate. But we are pretty sure that a brain never tastes of chocolate *even when its owner is experiencing the taste of chocolate*. (I doubt that the experiment has ever been done, but even if it had, all the scientist would experience would be his or her taste, not yours. Your taste would remain private, privileged only to you. Licking your brain would not give the scientist access to *your* taste.) Thus, we can be quite sure that *something besides brain events is involved in the event called "tasting"— namely the* experience *of tasting.* In addition to objective brain events, experiences involve private, subjective events. There is an "interiority" to subjectivity not available to the probing observation of objective onlookers. As Nagel expressed it: "Your experiences are inside your mind with a *kind of insideness* that is different from the way your brain is inside your head."[6] And he adds:

> If what happens in your experience is inside your mind in a way in which what happens in your brain is not, it looks as though your experiences and other mental states can't just be physical states of your brain. There has to be more to you than your body with its humming nervous system."[7]

A little later, he says:

> And there is no way that a large number of physical events in the brain, however complicated, could be the parts out of which a taste sensation was composed . . . Physical parts just can't add up to a mental whole.[8]

## DUALISM: MIND IS SEPARATE FROM BRAIN

According to Nagel's argument, it is clear that the identity theory—mind is nothing but brain—cannot be true. It follows, therefore, that mind must be something other than the brain's physical processes. And, as we saw earlier, dualism is one way philosophers have tried to account for this. Mind or consciousness is considered to be something that can subsist entirely without the aid of matter but is able to penetrate it and move it.

What could possibly be the mechanism by which mind transmitted a "force" to a material thing, thereby causing an effect? Similarly, how could, for example, the matter of the brain cause anything to happen in an immaterial mind? What would be the nature of their point of contact? Would it be physical or mental? Or both? If either physical or mental, the original problem remains; if both, then within that point how would the physical and the mental interact? The problem remains all the way down. Dualism appears to be incapable of extricating itself from this dilemma.

## DOUBLE-ASPECTISM: BRAINS ARE BOTH PHYSICAL AND MENTAL

Well, if identity materialism doesn't fit the bill, and dualism likewise fails to provide an explanation, how are we to account for the mind-brain relation? One interesting proposal is that although experiences such as feelings, thoughts, hopes, and desires do occur in the brain and are never separated from it, they are nevertheless *not physical* events in the brain. "This would mean that the grey mass of billions of nerve cells in your skull is *not just a physical object*. It has lots of physical properties . . . but it has *mental* processes going on in it as well."[9]

This is a very interesting position because (1) while claiming that mental events occur in the brain and depend on brain events, at the same time it denies that these *mental events are merely physical events;* and (2) it acknowledges the existence of mental events distinct (but not separate) from the matter of the brain while *rejecting dualism* (of separate substances). In other words, the "stuff" of which brains are made has two aspects to it, one of which accounts for objective physical events, the other for subjective mental events. This is known as the "dual-aspect" theory. The brain is an object with both physical and mental aspects, as Nagel said:

> When you bite into a chocolate bar, this produces in your brain a state or process with two aspects: a physical aspect involving various chemical and electrical changes, and a mental aspect—the flavor experience of chocolate. . . . If this were true, your brain itself would have an inside that could not be reached by an outside observer even if he cut it open. It would feel, or taste, a certain way to you to have that process going on in your brain. . . .
>
> There's something it's like from the inside to taste chocolate because there's something it's like from the inside to have your brain in the condition that is produced when you eat a chocolate bar.[10]

The double-aspect perspective on the mind-body problem will become a recurring theme throughout this book. We will meet it again later in a different guise when we come to discuss panpsychism, panexperientialism, and radical naturalism. The version of double-aspectism outlined here, based on Nagel's critique, sees mind as an additional, though intrinsic, aspect of matter in a structure as complex as the human brain. If this is the case, we have two options for understanding how this state of affairs came about.

The first is a form of emergentism, which basically states that the interiority, or consciousness, of brain matter is an emergent property and a product of ordinary matter at a certain level of evolutionary complexity. The second states that it is impossible that something like subjectivity or consciousness could ever evolve from matter that was wholly objective and nonconscious to begin with. In other words, *all* matter, not just brains, would have this dual-aspect of both subjectivity and objectivity; all matter would be both physical and mental in some degree all the way down. I will come back to this again in more detail in later chapters.

## IDEALISM: ALL IS MIND

One mind-body position I haven't considered in this chapter (though I touched on it earlier) is idealism. This metaphysical view claims that only mind, consciousness, or spirit is ultimately real. It is the exact reverse of materialism, which says that only matter or physical energy is real. According to idealism, not only is mind not produced by brains, but that brains—indeed, *all material objects*—are merely the creations of mind.

Given this view, then, the mind-body, or mind-brain, problem disappears because *everything is made of the same mind "stuff."* In reality, there is no body or brain distinct from the mind for consciousness to interact with. It's *all* mind.

Another form of idealism, emanationism, states that all forms of matter (and therefore bodies and brains) are emanated or poured forth from spirit and that matter is nothing more, ultimately, than a condensed form of spirit. This perspective is central to what has been called the "Perennial Philosophy"—from Plato and Plotinus down to present day New Age metaphysicians.

*Note to the reader:* the following discussion about free will and the ice cream cone is also found in my 2009 book, *Consciousness from Zombies to Angels.*

## The Problem of Free Will

At the risk of implying that philosophy of mind is a discipline obsessed with the gustatory wonders of the cocoa bean, let's stay with the taste sensation of chocolate a little while longer. Try this thought experiment: Suppose you are at the boardwalk with a friend and she buys two cones of ice cream—one is chocolate flavored, the other is vanilla. She invites you to take one. But before doing so, she insists that you make your choice *completely independently* of all considerations you have about preferences (yours or hers) for one taste or another, or for size, shape, texture, or anything else. Her instruction is simply either to make your choice *prior to* all considerations, or to put aside—"bracket out"—all such considerations that spring to mind, *and then choose.* You agree. And this raises three deeply interesting questions.

The first question is can you do so? Can you exercise a choice that is not determined by any of your conditioned preferences, beliefs, opinions, fears, hopes, wishes, and so on? The second question, once you have made your choice (let's say it was chocolate), is "Why did you choose chocolate?" At this point you may be tempted, by force of habit, to say something like, "Well, I prefer chocolate." And your friend will remind you that that is not what you agreed to do. You agreed to choose *prior to* any considerations or *after all considerations were bracketed.* So she takes back the cone and offers both to you again, with the original invitation to choose prior to or after all considerations are put aside. Feeling a little sheepish, you agree one more time, and you make your choice.

Now, since you successfully put aside all considerations and chose, it is clear that the answer to question one is "yes," you can choose independently of all considerations. This time you chose vanilla.

Again, your friend asks, "Why did you choose vanilla?"

And, feeling a little clever and creative now, you say, "Because this time I wanted to be different?" At which point, your friend immediately takes back the cone and points out that that is not what you agreed to do.

"Wanting to be different is just another consideration," she points out. "The agreement was that you would choose *independently of all considerations.* Is our original agreement back on?" One more time you agree, and she offers you both cones (which are beginning to drip down the sides by now).

And so the situation unfolds, and each time you choose she asks you why you chose (either chocolate or vanilla), and each time you answer "Because. . . ." And each time you answer "because" she quickly points out that you have broken the agreement. Eventually, frustrated and somewhat confused, you spontaneously make a choice, and when she asks why you made that particular choice, you equally spontaneously blurt out, *"because that's what I chose!"* Bingo! She let's you eat what's left of the ice cream cone.

"That's right," she says, "you chose because you chose. Period. Which means, does it not, that there was no 'because' determining your choosing. You chose because you chose. *Your choosing was its own cause.*"

A green light of insight flashes in your mind: "Oh, I get it, my choice is not determined by anything other than the choice itself. In other words, my choice is unconstrained, it is *free.*" In other words, making a choice is an act of free will, not determined by anything outside the agent who chooses.

Having got this far, your philosophical friend now asks you the third question: "The fact is that you chose chocolate. Could you have chosen vanilla?" You think about this for a moment. You want to be careful about your response. You think to yourself, "If I say, 'No, I couldn't have chosen vanilla,' that's the same as saying 'I *had* to choose chocolate.' But that would mean my choice wasn't free, which would be a contradiction."

So you say to her, "Yes, I could have chosen vanilla."

She replies, "But the fact is that you didn't choose vanilla, you chose chocolate. Why?"

Now sharp to the line of questioning, you respond, "For no particular reason. I simply chose chocolate because I chose chocolate." *For no particular reason.* You're feeling pretty smart now.

She has you repeat "for no particular reason."

"In other words," she continues, "there was no reason for your choice."

"That's right," you say, pleased with yourself.

"But," she comes back, "if there is *no reason* for your choice, isn't that the same as saying that what you call 'choice' *just happens?*"

Suddenly your insides have that old sinking feeling. You're beginning not to feel so smart after all. She underlines the point: "If choice 'just happens,' that's the same as saying no one is responsible for it, *not even you.* It's like saying 'it's raining,' or 'accidents just happen.' How can choice be something that 'just happens'? Surely the whole point of any choice is that *you* make it, that you are the agent?"

Choice means, as we saw earlier, that you are the agent, you are the cause—nothing else is. But now you are saying that because your choice is made for no particular reason (as you agreed), it "just happens," it has *no* cause. You are out of the picture of your own choice. How does that differ *experientially* from the situation where your choice is determined or conditioned? As far as you are concerned, logically if your "choices" just happen, if they are utterly random, you have no claim to agency. Similarly, if your choices don't just happen, if they are not random, they must be determined, and once again you have no claim to agency. Without agency, without the power or possibility to freely initiate action, what has become of your free will?

This is the core of the problem of free will: In a world of causes and determined effects, how can there be anything such as free will? On the one hand, it certainly feels that (barring extreme situations) we all have the experience of being free agents, able to exercise our own free will. Yet as soon as we explore its existential parameters we find that (1) free will means the self-as-agent is the cause; (2) but self-as-cause means without prior determination or consideration, that is, without any reason; (3) but an event that happens without any reason is the same as saying "it just happens"; (4) and that's the same as saying "it's an accident," which means no one, including you, is responsible; (5) but if you are not responsible for your choices, then that is the same as saying you are not the agent of your choices; (6) and that contradicts premise (1). Which leaves two options: Either (a) all your "choices" are effectively random, or (b) all your "choices" are effectively determined. Free will is refuted. It is an illusion; a persistent, universal illusion, but an illusion nonetheless—according to this analysis.

## SELF-AGENCY AS UNCAUSED CAUSE

If this analysis is correct, free will is an illusion. If free will is not an illusion, this analysis must be in error. Does the above analysis, then, contain an error?

Some philosophers (the determinists) say no, this analysis (or some variation of it) provides a devastating critique of the notion of free will. Other philosophers (the volitionists) insist that the analysis must be wrong because it flies in the face of one of our most intimate experiences: our ability to exercise volition. The volitionists rely on the notion that logic cannot override experience; that if logic and experience are in conflict, then experience must take priority, and so much the worse for logic. A third group, the rationalists, say that logic and experience cannot contradict one another. So if the experience of free will is a fact of our general experience of being healthy and whole human beings (which it clearly is), then it is not that logic as such is inferior, but that the logic of this particular argument must be faulty.

Where might the flaw be? Let's take another look at premise (2), which asserts that "self-as-cause means without prior determination or consideration, that is *without any reason*." Premise (3) then follows: "but an event that happens without any reason is the same as saying 'it just happens.'" As we saw in the chocolate-or-vanilla thought experiment, choice was *independent of all considerations,* which means it happened without any prior cause. But if the selection, the physical act of taking the chocolate cone, was the *effect* of the choice, then the choice must have been the *cause* of the selection (a standard axiom of logic is that causes always precede effects). That is, the selection did have a cause—namely, your choice. But the choice itself had no cause, it had no prior reason compelling it (as we saw).

What does it mean to say "the choice itself had no cause"? Well, according to the earlier analysis it means that the choice "just happened," that it was random—which hardly counts as choice at all. But to insist on this line of argument is to ignore premise (1), which asserts that "free will means the self-as-agent is the cause." Therefore, given this premise, it is not accurate to say that choice "just happens" without reason. There is a cause, there is a reason: the *self-as-agent.* But, and here is the important point: The self-as-agent does not provide a cause or reason *prior to* the act of choosing. The act of choice by the self-as-agent is purely creative, a spontaneous exercise of volition *right at the moment of choice.* In this particular case, in the act of choice, choice-as-effect coincides with self-as-cause. (That is, in this unique case, cause *does not* precede effect. They are synchronous.) And this amounts to saying that choice is uncaused by anything external to the existential act of choice itself. For this to be true, choice and self must coincide. There is no dualism of agent and choice. Agency *is* the act of choosing.

In fact, this line of analysis leads to an axiom: "In any case where cause and effect coincide in time, there is an identity of agency and choice." A corollary is that "identity of cause and effect *is* the self-as-agency." Self, as an occasion or instance of agency, *is* the creative act of choice. That is to say the very essence or being of self (or consciousness) is the act of choice. *Self exists only as choice.*

This is a profound conclusion. To really "get" this at an experiential level, not just intellectually, can result in a radical transformation in the consciousness of the subject. It reveals an existential reality where the self is experienced to be a true source of creative power. It means, in effect, that in some sense we are like gods. We are creative beings who from moment to moment can choose, and thus create, our way through time. And since our choosing affects (to some degree) the organization of the physical world around us, to *this degree* we do create our own reality. As conscious, choosing beings, we create (or can create, if we so choose) much of our relationship with physical reality. (We even have the paradoxical power to choose not to choose—to become, in effect, like mechanical robots; to be victims or slaves of circumstances.) And this means we are *responsible* beings. Fully realizing the depth of this responsibility reinforces our awareness of self-agency. It is a self-empowering act. German idealist Fichte referred to consciousness as "self-positing self," and a century later Whitehead introduced the notion of the self or subject as a self-creative agency positing itself from moment to moment to moment within the world of physical objects. (The ontological centrality of creative choice will be discussed in greater detail later in chapter 9, "Integrating Worldviews: Past Matter, Present Mind," where it plays a crucial role in Whitehead's solution to the mind-body problem.)

Thus, the error in the initial analysis was ignoring premise (1), self-as-agency is the cause of choice, and assuming that choice "just happens" because there is no *external* cause. There was a cause: the *internal*, or coincidental, agency of the self exercising the choice. Choice doesn't "just happen"; in fact, choice is the precise opposite of randomness. It is the injection of order into the flux of stochastic events. In short, choice is neither random nor determined—it is not random because it is a reduction of the random, and it is not determined because (as we saw) it was exercised prior to all considerations, external causes, and reasons.

However, a problem still remains. In the thought experiment described above, the agent (you) made your choice prior to all *conscious* considerations. It is entirely possible (and likely) that beneath the threshold of awareness all sorts of unconscious psychological and physiological dynamics are at work* *determining* your preferences and considerations. You may consciously bracket out all conscious considerations, but you cannot block out your *unconscious* biases. By definition, the contents and processes of the unconscious are not accessible to conscious awareness. (As soon as they rise to awareness, they are no longer unconscious.)

It remains possible, therefore, that your act of choosing the chocolate cone was not prior to all *unconscious* considerations. And you have no way of knowing whether your act of choice is *independent* of all such unconscious dynamics. Thus, the determinists argue, you have no way of refuting the claim that all your choices are determined by unconscious motivations and drives. This is true; but by the same token, the determinists have no way of confirming that any or all of your choices *are* determined by unconscious dynamics. The issue remains open.

The problem of free will, therefore, like the problem of other minds and the mind-body problem, remains unsolved. Plenty of work remains to engage philosophers of mind for the foreseeable future. However, it is my intention in this book to show that we do in fact have ways of solving these problems—ways that involve a radical alteration in our assumptions about the nature of reality and about our ways of knowing.

---

*See, for example, the discussion of "fringe consciousness" in chapter 4, "Meanings: Language, Energy and Consciousness."

## A Radical Way Out?

One promising line of inquiry makes a radical shift from "substance-thinking" to "process-thinking." As long as we try to figure out the mind-body problem, the other minds problem, and the problem of free will in terms of substances—whether material or mental—it seems the issues will remain unresolved. But by looking at the problems from the very different perspective of *process* (where minds and bodies are understood as *temporal* relations rather than merely spatial configurations), then a whole new array of possibilities open up for mind-body, mind-mind, and self-agency solutions.

But this shift from substance to process is so counter-intuitive ("counter-habitual" is more accurate), so much against the grain of our usual ways of thinking and visualizing, that it often takes some time for people to "get" it. Part of the problem is that our language is so steeped in substance-thinking—as if the world is a collection of *things* that move about in different configurations and relationships and not a series or network of *events* or processes out of which apparently individual "things" or "objects" arise and vanish, depending on the relative stability of nodes in the network of events.

When we switch to thinking of minds and bodies in terms of process—as patterns of events in time—the relationship between matter and mind becomes much easier to comprehend (as we will see in chapter 9, "Past Matter, Present Mind"). And given this shift in our fundamental ontological assumptions, the way opens for an equally radical epistemological shift—an opening to solve the problem of other minds through a new understanding of subjectivity and intersubjectivity.* Because this way of thinking involves such a radical shift, I will postpone discussion of it for later chapters.

It is now time to look more closely at the alternative worldview of panpsychism and at the long lineage of mind-in-matter, of consciousness all the way down. As we will see, this is an idea with a venerable history.

---

*I address this question in *Radical Knowing*.

# 6

Panpsychism

# A LONG LINEAGE OF MIND-IN-MATTER

How has humankind become so alienated from nature? There was a time when our ancestors moved with the animals and sang with the wild symphony of the natural world—the swoop of a hawk, the roar of a waterfall, the whisper of evening breezes, the kiss of moonlight. We lived *in* the world, responded to its *felt* and subtle messages, understood its deeper meanings. We not only communed with nature, we were in open communication with all its great variety of sounds and rhythms. In short, we understood and spoke the *language* of nature.

Throughout the long history of our hominid evolution, our ancestors lived and survived by moving through a world of unexpected happenings in nature. Prior to the development of speech, our forebears uttered spontaneous sounds such as gasps, sighs, screams, and cries as they encountered the contingencies of the wild.[1] At the sound of swishing wings of a swooping hawk, for instance, a sudden gasp of breath might have been the human body's instinctive response. The hawk's movement and sounds, immediately meaningful, spoke a language of gesture initiating a dialogue between animal and human. *Bodies in nature spoke to each other* long before the development of grammatical speech. Semantics preceded syntax.

Underlying the varieties of human speech, we share a common preverbal language of bodies embedded in nature. Our spoken words are derivative expressions of this deeper embodied language. And speech is most effective—as in poetry—when words arise, still connected, with their deeper embodied meanings. Sometime around 2000 BCE, with the invention of written alphabets, the connection between language and embodied meanings began to come loose. With reading and writing, words became static, frozen out of time, out of their lived context. Language became *silent;* it became progressively disconnected from the dance of natural communication, of bodies spontaneously responding to each other. And as literate civilization progressed, particularly with the spread of printed words since the fifteenth century, the silent gap between humans and the rest of nature deepened.

Literally out of touch and out of communication, modern civilization has left us aliens in our own landscape. In general we no longer feel or hear our once intimate connection with the land and its rooted, running, hopping, flying, swimming, burrowing, crawling creatures. Our bodies have all but fallen numb and dumb to our profound kinship with the stuff of the earth. We no longer hear its voice, no longer respond to its calling. The loss is mutual and profound: Not only are we disconnected and alone, we have inflicted the pathology of fragmentation and desolation on a great part of the world around us. In this time of "silence," during the centuries of alienation, we have created an Age of Ecological Crises.

Our hope, says philosopher David Abram, is to reinvigorate the language of the body, learn to let our muscles, sinews, blood, and bones sing again in harmony with the wild chorus of the land, sea, and air—to *feel* again the pulse of natural kinship. We need to open the vital channels between our words—even our written words—our bodies, and the articulate flesh of the world. We need to feel and respond to the deep intelligence of the matter of the planet and cosmos from which we are born. We need to pay attention to the stirrings of mind *in* matter, to the symphony of universal meaning—to the deep narrative of matter itself.

The "new" story we need to tell has deep roots and for many centuries has been known as *panpsychism.* Panpsychism is a cosmological and ontological theory that proposes all objective bodies (objects) in the universe, including those we usually classify as "inanimate," possess an interior, subjective reality (they are also subjects). In other words, there is something it feels like from within to be a body (of any kind). Panpsychism, thus, presents us with a view of nature consisting universally of materially real bodies with an interior or experiential reality. All bodies, therefore, are in some respects both material and psychic.

However, this material-cum-psychic reality should not be confused with standard dualism, as defined earlier: namely, two distinct substances existing in their own separate (but mysteriously interacting) domains. What is distinctive about panpsychism is that there is explicitly no separation between matter and mind. They are, rather, more like two aspects of the one thing, body, or "organism." But, again, this theory should not be confused with dual-aspectism or neutral monism, as in Spinoza, where mind and matter are understood as two aspects of some deeper underlying single ontological reality.

Although panpsychism is compatible with Spinozistic ontology (in fact this is a criticism often leveled at Spinoza's philosophy), it does not necessarily entail it. It is possible that the mind-matter coupling distinctive of panpsychism is intrinsic to the fundamental nature of reality and that there is no deeper "stuff." Reality, then, just *is* such that it requires both matter and mind *all the way down*. According to this view, there is only one fundamental ontological substratum, but it exists necessarily in two modes of being: the material and the mental.

Thus, panpsychism could be considered another variation of monism; but it is neither neatly materialist (purely physical) nor idealist (purely mental). Nor, as already noted, is it truly a dualism. It is an ontological position that has, as we shall see, a long heritage that embraces the paradoxical status of "dualistic-monism" or "nondual duality."

The long heritage of panpsychism, in fact, goes all the way back to the beginnings of Western philosophy and has precursors in many prephilosophical cosmologies, such as those found in animistic and pantheistic mythologies of shamanic cultures.

## The Orphic Influence

In *Homage to Pythagoras* Lindisfarne scholar Christopher Bamford observes that the Pythagorean religious-philosophical tradition—where philosophy was a way of life, practiced as a transformative discipline (*mathesis,* from which we get "mathematics")—was primarily about pattern or form, rather than about substance.[2] This distinction is fundamental to the thesis I am proposing here:

For nearly four hundred years, Cartesian-inspired science and philosophy have held the primacy of substance—resulting in an ontology and epistemology that are actually aberrations from a much longer tradition, stretching back into antiquity and beyond. This "other" tradition is based on the ontological primordiality of form, an underlying or intrinsic dynamic that informs and gives shape to material substance, and on an epistemology, a way of knowing, that involves a transformation in the being of the knower.

The early modern ontology of Francis Bacon and René Descartes is an aberration because it was based on an obsession with matter as inert and mechanical substance, a view that has continued to dominate modernist science and philosophy. In contrast, this "other" tradition has tended to regard matter either as possessing an inherent capacity for self-organization or as intrinsically sacred, possessing spirit or consciousness. It is a view of matter in which spontaneous pattern and form are intimations of a deeper and more elusive aspect of nature than the phenomena apparent to our sense perception.

This pre-Cartesian tradition has continued in an unbroken, though at times recessive or occluded, lineage right up to the present day. In contemporary mainstream science, echoes of it are to be found in works by physicists such as Werner Heisenberg,[3] David Bohm,[4] and Eugene Wigner,[5] psychologist Carl Jung,[6] biologists D'Arcy Thompson,[7] C. H. Waddington,[8] and Rupert Sheldrake,[9] molecular biologist Manfred Eigen,[10] biologist-anthropologist Gregory Bateson,[11] philosopher Martin Heidegger,[12] and mathematician G. Spencer-Brown,[13] as well as in the cutting-edge sciences of fractals, chaos, and complexity theories,[14] where pattern and form show up as intrinsic, self-organizing dynamics throughout nature.

In addition to these more mainstream "echoes" (which preserve traces of the ancient form-based ontology but not the ancient transformative epistemology), the primordiality of nonmaterial form and the spirit of epistemological transformation have continued in a hidden or underground esoteric stream, identified by Harvard scholar Eugene Taylor as the noetic or visionary tradition.[15]

Bamford traces this lineage back to Pythagoras and the Pythagoreans, pointing out that although Pythagoreanism is revolutionary, it is not original. By this, Bamford means that Pythagoras (ca. 578–510 BCE) himself was influenced by even older sciences from Egypt, Crete, Babylon (and possibly even India), where he spent many years traveling. However, whatever learning Pythagoras may have picked up from these other cultures, his primary influence appears to have been from the ancient Greek religious-mythological tradition and transformative discipline known as Orphism.

According to Bamford, by the time of Pythagoras no one knew anymore where the legendary, semi-mythological figure of Orpheus had come from. Mythologically, his origins go back to the beginnings of the world, in direct line of descent from the primordial god Chronos who created the world of time and by an act of self-reflection created the primal gods Chaos and Aether. According to the myth Orpheus was the son of the Muse Calliope and the god Apollo. His grandparents, therefore, would have been the gods Mnemosyne (Memory), mother of the Muses, and the great god Zeus.

As a "person," Orpheus is considered to be "the Greek representative of 'ancient theology,' the peer of Moses, Zoroaster, and Hermes Trismegistus,"[16] dating back to 1200 or 1500 BCE. Like the religions that followed these other prophet-magi, Orpheus is considered to have been a prophet (of the cult of Dionysus). What is distinctive about Orphism, however, is that Orpheus seems to have prescribed not merely a set of religious rites and myths, but emphasized a *transformative way of life,* whereby any individual could attain to a state of "transcendent purity synonymous with divinity."[17] Orphism was, therefore, also a healing art.

The Orphic transformation, which aligned human experience with that of the gods, resulted from a set of disciplines and rituals through which the individual "resonated" or responded sympathetically to the rhythms of the gods themselves. For, as Bamford points out, beginning with Chronos as the god of Infinite Time, the "First Principle or Principle of Principles," all the other gods were born from "a dynamic cosmogony of action in which action is anterior to time-space-movement-matter in any form."[18]

The Orphic gods, in other words, were conceived to be in some sense "rhythms," or "patterns of forces," undulations of forms and cosmic relationships—what Pythagoras came to call "numbers." By attuning with these rhythm-gods, the mortal human being in effect discovered a way to synchronize his or her own actions with the *timing* of the gods. As in all Orphic-Dionysian rituals, this rhythmical attunement was achieved through a combination of practices and disciplines, often involving ecstatic dances, chanting, ingestion of mood- and mind-altering plants, and deep contemplation of, and *participation in,* the Orphic mysteries.

But this Orphic tradition, dating back somewhere between one and two millennia before the common era, is itself an echo of an even more ancient, extremely archaic, tradition of ritual rooted in shamanic practices, reaching back into neolithic times and perhaps even back to Cro-Magnon and Neanderthal ancestors. In the shamanic traditions, too, transformation plays a central role where a consciousness of "participation mystique" is induced by chanting, dancing, and drumming—by sacred *rhythm.* With roots in shamanism, Orphism, therefore, dates back to a time before the separation of language and nature, to a time when the spoken or chanted word not only invoked the gods but, in some way, participated in their creation. According to Bamford:

> Orpheus dates back to an ancient time when words and things were not yet separated but were united in a kind of melodic chant. Naming, singing, was identical with creation, with making reality. Or, rather, in naming, the Gods spoke through the name. . . . In this sense, poetry was science; language was knowledge and power: At least in the mouth of the prophet-poet-shaman, language was the language of the Gods.[19]

And later, Bamford makes explicit the meaning of sympathetic resonance, of participatory rhythm:

> In other words, behind every sensible phenomenon there lies a reality of an animistic, super-sensible order, and just as one can make an open string vibrate by sounding its own note on a nearby instrument, so one may conjure up and communicate with a spirit by providing it with a song or tone.[20]

In the shamanic-Orphic tradition, therefore, we see that the ability of human consciousness to respond in rhythm with the gods in nature meant that the "objects" of nature were themselves *subjects* in which meaning and experience resided. Following the principle of sympathetic identity—only like responds to like—meaning in the human mind was responding to meaning in the ritual object. There was no separation between meaning and the sense-object. The "forms" of the human mind resonated with the "forms" inherent in matter. This was what Owen Barfield meant when he spoke of "original participation."[21] The world of nature, *matter itself,* was infused with meaning. And the shamanic-Orphic chants, songs, and poetry were the means by which the human mind could participate in the story of matter itself. But we lost this deep connection a long time ago—when we stopped listening, and nature and the gods fell silent.

Even by the time of Pythagoras, as Bamford noted, "it seemed as though meaning and object were coming apart, the Gods were growing silent, meaning seemed to be moving into another dimension."[22] In other words, form was being separated from matter. And by the time of Plato, this separation was almost complete. Pure forms had been shunted to a transcendent dimension. Nevertheless, the ancient shamanic-Orphic tradition of "form-within-substance," of "meaning within matter," persisted in a continuous lineage (sometimes hidden, sometimes explicit) right down through history. Only with Descartes was the Platonic separation finally completed. Meaning was removed from matter; the world of nature lost its inherent narrative and fell silent to the ears of civilized humanity. All meaning and experience, and therefore all *story,* were confined to the human mind or to the mind of God.

But even after Descartes, the visionary tradition of "narrative matter," of an inherently meaningful cosmos, persisted—albeit in a suppressed and esoteric form. And it is this lineage—in the history of Western philosophy, from before Descartes to those who came after him—the rest of this chapter explores. We pick up the story, after Orpheus, beginning with the "father of philosophy," Thales.

# The Panpsychist Lineage

In his essay on panpsychism in the *Encyclopedia of Philosophy,* Paul Edwards lists eminent thinkers from antiquity and from recent times who, in one way or another, have espoused an ontology in which mind is a quality or aspect intrinsic to matter or to the ultimate primordial substance.[23]* Among the earliest pre-Socratic philosophers the following endorsed some form of panpsychism.

**Thales** (ca. 625–545 BCE), generally considered to be the founder of the earliest philosophical school in the history of Western civilization, asserted that there was a single cosmic substance—*water,* the fountain of all living beings. Although Thales wrote no books, his teachings were passed on by oral tradition. Aristotle noted that Thales attributed souls to lifeless matter, a conjecture based on observations of lodestones (mag-

---

*The panpsychist trail, according to Edwards, includes "Thales, Anximenes, Empedocles, several of the Stoics, Plotinus, and Simplicius; numerous Italian and German Renaissance philosophers (including Paracelsus, Girolamo Cardano, Bernardino Telesio, Giordano Bruno, and Tommaso Campanella); G. W. Leibniz, F. W. J. von Schelling, Arthur Schopenhauer, Antonio Rosmini, W. K. Clifford, Harald Høffding, C. B. Renouvier, Eduard von Hartman, and Wilhelm Wundt; the German freethinkers Ernst Haeckel, Wilhelm Bölsche, and Bruno Wille; C. A. Strong, Erich Adickes, Erich Becher, Alfred Fouillée, C. S. Peirce, and F. C. S. Schiller; and, in our own day, A. N. Whitehead, Samuel Alexander, Bernadino Varisco, Paul Haeberlin, Aloys Wenzel, Charles Hartshorne, and the biologists Pierre Teilhard de Chardin, C. H. Waddington, Sewall Wright, and W. E. Agar."

To this list we may add also French philosopher Pierre-Louis Maupertuis (1698–1759), German scientist-philosopher Johann Wolfgang Goethe (1749–1832), German philosopher-psychologist Gustav Theodor Fechner (1801–1887), German Idealist metaphysician Rudolf Hermann Lotze (1817–1881), Russian philosopher Alexey A. Koslov (1831–1901; who actually called his system "Panpsychism"), American psychologist-philosopher William James (1842–1910), American philosopher Josiah Royce (1855–1916), French philosopher Henri Bergson (1859–1941), and contemporary American theologian-philosopher David Ray Griffin, as well as contemporary biologists Bernard Rensch and Charles Birch.

Surprisingly, British philosopher Francis Bacon (1561–1626), who opened the way for empirical-experimental science, expressed the belief that "all bodies whatsoever, though they have no sense . . . yet have perception. . . . And sometimes this perception, in some kind of bodies, is far more subtle [sic] than sense . . . And this perception is sometimes at a distance, as well upon the touch . . . [and] that which in these perceptions appeareth early, in the great effects cometh long after."[24]

nets) and amber rubbed with fur (producing static electricity). Thales is said to have held also that all things are full of gods.[25]

**Anaximander** (ca. 610–547 BCE). Typical of Presocratic thought, Thales' pupil Anaximander postulated a purely monistic ontology. For him, the ultimate was the boundless *apeiron*—"the infinite and eternal, perfectly homogeneous but utterly structureless and amorphous primary substance constituting everything that exists in the universe."[26] According to Anaximander, the *apeiron* was the source of everything, including the creation or emergence of all new forms, and to it everything ultimately returned. As the source of all forms, the *apeiron* was therefore the source of creative novelty; that is, it was intrinsically creative and self-organizing—similar to Giordano Bruno's *mater-materia* (mind-in-matter) or "intelligent matter."

**Anaximenes** (ca. 585–525 BCE), along with Thales and Anaximander, was one of the triumvirate of important Milesian philosophers. He believed that the fundamental substance was infinite like Anaximander's indeterminate *apeiron*, but unlike the *apeiron*, Anaximenes' fundamental substance was determinate—he said it was *air*. Always in motion, air forms all things by spontaneous changes due to condensation and rarefaction—for example, earth and stones are condensed air, and fire is rarefied air. And just as the human soul (psyche) is the breath or air that holds us together as living beings, "so do breath and air encompass the whole world."[27]

**Pythagoras** (ca. 578–510 BCE), said to be the first person to call himself a philosopher,[28] combined rational, mathematical science with religious mysticism as a methodology for penetrating the great mysteries of nature. He and his school, the Pythagoreans, taught that number and geometry were the essence of reality. In other words, behind the multiplicity of material forms in nature there lie hidden structures or forms that are essentially mathematical. By discovering these "forms" or "laws of harmony," philosophers could come to understand the inner forces of nature. Pythagoras insisted that perfection existed only in the transcendental realm of mathematical forms, accessible only to the mind, and that the world of material forms, accessible to the senses, was necessarily imperfect. This dichotomy of perfect mathematical forms and imperfect material forms influenced later generations of philosophers, such as Plato and his followers, and indeed may be seen as the origin of the entire Western tradition of metaphysical dualism.

The first intimation, then, of another realm different from or transcendent to the substantial world of nature came from Pythagoras. Actually, this "other realm," which Pythagoras recognized as "number," was taken to be the essence of matter. With this insight, Pythagoras revealed that the world of empirical forms, the world of sensory nature, was in essence an expression of the mental realm of mathematics. Matter, in his view, was inherently rational. Numbers, ratios, and geometrical forms were primary and gave shape to the visible world. So Pythagoras not only drew a distinction between the two realms, he was the first to see an intimate relationship between them.

Pythagoras's dualism was expressed in another way: as the opposites of the unlimited (*apeiron*) and the limited (*peras*). The unlimited *apeiron* was space, while the limited was the origin of number and geometrical shapes. When the unlimited is first limited, the result is unity, or a point. Next comes two (a line), followed by three (a plane), and then by four (a solid). There is also a trace of panpsychist monism in Pythagoras's philosophy, insofar as he spoke of the supreme mind or ultimate deity as the monad. The soul was the "spark of the monad," an immortal essence imprisoned in the body. He conceived of the universe as a living being, permeated and animated by the intelligence of the monad. This position qualifies him equally as a forerunner of dualism (soul as an "imprisoned essence" in the body) and as a panpsychist (intelligent soul permeates the material universe and is inseparable from it). This last insight, along with his view that nature, to its core, is ultimately composed of creative, self-generating dynamic forms, qualifies him for a place in the historical lineage of panpsychism.

As I will show, we can find a direct line of conceptual descent from Pythagoras's mathematical-material forms, to Plato's substance-Form, to Aristotle's hylomorphic matter-form, to Bruno's self-organizing, mind-in-matter, *mater-materia,* to Leibniz's monadology, and to Whitehead's explicit panpsychism.

Even **Heraclitus** (ca. 540–480 BCE), an unreserved critic of Pythagoras, shows a trace of panpsychism. Most famous from antiquity for stating that all things are one and always in flux, he said that fire is the fundamental element and that the "soul [is] a spark of the substance of the stars. . . . [The soul is] immortal and returns upon death to the all-soul to which it is related."[29]

> This order, which is the same in all things, no one of gods or men has made; but it was ever, is now, and ever shall be everliving Fire, fixed measures of it kindling and fixed measures of it going out.[30]

Heraclitus is the father of process philosophy, which, as we will see, is the fundamental ontology common to all panpsychism, especially the cosmology of Alfred North Whitehead.

With **Anaxagoras** (ca. 500–428 BCE), we come to the philosopher who introduced the term that was to form the basis of the etymology (if not philosophy) of a long tradition of nonmaterialist philosophies, such as Gnosticism, Neoplatonism, and the perennial visionary noetic tradition, in which mind, intelligence, or spirit was to play a major part. The word that Anaxagoras introduced was *nous*. However, reading extant fragments of Anaxagoras's work, he is seen to be both an explicit nonpanpsychist and a panpsychist. This apparent contradiction can be resolved by viewing the body of Anaxagoras's work from the perspective of an evolutionary cosmogenesis.

Anaxagoras states initially that "all things were together infinite both in number and in smallness" and that "in everything there is a portion of everything except Nous, and there are some things in which there is Nous (mind) also."[31] Clearly, he is saying that nous (mind) is not in *all* things. He goes on to explain why this must be so:

> All other things partake in a portion of everything, while Nous is infinite and self-ruled, and is mixed with nothing, but is alone, itself by itself. For if it were not by itself, but were mixed with anything else, it would partake in all things . . . and the things mixed with it would

hinder it, so that it would have power over nothing in the same way that it has now being alone by itself. . . . [Yet] Nous has power over all things. . . . Nous set in order all things that were to be and that were, and all things that are now. . . . But no thing is altogether separated off or distinguished from anything except Nous.[32]

Anaxagoras's cosmology is both holistic-holographic ("there is a portion of everything in everything") and infinite-particulate ("there is always a smaller," that is, the world is composed of infinitely small particles, "germs," or "seeds," as he called them). Combining these two postulates, he states that everything contains the seeds of everything else, *all the way down*. The smallest particle, therefore, contains the seeds of the entire universe. All forms that occur in the universe are the result of some readmixture of its constituent particles. And all qualitative distinctions are due to differences in mixtures. With one exception: *Spatial* distinctions, the separations between particles, are not due to rearrangements of particles but to the motive force of *nous*.

Nous, or mind, is the one exception to the "all in everything" rule. Nous, the "finest and the purest" of the infinite cosmic particles, does not mix with all the rest. Instead, these particles are the only self-moving entities, and because of them all other separations take place. It is due to the action of these mental particles that all other particles separate out from their original amorphous mixture. This "separating out" occurs via a process of revolutions, a sort of mind-induced centrifuge, which deposits the heavy-dense particles as earth and the less dense as water, air, and fire.

Anaxagoras, therefore, is telling us that nous is distinct and separate from all other things (the world of inert matter-particles), and this must be so because it is nous that is the power behind all separation in the world. In fact, "separation" is the original meaning of "nous": It is the principle of separation that gives rise to "other" in the world.[33] Thus, Anaxagoras appears to be postulating a fundamentally dualist ontology: mental, self-motivating, finely grained, nous particles on the one hand and grosser inert material particles on the other. From our perspective in history, this all looks very Cartesian (if we ignore the radical atomism). Nous is both separate and distinct from inert matter.

However, the monism of Anaxagoras' philosophy is reclaimed when we realize that he considers *all* particles to be essentially material, or physical. The difference is that only nous particles are capable of self-motion and therefore are the only ones with an intrinsic psychic component. By imparting their motion to the undifferentiated mixture of inert particles, nous particles induce separation and distinction between various mixtures and introduce "other" into the pluralistic world of forms. Thus, on the one hand, even if nous is itself particulate and material, it is separate from all other forms of matter.

On the other hand, there is a further twist to Anaxagoras's cosmology and ontology: Whereas, in the first instance, nous is separate from and gives rise to "other" (distinctive forms of matter), the second nous is dynamic; it is a motive power and thus initiates an *evolutionary* cosmos. Once nous has completed the initial task of cosmogenic separation and created the "other" mixtures, it *then* exists as a fine animating "mist" in all things that have separated off.

> But Nous has power over all things that are, and it is now where all the other things are, in the mass that surrounds the world, and in the things that have separated off and that are being separated off.[34]

What we get from Anaxagoras is a cosmogony that distinguishes between *ontological* separation of nous and "other," and cosmogenic, *evolutionary,* or *temporal* infusion of inert matter by nous. Once the separation is set in motion, it is as if nous then impregnates other matter with its own internal motive force. Even though certain mixtures of matter may be self-moving because of their complement of nous, it is still *nous* that is responsible for the motion and creativity of matter. This is very similar to Giordano Bruno's notion of *mater-materia,* which is a fusion of infinite "intelligent" matter with the cosmic mind. In fact, as the ex-Jesuit and Humanities scholar Ramon Mendoza points out,

It did not take Bruno too long to discover that Anaximander's fecund *apeiron* was intimately related to Anaxagoras' *nous*. His synthesis of the *apeiron* with *nous* paved the way for the fusion of boundless *mater-materia* with the cosmic mind and, consequently, also to a markedly monistic ontology.[35]

To sum up: Anaxagoras begins as a monist (everything is particulate and material), slips into dualism (only the finest "mist" of particles have self-motion or mind), but quickly pulls himself out by proposing a panpsychist evolutionary perspective (nous or mind infuses all material forms and mixtures with a complement of self-motion).

There is, therefore, an important distinction between Anaxagoras's and Descartes's forms of dualism. In Descartes's case, as repeatedly emphasized here, his dualism is predicated on a distinction in kind between "spatial" and "nonspatial" ontological entities—namely, extended matter and nonextended minds, respectively. In Anaxagoras' case, however, *both* nous (mind) particles and inert material particles are spatial. They are all *physical* in the Cartesian sense, since they occupy some portion of space—even if it is infinitesimal. The essential difference, therefore, is not between physical and mental entities. What distinguishes nous particles from inert particles is not a difference between matter and mind, but a difference between one kind of (self-moving) physical particle and another kind of (inert) physical particle.

However, and this is the important point for panpsychism: One of these two kinds of physical particles has *the power of self-motion*. Given the ability for self-motion, the "mist" of nous particles meets the criterion for panpsychism as long as these self-motivating particles are universally "in the things that have separated off and that are being separated off." If *all* mixtures, no matter how small or how large, have a complement of nous, then all objects will be ostensibly mental, and panpsychism would hold.

So far we have seen how the Presocratics emphasized some form of ontological monism: For Thales the single primary substance was water, for Anaximander it was the indeterminate *apeiron*, for Anaximenes it was air, for Pythagoras it was number, for Heraclitus it was fire, and for Anaxagoras it was particulate matter. Typically, these philosophers explained multiplicity of forms and change as due to variations of concentrations of the specific primary substance.

The first philosopher to replace the Presocratic One with a universe in which change was due to combinations of more than one element was **Empedocles** (ca. 490–435 BCE). He proposed that the world evolved through a four-stage cycle based on four irreducible elements: earth, water, air and fire. All changes were governed by two fundamental forces—Love and Strife—and the four stages they followed were (1) the elements are in perfect harmony due to the attractive power of love; (2) strife enters the world and begins to pull asunder harmonious and ordered combinations; (3) strife dominates, and the combinations of elements completely decay; and (4) love reenters the world and begins to rebuild unified combinations again. Empedocles' panpsychism is revealed in his understanding of love as a universal force, a principle of organization present throughout the universe, acting from within, and on, all bodies.

Following Pythagoras' notion of ideal mathematical forms, **Plato** (ca. 427–347 BCE) proposed a more definite dualism: He agreed that the world of nature is a manifestation of a domain of ideal essences, which he called the realm of "Pure Ideas" or "Ideal Forms," and he denied that the ideal forms are themselves to be found in the world of matter. Perfection exists, Plato said, only in the domain of Forms or Ideas, a purely transcendent, metaphysical realm. With Platonic dualism, then, we have a clear statement of different domains of reality: the world of perfect Forms, and the world of imperfect matter. In his famous allegory of "The Cave," Plato said that the world of the senses, the world of material shapes, is merely an imperfect reflection of the perfection of the transcendent world of Ideas.

Not only did Plato prepare the ground for Western dualism, but by claiming that the only true reality was the domain of Forms or Ideas, he also opened the way for the Western philosophical tradition of idealism. By relegating the world of matter to an inferior ontological level, Plato began a trend that found favor especially in dualistic Neoplatonic,

Gnostic, and Christian traditions that regarded the world of matter as somehow degrading or even corrupting. (This reading of Plato has been challenged by Ken Wilber, however.*) In any event, Plato's philosophy resulted in a decisive move away from the various monistic materialisms of the Presocratics.

Plato's pupil, **Aristotle** (384–322 BCE) agreed that perfection did not exist in the sublunar world but that it did in the supralunar world. He believed in a physical dualism: that bodies in the celestial sphere moved in perfect trajectories, whereas those on Earth did not. However, Aristotle emphatically disagreed with Plato's metaphysical dualism. He denied that the realm of forms was transcendent to the world of matter. Although, never quite returning Greek philosophy to the ontological monism of the Presocratics, Aristotle did propose a kind of "dualistic-monism." For fundamental to Aristotle's metaphysics was his notion of *hylomorphism*—

---

*According to Ken Wilber in *Sex, Ecology, Spirituality: The Spirit of Evolution*, this conventional interpretation of Plato has got it backward. He makes a strong case that a major flaw in the Western intellectual tradition has been a badly distorted view of Plato and a misplaced emphasis on Aristotle.

An open and unbiased examination of Plato's work, says Wilber, shows a balanced recognition of the value of a downward orientation toward the world of matter (the "descending" involution of spirit into matter), along with an upward orientation toward the transcendent world of the divine One (the "ascending" evolution of matter into spirit). Platonism, therefore, includes *both* transcendence and immanence.

Wilber says it is a gross misreading of Plato to characterize his philosophy as "other-worldly," aimed solely beyond "this world." Such a reading completely misses the importance Plato placed on the *creative* aspect of the divine One, described by Plotinus as an "effulgence," a pouring forth or overflowing, of the One's own being into the world. The created—or *emanated*—world, from the World Soul to matter itself, is, therefore, intrinsically divine. The only way "up," toward transcendence, is by acknowledging, realizing, and honoring the *already* embeddedness of Spirit in souls, minds, bodies, and matter.

On this view, neither Plato nor Plotinus (and therefore not the Neoplatonic tradition) devalued matter in general, or flesh in particular. This mischaracterizing of Platonism has resulted in the history of Western philosophy being what Wilber has called (after Whitehead) a series of "fractured footnotes" to Plato. Wilber does not deny that for large slices of its history, Western thought has been oriented toward the transcendent—but *this has been due to a seriously one-sided reading of Plato*. The flaw of the "fractured footnotes" is not Plato's, it is the fault of those who followed him (Plotinus and other Neoplatonists excepted, of course).

forms inseparable from matter, and if there are ideal forms, they are part of the physical. Thus, although Aristotle did postulate two different metaphysical principles, a dualism of matter and form, he also insisted that they were always inseparable and constituted a kind of dualistic monism.

What is interesting about the doctrine of hylomorphism is just this paradox of "dualistic monism." Such a "dualism" opens the way for a revolutionary conception of the mind-body relation, one that avoids the absurdities of Cartesian substance dualism and the logical perplexities of conventional materialistic emergentism. Its "monism" is accounted for by the fact that such a model does not make an ontological separation between matter and nonphysical mind. In Aristotle's hylomorphic metaphysic, both matter and form are physical—but Aristotelian physics is decisively different from the mechanistic paradigm dominating modern physics and our understanding of matter today.

For example, central to Aristotle's physics is a much broader notion of causality, with four types of causes: material cause, formal cause, efficient cause, and final cause. Aristotle's cosmology is inherently teleological. It presents a view of matter-form that is intrinsically purposeful, both in-forming itself and drawn to a final goal. By contrast, modern physical science recognizes only one form of causality, namely Aristotle's efficient cause—that is, mechanical "bump or pull" causality of energetic causes and effects.

Although he uses terms similar to Plato's substance and Form, Aristotle's form is not separate from matter—physical reality is always teleological "matter-form." In Aristotelian hylomorphic physics, the formal or morphic cause, that which gives shape to matter, is always and inevitably associated with matter—*morph* is essential to *hyle*.

However, Aristotle's hylomorphism reveals a residue of Platonic dualism by continuing to view matter as merely a passive receptacle or receptive substratum of form. For Aristotle, matter was powerless in itself, and were it not for the inevitable presence of form, or the in-forming principle, matter was virtually nothing in itself. Aristotelian matter was effectively mere *potentia,* deriving its actuality only through the activity of form. In Aristotle's dualism, form was "act," or the active principle, while matter was potential, the passive principle. Together, act plus potentia resulted in actuality. Given this radically passive conception of matter, Aristotle was forced to define it in purely negative terms: "*neque quid, neque quale, neque quantum, neque aliud quid ex quo res determinatur*' (neither a thing, nor a quality, nor a quantity, nor any other thing by which anything can be determined)."[36]

Besides Aristotle's hylomorphic theory of inseparable matter and form, we can trace the continuity of the panpsychist lineage during the next two to three centuries after Empedocles to several of the Stoic philosophers, followers of **Zeno the Stoic** (ca. 340–265 BCE). Only fragments of the more than twenty books written by Zeno the Stoic remain, but among these we notice elements of the panpsychist worldview. For instance, "The parts of the world are sensing. The world does not lack feeling" could be straight out of Whitehead, as will become clear in the next few chapters. And "Now the soul feels with the body in sickness or under the knife, and the body feels with the soul turning red when the soul is ashamed and pale when the soul is afraid. Therefore the soul is the body"[37] expresses the essence of the intimate psychosomatic relationship implicit in the mind-body holism of panpsychism.

After the Stoics, the next most significant figure in Western philosophy to espouse a panpsychist metaphysic is **Plotinus** (205–270 CE). And with Plotinus we come to a watershed in Western cosmology and ontology. For the first time a characteristically Indian or Vedantist worldview becomes a major force in Western thought. Scholars are undecided about whether Plotinus ever actually encountered Vedic teachings, although many agree that he desired to explore Indian and Persian philosophies. In fact, he specifically enlisted with Emperor Gordianus's army to invade Persia so that he might have access to Aryan and Vedic knowledge. However, his stay in Persia was short-lived due to the assassination of the emperor.

Nevertheless, whether through some direct or indirect Indian influence or independently, Plotinus came up with a religious philosophy remarkably consonant with fundamental Hindu cosmology and ontology. Plotinus was the first Western philosopher to explicitly propose an emphatic spiritual monism. Previously the various monisms of the Presocratics were typically matter based in some form or another—water, *apeiron*, air, or fire. And even the nascent idealism of Pythagoras's number and geometrical essences, and the explicit idealism of Plato's transcendental Forms, were pluralistic. Although Plotinus—a founder of Neoplatonism—was clearly inspired by Plato, he went much further in developing an idealism of spiritual monism.

For my purposes—elucidating an ontology adequate to an epistemology of consciousness—what is significant about Plotinus is that he develops a version of idealism that is also thoroughly realist, in that it does not deny the reality of the material world. One of the most interesting aspects of Plotinus's cosmology is that it goes much further than an account of spirit and matter, offering the first Western vision of a "continuum ontology," with gradations or levels in a hierarchy of being. This "great chain of being" reaches from matter, at one end, all the way through organic, living bodies, minds, souls, and spirit—finally transcending all categories of sensing and knowing into a thoroughly ineffable "One."

Whereas all the panpsychist ontologies I have looked at so far postulate matter as a primary datum, albeit coupled with mind as a self-motivating, self-organizing, and self-informing principle, Plotinus describes a cosmology in which matter is a late consequent of spirit. Therefore, on the one hand Plotinus is clear that matter does not have ontological primacy, while on the other hand, when matter does appear in his scheme, it is thoroughly infused with spirit. In this sense Plotinus's idealism is also a form of panpsychism. However, whereas most of the models we've looked at so far are *ontological* panpsychisms, Plotinus's is a *consequent* panpsychism.

I'll summarize Plotinus's model to help clarify what I mean by "consequent panpsychism." I should point out, however, that, of all the philosophies I've looked at so far, Plotinus's most explicitly qualifies as true "epistemotherapy," or perhaps "epistemo-liberation"—a transcending of psychospiritual constraints through a transformation in knowing and experience. (Plotinus was not the first to propose a philosophy of transformation; this was also the focus of the teachings of Pythagoras and Plato, for instance. But for Plotinus, psychospiritual transformation was central.) Such a transformative approach to philosophy is a major thesis of this book: Any healing of the ontological split between mind and matter will involve an effective epistemotherapy—engaging in an adequate epistemology in such a way that the consciousness, the experiential being, of the investigator is radically transformed.

The primary motivation behind Plotinus's teaching was to show people the way back to the source from which they, and everything else, came.[38] This source is the "One," which is beyond all limitation, beyond all determination, and thus beyond all possibility of sensory perception or rational definition and description. The One is even beyond being. In order to be able to refer to it at all, as the source of everything else, Plotinus was forced to name it—but clearly only as a heuristic provision. He might simply have called it the "Beyond," the "Source," or the "Unnamable." Once the path back to the source has been completed, even the designation "One" must be dropped.

The One is thus utterly transcendent. However, although (or perhaps because) it is unconstrained and unlimited, the One naturally and necessarily expresses itself in an outpouring of itself. It is transcendent but also necessarily immanent. To help us understand this apparent paradox, Plotinus used the metaphor of "emanation": As the Sun is transcendent to (above and beyond) the Earth, it continually radiates its light, bathing the Earth and everything on it. Just as it is the nature of the Sun to radiate, the transcendent One naturally emanates through a series of stages or levels, at each stage moving farther from the original unity toward greater multiplicity.

The first stage of emanation is the nous or divine intelligence, a reflection of unity in multiplicity. The multiplicity, here, is the level or domain of Platonic Forms, still prior to space-time. At this level all knowing involves total identification of the knower with what is known. It is a blending of knowing and being, a fusion of epistemology and ontology.

Next, the nous further differentiates into the level of soul, or world soul (anima mundi). This is similar to Plato's "demiurge," the primordial active principle of nature that generates forms and patterns in the world of space-time. The world soul is the immanent self-organizing activity of the entire natural world, including humans, other animals, plants, minerals—all elements of the material universe. It is at this level that Plotinus's spiritual monism encompasses panpsychism: All the individual things of the natural world are imbued with soul, in fact, derive their forms and their being from the world soul. "The world soul contains the world as its body. Time is the record of the world soul's attempt to embody in matter the fullness of eternal and infinite being."[39] Thus,

Plotinus's panpsychism derives from the *panentheism* implicit in his form of idealism.* The material world, ultimately, exists *in* the effulgence of spirit. Matter is a consequence of emanating spirit and is thoroughly imbued with soul: hence, "consequent panpsychism."

The final stage of the divine emanation is when spirit, through the world soul, devolves into matter itself. This is the hierarchical level of maximum multiplicity, and is therefore the stage farthest removed from the original unity of the divine One. In this sense, since Plotinus equates the One with the Good, matter is regarded as the negation, even the opposite, of the Good. In his essay "Plotinus" in *The Concise Encyclopedia of Western Philosophy and Philosophers,* A. Hilary Armstrong sums up the position of matter in Plotinus's hierarchical ontology:

> Matter itself, though it proceeds like all else from the Good, is the principle of evil because it is the absolute limit, the utter negation and deficiency of being that marks the end of the descent from the Good through the successive levels of reality.[40]

However, as Armstrong goes on to point out, this characterization of matter as "evil" should not be taken as a rejection by Plotinus of the intrinsic worth or value of the material world. Its "evil" is relative to the limitless goodness of the transcendental One. It is only "evil" in that matter, were it to exist by itself devoid of form, would be, in fact (contrary to our usual way of understanding things), the "closest approach to nonbeing."[41] In fact, despite its lowly position in the great chain of being, the material universe (certainly in the celestial realms) is considered by Plotinus to be "good and beautiful as a living structure of forms, and the best possible work of the soul."[42]

Three features of Plotinus's cosmic system should be noted at this point. First, as the One emanates, its relationship with all subsequent

---

*"Panentheism" ("all is *in* god") differs from "pantheism" ("all *is* god") in that the former refers to the world existing *in* spirit or god, whereas the latter refers to an *identification* of god and world. In pantheism, as in Spinoza, nature *is* god; the divine is wholly immanent in nature. In panentheism, as in Plotinus, nature is *in* god; the divine is both immanent in and transcendent to nature.

stages is *evolutionary*. Second, the evolutionary descent of spirit into matter—"involution" would be a better term—is only half the story. Having devolved or "involved" itself with material forms, the play of spirit in the world now turns upward. Following its involutionary descent into matter, the whole thrust of spirit-in-matter is to liberate itself from material constraints and multiplicity and to return to its original unity, its source in the One. "This double rhythm of outgoing and return runs through the whole of Plotinus's universe."[43]

The third point about Plotinus's system is perhaps the most difficult for Western-trained minds to grasp. The entire process of the One becoming the many and the many becoming the One—the whole sweep of involution and evolution—does not take place in time. It is a logical, rather than a chronological, sequence. All levels of being are present, *permanently,* simultaneously in everything. This is a metaphysic of paradoxical timeless evolution, more properly envisioned as "logovolution" or "onvolution"—the spontaneous subdivision of the *logos* or *being* into multiplicity. Humans, as with all material forms, long to reunite with the eternal forms of the world soul, with the divine intelligence of the nous (or logos), and ultimately with the unimaginable, utterly ineffable, wholly transcendent One.

With our specific combination of material forms and spiritual essence we have minds able to think and contemplate. We can choose to either remain engaged at the lower level of matter and body or to follow a disciplined spiritual path toward enlightenment and liberation at higher levels of consciousness. If we choose the path of consciousness evolution, according to Plotinus, we will pass through various levels of experience and knowing until we reach the level where our way of knowing becomes indistinguishable from the nature of the being known. This is the epistemological-ontological fusion of subject and object I mentioned earlier, the ultimate "nondual," which I examine in more detail in *Radical Knowing.*

Such fusion of knowing and being is called "transformation," where the essence of the knower, the knower's very being, undergoes an evolutionary shift of state in order to blend with "that being known." Such transformation, which is essentially a spiritual or religious experience, is radically different from ordinary, intellectual philosophical knowledge. The knower is radically transformed in the process of growth in knowing. This was precisely the motivation and objective underlying the kind of spiritual philosophy expressed in Plotinus's cosmological system. It is also the kind of epistemological shift that, according to the view proposed in this book, will be required for philosophers of mind to crack the hard ontological problem of mind-body relationship and to bridge the epistemological explanatory gap, and for scientists to break the "mind barrier" and develop a true science of consciousness.

## Neoplatonism and the Panpsychist Lineage

Plotinus's influence continued for several centuries in the form of Neoplatonism, a school of mystical philosophy that incorporates and synthesizes elements from many philosophical and spiritual traditions, such as the works of Pythagoras and the Pythagoreans, Plato, Aristotle, and their respective followers, as well as influences from early Greek and Oriental polytheism, alchemy, astrology, and Hermetic magic practices.

Although Plotinus is customarily identified as the founder of Neoplatonism, scholars have pointed out that, like all philosophical schools, deciding on any exact date or person, in what is an evolutionary process, is always to some extent arbitrary. For instance, among Plotinus's precursors (obviously, besides Plato himself) was **Xenocrates** (396–314 BCE), head of Plato's Academy from 339 BCE. Five centuries before Plotinus, he had already identified the supreme god with the primal unity. Xenocrates, thus, not Plotinus, may be regarded as the first Western philosopher to have proposed a theological or spiritual monism.

**Numenius of Apamea,** a second-century CE neo-Pythagorean philosopher, is considered by some scholars to be the true founder of Neoplatonism. His teachings prefigure much of the theologically based continuum ontology of Plotinus. For example, he spoke of an absolutely transcendent god, one of three levels of divinity. The first transcendent god is a kind of cross between Pythagorean numbers and Platonic Forms. The next god creates the world in accordance with the number-forms. And the third god is the ruler of the created world. Beneath these is a hierarchy of divine and demonic beings, and inferior to these is the human being composed of soul and body, with the hierarchy ending finally in "prime matter," associated with nonbeing.[44]

Around the time of Christ, a Jewish philosopher, **Philo Judaeus** (30 BCE–50 CE) anticipated Plotinus's trinity of the utterly transcendent One, the nous, and the world soul by proposing what he called "negative theology," where God is so completely beyond any conceptual reach that all that can be said is what God is not. Whereas Plotinus's One relates to the world of multiplicity via a hierarchy of nous, world soul, and material forms, Philo had previously presented a hierarchy of God, Logos, world. In addition, Philo, like Plotinus, said that the way to know the utterly nonconceptual divine is through nonconceptual rapture, a wholly feeling-based epistemology.

**Ammonius Saccas** (ca. 175–242 CE), also sometimes considered to be the founder of Neoplatonism, was the teacher of Plotinus and other third-century "founding" Neoplatonists, such as Origen and Longius. After Plotinus other significant Neoplatonists, preserving the lineage of idealist consequent panpsychism, include Plotinus's disciple and biographer **Porphyry** (ca. 232–304 CE), **Proclus** (410–485 CE), who explicitly derived matter from the One, and **Simplicius** (fl. 527–565 CE), who attempted to reconcile Stoic philosophy with Neoplatonism. Even **St. Augustine** (354–430 CE), the great early medieval Christian theologian, was at one time a Neoplatonist. In the ninth century the Irish theologian-philosopher **John Scotus Erigena** (810–877) elaborated a Neoplatonist theophany of emanation and return, which was in essence panentheistic and therefore a form of consequent panpsychism. Thus Neoplatonism continued to be an influential stream in the development of Western thought, via its impact on Christianity, right up to the seventeenth century, and, in fact, even into our own time.

For about five hundred years, from around the middle of the fifth century to the tenth, Europe slipped into the long night of the Dark Ages, when widespread contact with Greek philosophy was lost. Then, in the twelfth, thirteenth, and fourteenth centuries, following the rediscovery of Greek learning, in translations of the works of Plato and Aristotle by

Arab scholars such as **Avicenna** (980–1037) and **Averroës** (1126–1198), new waves of intellectual excitement began to emerge in Europe. Arab philosophers also contributed to the Neoplatonic stream through an accident of history. Earlier, in the ninth century in Syria, the School of Baghdad, intent on translating Aristotle's works, mistakenly included portions of Plotinus's *Enneads* and portions of books by Proclus. In the late thirteenth and early fourteenth centuries the German mystic **Meister Eckhart** (1260–1372), although trained as a Dominican Aristotelian scholar, was influenced by the Neoplatonism of Plotinus, Augustine, and Scotus Erigena.

Many other names could be added to the long Neoplatonic-panpsychist trail,* which continued into the flowering of the European Renaissance during the fifteenth and sixteenth centuries—men such as **Marsilius Ficino** (1433–1499), a translator of Plato and Plotinus who attempted to unite Platonic and Christian thought; as well as Paracelsus, Giordano Bruno, and Tommaso Campanella, about whom I should give more than a passing mention. **Tommaso Campanella** (1568–1639*)* is another generally unsung Renaissance great whose philosophical insights foreshadowed Descartes's famous method leading to the *cogito*. Like his fellow Dominican, Bruno, Campanella was accused of heresy and was

---

*Ken Wilber offers his own version of the Neoplatonist lineage, emphasizing its sustained impact on Western philosophy, in fact on Western civilization: "This general notion—a multidimensional Kosmos interwoven by Ascending and Descending patterns of Love (Eros and Agape)—would become a dominant theme of all Neoplatonic schools, and exert a profound influence on virtually all subsequent thought, up to (and beyond) the Enlightenment. Through Augustine and Dionysius, it would permeate all of Christianity, in one form or another, from Boethius to Jakob Boehme, from the Victorine mystics (Hugh and Richard) to Saint Catherine and Dame Julian, from Saint Theresa and Saint John of the Cross to Tauler and Eckhart. Through Nicholas Cusanus and Giordano Bruno it would help jolt the Middle Ages into the Renaissance. Through Novalis and Schelling, it would be the roots of Romantic and Idealist Rebellion against the flatland aspects of Enlightenment. It would find its way into Leibniz and Spinoza and Schopenhauer, and make its way to Emerson and James and Jung. Even Locke would operate within its broad framework, though he would collapse the frame almost beyond recognition. Indeed, when Lovejoy traces the influence of the Great Chain, and refers to it as 'the dominant official philosophy of the greater part of civilized mankind throughout most of its history', the hand of Plotinus lurks, virtually without exception, there in the background."[45]

victimized by the Inquisition, imprisoned for life, and released only when deemed insane. The core of Campanella's epistemology was the notion that the only trustworthy datum of experience is the feeling of one's own existence, a feeling that withstands any rational doubt. Such self-certainty, when analyzed, yields knowledge both of God and the world.

But unlike Descartes's *cogito,* Campanella's Neoplatonist leanings led him, not to substance dualism, but to a panentheistic-panpsychist worldview. Instead of concluding that matter was inert, insentient extended substance and that mind was thinking-feeling nonextended substance, Campanella proposed a continuum ontology, with reality graded in a hierarchy from matter to God. "All things possess in their different degrees, the 'primalities' of knowledge, power, and love."[46]

**Paracelsus** (1493–1541), born Theophrastus Bombastus of Hohenheim, was a physician who was also a scholar of alchemy, the Kabbalah, Neoplatonism, and Gnosticism. He practiced the Hermetic worldview in his medicine, following the doctrine of "as above, so below," the view that human life is a microcosm of the macrocosm. His panpsychism is expressed in the view that both the macrocosm and the microcosm are essentially dynamic, with an intrinsic striving toward creativity.

Interestingly, instead of the Neoplatonic spiritual nous, Paracelsus's corresponding first stage of creation was "ultimate matter" that, through separation, becomes prime matter, the raw material for all other things in the world of nature. Thus his position could be viewed as a form of subtle materialism. However, his entire system was ultimately neither materialist (not even in the radical panpsychist sense) nor dualist, but a form of idealist or spiritual monism familiar to all monotheistic religions; for Paracelsus believed that the universe of ultimate and primary matter was created by God.

**Giordano Bruno** (1548–1600) has been variously recognized as a gifted philosopher, cosmologist, astrologer, poet, magus, a heretic, a martyr, the first of the moderns, and a scientific genius whose brilliance has mostly gone unrecognized throughout history. He began his career as a Dominican monk in Italy but soon fell into disfavor with his superiors, and even as a teenager was threatened with the Inquisition for daring to challenge Church dogma. His rebellious nature led to his excommunication, and he spent the rest of his life staying one step ahead of the Inquisition, roaming throughout the great cities of Europe, where he taught in their leading universities, including Paris and Oxford.

His central driving ambition in life seems to have been a desire to overturn Aristotle's metaphysical hold on the minds of Europe's intellectuals. And to the extent that Aristotelianism had long become the foundation of Catholic theology, his threat to Aristotle's teachings was also a threat to the Church. His main point of contention was Aristotle's outdated Ptolemaic cosmology that placed Earth at the center of the universe. Earlier in the sixteenth century, a generation or so before Bruno, Copernicus had already challenged the Ptolemaic geocentricism and had declared that the Sun was the center of the universe. Bruno, far more audacious, insisted that not even the Sun was at the center, because there was no center at all.

In Bruno's acentric cosmology the universe was both boundless and eternal, coterminous with God. In fact, the implication of this aspect of his cosmology was more of a threat to Church dogma and authority than even the outrageous revolutionary vision of the acentric universe. For if the universe was coeternal with God, it was merely a short step to pantheism, which says that the universe, or nature, *is* God. In fact, Bruno did not explicitly avow pantheism, but his cosmology was very clearly panpsychist.

For Bruno the only acceptable ontology was a pure monism, and the nature of this ultimate was entirely in accord with the radical naturalism that I outlined previously for panpsychism. He viewed the world as consisting of *mater-materia,* a form of "intelligent matter," which in its highest form amounted to the Cosmic Mind (not unlike Plotinus's world soul). But the Cosmic Mind necessarily had a Cosmic Body, since everything that exists is made up of infinitesimal monads. He distinguished between three kinds of monads: God, the monad of monads; souls, and indivisible atoms.

Bruno's writings had a decisive influence on many later philosophers in the lineage of panpsychism (and on many who would never have considered themselves such). Among the most notable of these were Spinoza and Leibniz. (I will return to Bruno's remarkable legacy in chapter 10, "Stories Matter, Matter Stories.")

## Leibniz, Spinoza, and Chinese Influence

Although Spinoza was an older contemporary, I'll turn first to Leibniz, for his impact on philosophical panpsychism has been significantly greater. Until now I have discussed panpsychism within the context of a paradoxical ontological category: "dualistic monism" or "nondual dualism." It is possible, however, to interpret panpsychism as neither a form of monism nor as a form of dualism, but as a third option: pluralism.

**Gottfried Leibniz** (1646–1716), a German philosopher, largely self-taught, developed Bruno's concept of "monads" in *The Monadology.*[47] For Leibniz the universe consisted of an indefinite number of indivisible units. The most novel aspect of Leibniz's ontology is his notion that the indivisible monads are not physical in the Cartesian sense—extended in space—but each is primarily a center of force or action.*

Thus, Leibniz presents an ontology radically at odds with Descartes's. Not only does Leibniz replace extension with force as the ultimate nature of reality, but in doing so he avoids the problematic dualism of Cartesian extended substance (matter) and nonextended substance (mind). However, since force is nonextended, it is also nonphysical (in Cartesian terms). How, then, do Leibnizian nonphysical monads result in the real world of physical space and time? On the face of it, this seems to be the kind of problem confronting idealism: How can pure (nonphysical) spirit account for physical reality? But there is yet another question: How do monads as units of force account for minds? This, of course, is not a problem for idealism. But how do we get either minds or matter out of pure force? Leibniz provides an ingenious solution.

First of all, since monads lack extension they do not occupy space; they are *inextensional.* That is to say, whatever is not extensional must be *intensional,* having the characteristic of intentionality, and intentionality is a characteristic of mind. Leibniz described his monads as centers of feeling, apperception, and perception. Every monad has an "interior" state,

---

*Today some theorists might call these indivisible units of force/action "quanta." See, for example, Arthur Young's *The Reflexive Universe,* where he posits the photon or the "quantum of action" as the ultimate constituent of the world.

an awareness of itself, at least in some rudimentary form, and this is its "apperception." When it is aware of other monads, this is "perception."

In other words, mind is intrinsic to monads because, as units of force, they are centers of *feeling*. In abstraction force is either a mathematical construct or it is conceived as a form of energy. But energy occupies space. Force, by contrast—for example, in acceleration or gravitation—is primarily a *felt* reality. So, we get mind from force because force is essentially a felt, or experienced, phenomenon. But what about matter? What about space and time?

Again, Leibniz presents a neat solution: Space is the "order of possible co-existences" of monads. That is, space is a phenomenon relative to the perceived configuration of monads. Thus, in complete disagreement with Newton's absolute space, Leibniz's space is a derivative of felt experience or perception: It has only a phenomenal existence. Similarly with time, which is the "order of possibilities [of monads] which cannot co-exist."[49] Monads that cannot coexist simultaneously, then, must exist successively, and perception of such successive configurations is what gives rise to the experience of time. Time, therefore, like space, is a derivative phenomenon of feeling or perception. When units of force cannot feel each other simultaneously, they experience succession, and we call this "time"; when units of force can feel each other simultaneously, they experience spatial relationship, and we call this "space."

W. L. Reese points out that Leibniz's conception of time is fundamentally relative—relative both to relationships between monads, and relative to the "world line" of individual monads. For each monad, as a bundle of force, constantly strives forward toward self-development, toward its own future.

> There are different times because each monad is in process of development; it burgeons with the future in co-ordination with all other monads; and this power to extract its being out of itself is perhaps why Leibniz calls the monads also "entelechies."[48]

In chapter 10, I will return to the significance of "entelechy" as part of the solution to the mind-body problem proposed here. For now, it will be sufficient to note that Leibniz's metaphysics lends itself naturally both to a process-oriented ontology and to the notion of an "interior" force or urge in all monads or forms of matter.

So, we have Leibniz's solution for deriving space, time, and mind from force, but what about matter? Again, the solution is relatively straightforward. Central to Leibniz's metaphysics are a number of principles and laws, and two of these are what he calls (1) "the principle of identity of indiscernibles" (any two things with exactly the same properties are the same thing) and (2) "the principle of sufficient reason" (which holds that nothing occurs without a reason, and the corollary, which we find in Whitehead, that any sufficient reason must also be a concrete actuality). Leibniz also posits (3) "the law of continuity" (which states, in essence, that "everything takes place by degrees"). Now, if we accept the principle of the identity of indiscernibles and the law of continuity, we get an ontology in which any discernible differences between monads results in a *graded hierarchy* of monads.

This graded hierarchy runs from those monads infinitely close to insentience to an all-encompassing, supreme monad, which we may call God, or the "monad of all monads" (as Bruno called it). We now have an ontological model in which the innumerable monads, or indivisible bundles of force, are arranged in nested systems of hierarchies within hierarchies. At the lowest, least complex, levels the monads are little more than bundles of pure force, with very low-grade feeling. At higher levels of complexity, the nested hierarchies of monads or bundles of force form "colonies" or "societies" with high grades of feeling and perception. They thus create a greater phenomenal space, a greater configuration of extension, and this is perceived and experienced as the solidity of material forms.

Leibniz, thus, employs the notion of graded hierarchies of monads to distinguish between mind (or soul) and matter (or body), without falling into the trap of Cartesian dualism. Mind and body are not two separate and distinct substances, they are composed of the same ontological "stuff" or, rather, force—just different hierarchical configurations of it. For Leibniz, the "soul [is] a monad of higher grade controlling a colony of monads of lower grade; the ruling monad is the entelechy of the body."[50]

We have in Leibniz, I believe, the first formulation of a process ontology and cosmology that, while being monistic (in that the ultimate "stuff" is a single *type* of force-filled monad) is also pluralistic (in that there are innumerable *tokens* or instances of the single type). It is also an ontology that, for the first time since Descartes (and subsequently his followers), provides a solution to the relationship between mind and body.

There is one problem, however.

According to Leibniz, "The monads have no windows by which anything may go in or out." This impenetrableness of the monads follows directly from their structureless simplicity and indivisibility. Being "windowless," the monads cannot exchange or communicate anything about their internal states. Thus, since each monad is a unit of self-propelling force, and since monads cannot communicate their intentions, there is no way for any one of them to coordinate its activity with any other one. Each monad would have an independent career, so to speak. This is a recipe for utter cosmic chaos and anarchy.

This time Leibniz's solution is more theological than philosophical: God prevents the chaos of innumerable, independent self-propelled monads by arranging things according to a "preestablished harmony." Whenever philosophers appeal to divine intervention or cause as the "sufficient reason" for some state of affairs, they have yielded the domain of explanation for the miraculous. If, however, God is understood in a pantheistic sense, equated with the world of natural phenomena, the solution may yet be compatible with metaphysical and even scientific explanation. For if by "God" we mean the highest level of the nested system of hierarchies, the all-encompassing sentient monad, then we have not taken recourse to something outside, or transcendental to, the system.

And Leibniz may be interpreted along these lines. For in some sense his monadology anticipated by more than two hundred years some of the basic tenets of general systems theory and "holism"—a philosophical-scientific approach that views the world as a collection of interdependent systems of parts nested within wholes. (One major difference, however, between Leibniz's holism and contemporary systems theory is that, for Leibniz, the *entire* hierarchy possesses sentience or experience in some degree—consciousness is intrinsic. For systems theorists consciousness is an *emergent* property of otherwise insentient, organized matter.)

For Leibniz each nested system of monads derives its individuality from the experience of the dominant monad. In contrast to such holistic systems of monads, Leibniz also recognized that matter may be arranged in aggregates of monads, which have no unifying dominant monad. Aggregates are not individuals—they are divisible into their constituent parts without any loss of a higher unity or monad. There is more than a superficial resemblance, for example, between Leibniz's monads and Arthur Koestler's double-aspect Janus-faced "holons"[51]—a concept that is gaining currency in modern holistic and systems theories, and also, most notably, in the hierarchic-integral evolutionary spiritual model developed by Ken Wilber.[52]

In Leibnizian panpsychism, nature is believed to be permeated by an "interior" psychic aspect that accompanies matter at all levels, from the simplest elementary particles to the most complex brains. Yet it is important to distinguish, as Leibniz does, between matter as systems of individual monads and as aggregational societies of monads. Whereas all individual and holistic systems of monads (organisms) have experience, aggregates as such (e.g., rocks, clouds, or oceans) do not have experience (though their individual constituents do).

In another form of panpsychism, usually conceived of as "animism" or "pantheism," everything is alive—aggregates as well as individuals—with spirit or experience. All matter (including trees, rocks, oceans, winds) is conscious to some degree or in some respect. In the Western tradition, the philosopher who comes closest to espousing such a view is Spinoza.

**Baruch Spinoza** (1632–1677) was a Jewish philosopher of Spanish-Portuguese descent, born in Amsterdam. Because the essence of his philosophy was the "Single Substance" he variously called "Nature" or "God,"[53] he was charged with atheism and, in 1656, was banned from the synagogue. He spent most of his adult life working as a lens grinder, living in near-poverty by choice rather than compromise his intellectual independence.

Although his philosophy was very different from Descartes's, in many respects Spinoza's lifework was a systematic elaboration of the Cartesian method. The ultimate substance, or God, was absolutely infinite in all respects, and therefore had an infinite number of attributes. However, human beings were limited to knowing only two of these attributes: Cartesian extension and thought.

The essential nature of Spinoza's "One Substance" is difficult to clarify, and philosophers have been arguing over it for centuries. However, since he was clearly determined to establish an ultimate self-sufficient "substance," and since this substance was "rational," we may be excused for interpreting Spinoza's "substance" as a form of panpsychism (or "holistic monism")—with the attribute of rationality or mind present everywhere, without exception, in nature. Certainly his philosophy supported pantheism, where god is equated with nature.

Spinoza's philosophy has often been compared with Chinese Taoism,* and although there is some validity to this comparison, there are also decisive differences. Whereas Taoism is a philosophy of change, Spinoza's cosmos lacks this emphasis. Spinoza's cosmology is, furthermore, completely determinist and rational, whereas Taoism is typically regarded in the West as a celebration of irrationalism,[54] of synchronistic meanings and systemic causality, and decidedly not in favor of the mechanistic, linear-type of causality associated with determinism (but see Hansen, *A Daoist Theory of Chinese Thought,* 1992).†

It is debatable whether we should include Spinoza and/or Taoism under the heading "idealism" (psychic monism) or "panpsychism." Clearly, both Spinozist and Taoist philosophies are monistic, but exactly what the ultimate nature of this monistic "entity" is is not clear.

Taoists say, "The Tao that can be named is not the nameless Tao"; it is beyond all classification and categorization. To call it "psychic" or

---

*Although Spinoza's writings show no evidence of familiarity with ancient Chinese texts, we do know that he spent time with Leibniz and that Leibniz was interested in, and had studied, via Jesuit translations, the works of the twelfth-century neo-Confucian philosopher Chu Hsi (Needham, 1977, p. 291).

†A different interpretation of Taoism has been put forward by Chad Hansen in *A Daoist Theory of Chinese Thought.* Hansen argues that it has been a long-standing Western misunderstanding of "Daoism" (he uses the newer transliteration of Chinese)—a historical consequence of our initial acquaintance with Chinese philosophy through the works of the neo-Confucianists—that it is mystical and irrational. On the contrary, according to Hansen, "Daoism" is inherently rational. Although Hansen makes a detailed and scholarly defense of this position, I am unconvinced that the best approach to knowing Taoism is by application of the metaphor of computers (as Hansen implies). Hansen appears to miss the deep *experiential,* and extrarational, nature of Lao Tzu and Chuang Tzu.

"spiritual" might seem to attribute to the Tao an essence that was never intended by the founders of Taoism. Yet it is also clear that this Ultimate was neither material substance nor physical energy. The Tao, if we can say anything about it, is definitely not material or corporeal. Nor is it the mere absence of actual, manifest physical reality, the "void," so it should not be equated with the "quantum vacuum potential" of modern physics. If anything, the Tao is best expressed as a principle, a homeodynamic principle,* the source of all order and organization in the universe (and, since it is the ultimate source, we must assume the Tao is also the source of all entropy and disorder in the universe, too).

Since the Tao is clearly monistic, yet not easily identified as either material or psychic, perhaps we would do better to investigate the possibility of a fourth metaphysical category—beyond dualism, idealism, and materialism—which may serve as a foundation upon which to build a science of consciousness. This fourth category avoids the pitfalls of substance by positing activity or action as the basis of the universe.† For now, we may identify the fourth category as "process philosophy"—and leave it open whether it is a monism, a dualism, or a pluralism.

## The Romantic Vision

In this chapter I have been concerned with tracing the earliest roots of panpsychism; and from this compressed and brief overview of its historical lineage we can see that its roots stretch back in time to the beginnings of Western philosophy—to Pythagoras, Anaximander, and Thales—and

---

*I prefer the term "homeodynamic" as a synonym for the more common term "homeostatic," which refers to processes that restore balance (as, for instance, in the operation of a thermostat, which tends to stabilize temperature around a fixed point). However, since it is a *process,* the notion of "stasis"—meaning without movement—is inappropriate. "Homeo-*stable*" would be preferable to homeostasis, since stability, like balance, implies a continual process of fine adjustment. When talking about the Tao, which is regarded as the source of all changes through the interplay of *yin* and *yang,* the dynamic character of balance-through-change is stressed—hence the choice of "homeodynamic" as a descriptor.

†This, as we've seen, was Leibniz's position. And in a kind of blending of Leibniz's "force" with Spinoza's implicit "pluralistic-dual-aspect-monism," David Bohm has proposed an ontology he calls "holomovement."[55]

beyond, into the prehistorical mists of Orphic mythology and shamanic visions, to a relationship with the living world before meanings and words were separated from objects, a time when the evocative power of poetic incantation connected our ancestors to the deep rhythms of nature. We saw how the lineage found expression in the strong current of Neoplatonic thought through the earliest centuries of the common era, and flowed on through the Dark Ages in the guise of esoteric Christianity and the Hermetic traditions, then into the Renaissance and late Middle Ages, even influencing some of the founders of modernism, such as Spinoza and Leibniz.

Although I have chosen not to pursue the lineage beyond that point in this chapter, for the sake of completeness I should point out that its influence continued on through the seventeenth- and eighteenth-century Enlightenment, right up to the present day. Most of this book will focus on the more recent contributions to this stream of thought in the works of philosophers such as Henri Bergson, A. N. Whitehead, and David Ray Griffin.

But before concluding this chapter with a look at arguments against panpsychism and Neoplatonic idealism, I want to single out two figures from the eighteenth-century Romantic movement that arose as a counterpoint to the extreme rationalism of the Enlightenment.

**Johann Wolfgang von Goethe** (1749–1832), a German interdisciplinary poet-scientist, was influenced by Spinoza's pantheism and Leibniz's panpsychism.[56] His most notable scientific contributions were in the diverse fields of anatomy, mineralogy, meteorology, biology, zoology, comparative morphology, and optics—including an empirical theory of color to rival Newton's purely mathematical theory of the spectrum.[57] Goethe placed great importance on exact observation of phenomena, having confidence in sensory experience as an effective way of knowing, as a phenomenological epistemology. His methodology emphasized critical inquiry based on precise observation of particulars, noting their conditions, effects, coherence, and variety and, from these, discovering general laws of formation. His pantheism is explicit in the following:

> In observing the cosmic structure from its broadest expanse down to its minutest parts, we cannot escape the impression that underlying the whole is the idea that God is operative in Nature and Nature in God.[58]

Goethe, in turn, later influenced philosophers in the Romantic tradition such as Friedrich Schelling (1775–1854), Ferdinand Canning Scott Schiller (1864–1917), and Rudolf Steiner (1861–1925).

**Samuel Taylor Coleridge** (1772–1834), a poet and leader of the English Romantic movement, was adamantly opposed to most eighteenth-century Enlightenment philosophers, where emphasis was on a mechanistic materialist ontology, a world to be explained in terms of "insentient matter acted on by external forces." Coleridge dismissed this as an "obsession with matter" and proposed instead an ontology much more in accord with Leibniz's notion of monads of pure force.[59] Coleridge, in fact, anticipated the ontology of process philosophy, where time and action are fundamental to the nature of the world.[60] Process ontology offers a radical approach to understanding the mysterious relationship between matter and mind, and opens the way for a solution to the long-standing mind-body problem.

Coleridge's process metaphysic is evident in the following:

> As soon as this gross prejudice [of matter as the primary datum] is cured by the appropriate discipline, and the Mind is familiarized to the contemplation of Matter as a product in time, the resulting phenomenon of the equilibrium of two antagonist forces, Attraction and Repulsion . . . the idea of creation alone remains.[61]

The idea that "creation alone remains" is, as we shall see, an anticipation of Whitehead's process cosmology where the fundamental constituents of reality are "actual occasions" that are, in essence, pure creative acts resulting from "moments of experience."

Coleridge's emphasis on creation as the result of the striving toward equilibrium of two opposing, or complementary, forces points us also in the direction of Neoplatonic cosmology where duality emerges from the One and strives to return to the common single source. Identifying the neo-Pythagorean strain in Coleridge, Christopher Bamford observes that Coleridge is a "transcendental philosopher" who, unlike Descartes, does not say "Give me matter and motion and I will construct you the universe," but who says, rather:

Grant me a nature having two contrary forces, one of which tends to expand infinitely [spatial extension as physical process], while the other strives to apprehend or find itself in this infinity [perception, feeling, psychic process], and I will call up the world of intelligences with the whole system of their representations to arise before you." In other words: Every power in nature and in spirit must evolve an opposite as the sole means and conditions of its manifestation: and all opposition is a tendency to reunion.[62]

Coleridge's ontology, with its explicit rejection of outright absolute materialism, of insentient matter, along with its implicit process-based panpsychism, is, therefore, a good example of a worldview that brings together the influences of Leibniz's force-based monadology and the Neoplatonic idea of emanation and return.

With Goethe and Coleridge presented as representatives of the Romantic reactionary phase of the panpsychist lineage, bringing us up to the threshold of modern times, I will now move on to an analysis of arguments against panpsychism and against Neoplatonic idealism.

## Problem with Panpsychism?

In my discussion of Plotinus's mystical philosophy, I noted three points that I feel require further analysis with regard to the cosmological and ontological story I wish to develop in this book. The three points are: (1) the distinction between ontological and consequent panpsychism; (2) the implication that knowledge of the deep relationship between consciousness and matter will require a transformative methodology in which epistemology and ontology—knowing and being—are fused; and (3) that the emanationist "process," the outpouring of spirit becoming matter and its drive to return to pure spirit, is timeless. It is "evolution out of time," a logical rather than a chronological sequence, which I referred to as "onvolution"—meaning the "unfolding of being"—a term I will explain more fully later.

Examination of these three issues will involve, as we shall see, a critique of panpsychism and idealism, a call for a radically different epistemology based on feeling rather than merely conceptual thought, and a

reassessment of the role of time in our understanding of both consciousness and matter. I'll begin with consequent panpsychism.

Ontological panpsychism, to restate the view expressed earlier in this
chapter, is a metaphysical position that states that fundamental and ultimate reality consists of intrinsically psychic matter. Wherever there is
matter, at all levels of complexity, there is also mind. The raw "stuff" of
the world is both physical and mental, both objective and subjective. This
position, as critics such as Thomas Nagel[63] and Colin McGinn[64] have indicated, entails a covert dualism or is logically absurd.* One of the advantages
of consequent panpsychism, however, is that it avoids this residue of dualism by starting off with a metaphysical assumption of monistic idealism.

The argument against ontological panpsychism runs like this: If
mind is inherent in matter, as the panpsychist position states, then either
mind is distinct from matter, or it is not. This opens three options: (1) If
it is distinct, then we have a form of dualism. If mind and matter are not
distinct, then we are left with two monistic possibilities: Either (2) mind
is a form or product of matter (only some states of matter will possess or
exhibit mind—as in materialist emergentism); or (3) matter is a state of
mind (as in emanationist idealism).

The second of these two options, emergent materialism, is incompatible with panpsychism; for panpsychism, *all* matter possesses mind. Thus,
the critique goes, panpsychism claims that either all matter possesses mind
*essentially distinct* from matter, option (1), ultimately a form of dualism; or
that all-pervasive mind *is not distinct,* option (3), emanationist idealism.
If it is a form of dualism, sooner or later we will confront the inevitable
problem of interaction: How could a nonmaterial mind or nonphysical
dynamic form interact with matter to move or shape it?†

If residual or covert dualism is a problem shadowing ontological panpsychism, that leaves us with *consequent* panpsychism—option (3): panpsychism
as a form of idealism. As we have seen, this is the kind of panpsychism we
get from Plotinus and the Neoplatonist lineage. (And from many versions

---

*See chapter 8, "Panexperientialism: Consciousness All the Way Down?" for an analysis
of McGinn's critique.
†I address this problem, and propose a solution, in chapters 9, "Past Matter, Present
Mind" and 10, "Stories Matter, Matter Stories."

of idealist Hindu cosmology, too. In fact, idealism, given its basic ontological premise of primary and universal consciousness, necessarily entails consequent panpsychism.) Spiritual idealism, then, the emanationist theory of reality, offers us a consequent panpsychism that avoids the residue of mind-matter dualism allegedly hidden in ontological panpsychism. It is "consequent" because matter is itself a devolved form of spirit or consciousness. However, as with all forms of idealism, a problem remains here, too.

In previous chapters I highlighted the key problems with dualism (interaction), materialism (emergence), and with idealism (existence of objective material world). I can now make the idealist problem more explicit.

## Problem with the Perennial Philosophy?

The perennial philosophy,* variations of a worldview that spans millennia and cultures, is essentially the ontology of idealism. Idealism states that only pure spirit or consciousness is ultimately real, or that spirit/

---

*Anthony Freeman, editor of the *Journal of Consciousness Studies,* asks "Am I the only person to find the term "the perennial philosophy" irritating? It seems to imply a deposit of timeless truth that puts it above the culture-bound pronouncements of all other philosophies. And I just don't buy that."

I've never found the phrase irritating, and until Freeman pointed it out, I must confess I've tended to take it as shorthand for idealism. I've accepted it as part of our intellectual history ever since Leibniz popularized the phrase in the seventeenth century. (Leibniz did not claim to have invented the term, but said he found it in the writings of sixteenth-century theologian Augustine Steuch. [I'm grateful to W. Thackara for this historical nugget.])

It seems to me that the term has undergone some evolution since Leibniz's time. When he used it he was referring to a worldview (essentially idealism) that has been around since the dawn of philosophy, and keeps reappearing in one form or another from age to age and across cultures. For Leibniz, then, "perennial" refers to historical longevity and cross-cultural persistence.

However, since Aldous Huxley published his book by that name (in the 1940s), the term seems to have taken on an ahistorical meaning. Now it seems to refer to the *content* of the philosophy—a content that, as Freeman says, is supposed to transcend the vagaries of culture and history. To speak of the "perennial philosophy" today is to refer to a belief system that purports to derive its content from a form of experience (mystical) that transcends time, space, and all duality. And—if we are to believe that the sages and mystics have accurately reported their experiences—such content represents

*(continued on page 140)*

consciousness is the source of all reality—including the entire material world. My question is: If reality begins with pure spirit or pure consciousness, *how* does it become matter? It seems we have two broad possible solutions. Either (1) maya hypothesis: The material world is an illusion (*maya*), made up of "dream stuff" with no reality independent of mind; or (2) emanationism: The material world issues forth from spirit and is, so to speak, a dense form of spirit.

## THE MAYA HYPOTHESIS

As we saw in chapter 3, if we go with option (1)—matter is illusory—then we are still left with the problem of accounting for the persistence of realism as a *pragmatic* necessity for biological survival and for psychological sanity. We just don't live as though the material world is an illusion (we wouldn't survive very long if, for instance, we treated trucks on the highway or poisonous substances as mere illusions). Even enlightened beings must "follow the rules" or suffer the consequences. (Certainly the literature is full of accounts of gurus, sages, shamans, psychics, and assorted other gifted folk

---

(*continued from page 139*)
absolute truth (or, at least, a form of truth that is impervious to any rational, cultural, or historical critique).

When I use the term, I'm not assuming that the content of the perennial philosophy is necessarily true. I'm referring to its longevity as a transcultural phenomenon, and essentially using it as a synonym for idealism.

But Freeman's comment raises two questions for me:

(1) Could materialists and/or dualists (not to mention panpsychists) likewise make a claim that their particular brand of ontology is also perennial? After all, in the West at least, we can trace a form of ontological dualism back to Pythagoras and later Plato, and a form of materialism back to Democritus. The Eastern traditions are not without their ancient materialists and dualists, either. (And in this book I make a strong case for the long lineage of panpsychism stretching back beyond the Presocratics through the Orphics to shamanic roots.) So, will the real "perennial philosophy" please stand up!

(2) Does using the term "perennial philosophy" give (inadvertently or otherwise) a kind of sanction and endorsement to idealism, privileging it over other ontologies? Does it imply not only a unique longevity to a particular worldview (which is questionable), but also that its longevity is due to its unique expression of ultimate truth?

If Freeman has been picking up on (2), then I'm not surprised at his "irritation." This implication does seem to assume an awful lot.

defying the laws of nature as understood in Cartesian-Newtonian science, but these accounts are noteworthy because they are *anomalies*. It is precisely the anomalous nature of such reports that requires explanation. The fact remains that even these people, *most of the time,* act *as though* the physical world is real. Why? When people act or behave in a way that is inconsistent with what they claim, philosophers call this a "performative contradiction.") So the maya hypothesis is *pragmatically* problematic for idealism (even if it may be philosophically irrefutable).

## EMANATIONISM

However, if we take option (2)—matter emanates from spirit—the situation is problematic even philosophically. If matter is "devolved" spirit, a dense concentration of spirit, soul, or mind, we have either (A) a covert materialism or (B) a covert dualism.

Let's take (A): If we accept that the maya hypothesis is problematic, then we may assume that realism is true in some sense. Matter is real; it really *is* physical. But if matter is real, if it is really physical, and is a devolved form of soul and spirit, then spirit, too, must in some way be physical.* Option (A) leads us onto one horn of a dilemma, namely, *spirit is physical*—even if it is a *very, very subtle form of matter-energy.*† But this is not at all how spirit is portrayed in religious and philosophical idealism, for instance in the cosmological model of Plotinus or Hindu models where *nirguna* Brahman is the ultimate, without all qualities and attributes.

However, if we wish to avoid option (A)—the covert materialism of physical spirit—we end up on the other spike of the dilemma. Option (B) leads us to say that if both spirit and matter are real, that spirit really *is* spiritual and that matter really is *physical,* then at what point in the devolutionary process, and just *how,* does spirit impress form on matter or

---

*According to the axiom "only like begets like," if matter comes from spirit then "spirit" itself must be (or contain) some form or trace of matter. But "physical spirit" is a contradiction.

†If we argue that it is possible for spirit to be a form of physical energy radically different from what current physics deals with—a form of physical energy that entails consciousness intrinsically—then we are not talking absolute idealism, we are talking panpsychism or radical naturalism.

"impregnate" matter? It is the old problem of interaction familiar from our attempts to make sense of dualism. And for a very good reason: Option (B) is covert dualism. Clearly, option B is not really an option for idealism (spiritual or psychic monism) because it involves a *dualism* of spirit and matter.

As presented, this critique amounts to a *reductio ad absurdum* of idealism, impaling it on the horns of a dilemma. If there is a way out, it will depend more on a leap of epistemological faith than on any empirical evidence or logical reasoning. It may be, for example, if the maya hypothesis is correct, that the above analysis that appears to deconstruct idealism only *appears* to do so because I am trapped in the very illusion I am attempting to unveil. It may be that with a different epistemology, with a different way of knowing beyond my senses and my rational faculties, the paradoxical nature of idealism would be experienced as wholly unmysterious. Or that even if the mystery remained, I would "see" that that is just the way *it is*. But if we want to *talk* about or *explain* idealism, we remain at the level of expository discourse—and here, pragmatism and rationality still count. Philosophically, idealism is stuck.

## Breaking the Eternal Tangled Loop

If reason and empiricism alone cannot resolve for us the problem of choosing among ontologies—dualism, materialism, or idealism—what other epistemological method is available to us? Intuition? Feeling?

At this point I can introduce the "Ep-On bootstrap principle." It has various formulations, such as: "Our choice of epistemology (Ep) is constrained by our ontology (On), and vice versa," or more simply, "epistemology and ontology codetermine each other." Eventually, as I will argue later, "knowing becomes being."

Given this principle, some interesting epistemological problems emerge. Take, for instance, absolute idealism: Since this ontology denies the reality of matter, it rules out the legitimacy of (sensory) empiricism as a way of reliable knowing. If all material forms are illusions, then our sense organs, too, must be illusory and would never give access to truth or reality.

If, however, absolute materialism were true, and all matter is intrinsically insentient, then the epistemological legitimacy of rationality is undermined. For if matter is intrinsically, wholly insentient, it seems inconceivable that any mental function such as reason (the apprehension of *experienced* coherence between concepts) could ever emerge. Yet we undoubtedly do have reason and experience. So absolute materialism must be false (as Campanella and Descartes brilliantly showed).

In the case of absolute idealism, ontology rules out an epistemology (can't have sense-based truth), in the case of absolute materialism, epistemology rules out an ontology (reality without experience)—this latter case is, of course, a restatement of the Campanella-Cartesian insight.

What about dualism? If we take absolute dualism to be true (that is, Cartesian dualism of absolutely separate and distinct ontological domains of matter and mind), we have the following problem: Reason, being wholly separate from matter, can give us no knowledge of matter. It is the old problem of mind-body interaction once again. How can nonphysical reason ever interact with matter to gain knowledge or information about it? What would be the nature of the point of transfer where information in matter is communicated to reason? Similarly, the Cartesian body alone can be of no help: How could insentient material bodies ever produce legitimate empiricism? For who, or what, would *experience* the perceptual event at the end of the chain of sensory events, without crossing the explanatory gap? Dualism is, thus, doubly problematic. On the one hand it undercuts the legitimacy of reason, on the other it removes the possibility of empiricism.

Where, then, does all this leave us? The more we explore the relationship between epistemology and ontology, the more it seems to get lost in a tangled loop—where epistemology guides our choice of ontology, but ontology determines our choice of epistemology—and does not appear to leave open a way for us to know the nature of reality. Can we break out of this Escher-like eternal loop?

One school of thought tends to the view that we cannot make the break in any systematic or foundational way. All we can do is simply begin with a set of *assumptions*. For example, we may start with the ontological assumption that matter is primary, or that consciousness is primary, or whatever, and see where it takes us. But how can we evaluate or choose between ontological assumptions? With this, we are back in the same tangled, eternal loop. We cannot, it seems, break the "Escher loop" and work from epistemology to ontology, or vice versa.

It is precisely this dilemma that suggests to me we need a kind of "bootstrap" epistemology-ontology (Ep-On, for short). By "bootstrap" I mean an Ep-On relationship that is so internally consistent it can pull itself out of the tangle and break the eternal loop by a sort of Moebius-like short-circuit. Of all the ontologies we've considered so far, only one, it seems to me, meets the Ep-On bootstrap criterion: panpsychism.

For if, as this worldview states, matter is intrinsically sentient, then all matter *feels,* including all the matter of our bodies, not just certain tissues and cells belonging to our nervous system. Our whole bodies feel, or, if you like, are pervaded by experience or consciousness. Therefore, somatic feeling is available to us as an alternative to the epistemologies of reason and sensory empiricism.

My inclination, therefore, is to go with *feeling,* with a form of knowing that arises from paying deeper and more sensitive attention to messages from my body as it interacts with the world around me. Such "feeling tones," of course, are not isolated from the rest of my experience, including my consciousness of whatever evidence is revealed to me by my senses, and whatever tracks I can find through the maze of available information with the help of reason. Intuition, too, the form of knowing that seems gratuitous or a gift of grace—that seems to come from "somewhere else," through a different shaft of knowing—plays a significant part.

And when I "listen" with all these antennae on alert, I am drawn not to dualism, nor to idealism, but to materialism. However, the "materialism" I am drawn to is not that which dominates current philosophical and scientific thinking. It is not the absolute materialism of inert matter, but a "radical materialism"—or radical naturalism—according to which matter, or nature, is itself experiential. It is a radical naturalism in which matter intrinsically feels—an ontological position that makes no separation between mind and matter, between consciousness and the physical world. And this ontology, as I have been emphasizing in this chapter, has a long, long lineage in Western philosophy, where it has conventionally been called "panpsychism." For reasons I will make clearer later, theologian-philosopher David Ray Griffin prefers the term "panexperientialism."

Of the three points mentioned above that required more discussion, I have so far covered the first two: (1) the distinction between ontological and consequent panpsychism, and (2) the need for a radically different epistemology based on feeling rather than conceptual thought if we are to break the tangled epistemology-ontology loop. That leaves point (3): the timelessness of emanationist evolution.

We have seen in this chapter, particularly in the story of Neoplatonism, a close historical relationship between the ontologies of idealism and panpsychism. However, whereas emanationist idealism—as found in those "perennial philosophies" that include the metaphor of the "great chain of being"—is explicitly atemporal, panpsychism, as developed by Giordano Bruno, Gottfried Leibniz, Henri Bergson, A. N. Whitehead, Teilhard de Chardin, Charles Hartshorne, and David Ray Griffin, is uncompromisingly temporal. The panpsychism, or panexperientialism, advocated by these philosophers is intimately bound to their process-based ontologies.

In the next chapter, then, I will turn to the postmodern philosophy of the twentieth century's greatest process philosopher: Alfred North Whitehead.

*Note to readers:* The next three chapters are the philosophical core of the book, exploring in some detail technical arguments for the validity of the panpsychist worldview—for consciousness all the way down. If you have little patience for philosophical subtleties, or if you find these chapters tough going, you can skip through them quickly (e.g., reading the first few and final pages of each, as well as the subheadings) and move on to chapter 10, "Conclusion: Stories Matter, Matter Stories." Of course, if philosophy excites you, and you enjoy engaging with its finer details, these chapters will (I hope) be both stimulating and rewarding.

# PART III

# SOLUTION

## POSTMODERN PROMISE

# 7

Resolution

# WHITEHEAD'S POSTMODERN COSMOLOGY

Our world once resonated with "sympathies" and "correspondences"—an unseen web of interconnections and harmonies linked macrocosm and microcosm through the great chain of being. Medieval philosophers lived in such a world, a world where the guiding paradigm was "organism," a world pulsing with life and significance.

That all changed with the advent of modernism, particularly with Descartes's radical division of nature into mind and insentient matter. Together with Bacon's emphasis on sensory empiricism, it was a relatively short step to the Newtonian worldview guided by the paradigm of mechanism, where all that was real was determined by physical data detected by our physical senses.

In previous chapters, we saw that sometime around the middle of this century the limitations of the modernist worldview became critical, particularly when the shortcomings of logical positivism and behaviorism were finally recognized. These limitations became even more acute as a result of discoveries associated with relativity theory and quantum physics.

One reaction, sometimes called "deconstructive postmodernism," was to acknowledge the inadequacy of reason, philosophy, and science to give us a coherent and final answer to cosmological questions such as the nature of reality, of matter, and of mind. The best we could hope for, according to this view, is to "deconstruct" our ways of thinking and talk-ing about the world, and to be content with conceptual relativism, that all our knowledge must necessarily be determined by our linguistic, social, historical, and cultural contexts. There is no "reality," says this decon-structive postmodernist view; there is, rather, a multiplicity of "realities" depending on our context and perspective.

However, the same set of circumstances that led to the decline of modernism prompted an altogether different reaction, known as "con-structive postmodernism."[1] According to supporters of this view, the fail-ures of the modernist project—which resulted in the crises in philosophy, science, and society noted earlier—reveals the need for a deep shift in our conceptions and perceptions of the world. To move beyond the pathologi-cal schisms of modernism to a true *post*modernism, we need a radical revi-sion of our ontology and cosmology. We need a vision of nature in which all parts of the ecological-cosmological system are innately meaningful, in which sentience or experience is all-pervasive, resulting in a profound sense that the world is itself sacred. The postmodern program, according to this perspective, is for us to develop a new science, a sacred science, in which meanings, values, purposes, and consciousness itself are integral.

The two forms of postmodernism could hardly be more different. Yet they share a common root in the bankruptcy of modernism, with its stated ideal of certain knowledge about the world. When Locke, followed by Hume and then Kant, showed that neither empiricism nor rationalism, nor both combined, could guarantee certain knowledge, that our minds could never know the world as it is in itself, philosophy retreated from the grand scheme of metaphysics, ontology, and cosmology, into episte-mology. If we couldn't know the world, then at least we could investigate the instrument of knowing that has failed us. Following Kant, who is sometimes regarded as the first or seminal postmodernist, the primacy of epistemology was established. The study of *how* we know took precedence over *what* we know to exist.

What is interesting about both forms of postmodernism today is their different reactions to epistemology and its failure to achieve certainty. On the one hand, the deconstructionists decry the futility of epistemology because it can never provide a firm foundation for certain knowledge;

therefore, we should leave aside all questions about how we can know mind and matter and concentrate on the contexts of our linguistic utterances. On the other hand, the constructive postmodernists, also recognizing the impossibility of a secure and certain epistemological foundation, declare that therefore this is all the more reason for reinvigorating our efforts at creatively constructing coherent systems of ontology and cosmology.

If we can propose a coherent cosmology, or "likely story" as Plato called it, one that includes the storyteller within the story itself, then we may begin to understand the relationship between the knower and what is known, between how we can know anything at all about the world and the necessary nature of the world itself. We would have a worldview that accounts for the possibility of *any* worldview—a world intrinsically knowable because it is a world that intrinsically knows.

Furthermore, in such a cosmology the implicit shift is not merely to a comprehensive account of *how* and *what* we know, but also—when the profound participatory relationship between knowing and being is fully engaged—to a deep inquiry into *who* knows. Inevitably, a rigorous and disciplined investigation of the relationship between knower and known involves a transformation of the investigator. And although such transformation typically involves nonrational and nonsensory ways of knowing, postmodern philosophers in the tradition of Whitehead recognize the vast potential of reason itself to reveal the nature of the world and of ourselves.

## Cosmology First

The speculative process philosophy of Alfred North Whitehead is perhaps the most rigorous attempt at constructing such a postmodern cosmology. For Whitehead, cosmology or ontology is primary. He avoids the "foundationalist" epistemological ideal of modernism: First deciding how we (can) know, before deciding what we (can) know.

Whiteheadians reject the irrationalism of the deconstructionists. Although they agree that we cannot have the certainty the modernists hoped for (and sometimes claimed), that is no excuse for falling into nihilistic relativism and a rejection of all metaphysics. On the contrary, they declare that we are, therefore, liberated to use our rational faculties creatively. Instead of avoiding ontological and cosmological questions altogether, we can—and should—creatively construct coherent and internally consistent systems of thought and continually question the inevitable assumptions underlying these systems.

This, says Whitehead, is the true rationalism: the rigorous and creative application of reason to the most profound ontological-cosmological questions—even though we may never (indeed, will never) finish the project. And if we begin this work, as we must, from within the modernist paradigm, we will sooner or later realize that radical changes have to be made if we are to truly move into the proposed new postmodern paradigm. Foremost among these, according to Whitehead, are:

- A deep and rigorous rational questioning of assumptions underlying conceptual expression of all experiences, including the nature of the experiencing entity itself;
- Development of a realist ontology that acknowledges the existence of a real world;
- Development of a realist ontology that contains within it an adequate account of experiencing subjects—that is, subjectivity and experience are real;
- Development of a rational realist ontology/cosmology that accounts for self-causation as well as efficient causation (i.e., accounts for the relationship between freedom and determinism);
- Development of a realist cosmology that accounts for ontological interdependence and wholeness, while at the same time accounting for "individuals";
- Development of a rational realist cosmology that accounts for purposive organisms and mechanical, determined relations between objects;
- Development of a process cosmology where "events" not "things," and relations and *relata,* not separate objects, are fundamental. Such a cosmology would account for the ontological relationship between process and substance, between subjectivity and objectivity.

In the latter phase of his long career, Whitehead laid out a detailed program for a new speculative philosophy in which he thoroughly addressed these criteria. I have already addressed the first of these: a rational questioning of assumptions in philosophy, science, and in society. Central to Whitehead's approach to cosmology is an explicit emphasis on the application of reason. It may never get us to a final answer, but we should always look for how we can apply it to bring us to a more coherent understanding of the world and of our place in it.

And the first task of reason, according to Whitehead, is to assent to the reality of the world with a conviction and commitment that reason can give us knowledge of it as it is in itself—if only ever-provisional. This, of course, flies in the face of Kant's monumental critique of reason, and his "Copernican revolution" in philosophy that unambiguously affirmed the impossibility of our ever knowing the nature of the world as it is in itself (including the knower). Whitehead emphatically disagreed, and he was not shy about criticizing Kant for leading philosophy badly astray for two hundred years. He frequently stated that his task was an attempt to return philosophy to its pre-Kantian glory.[2] There is a real world, and we *can* know it, says Whitehead, just as our commonsense presupposes. However, he does not advocate naive realism that unquestioningly accepts reality as it appears to our senses. It is the job of philosophy and science to identify mere appearances and to examine or bypass them to get at reality itself.

Whitehead's radical proposal was that we need to be bold in our ontology such that it would lead to an epistemology by which we could know reality in itself, and not just the appearances constructed by our categorizing minds. His solution was to propose that the fundamental nature of the world is not materialist "substance," nor Cartesian dual substances of matter and mind, nor Berkeley's mind-only idealism. The world is not composed of "things" but of "events," or processes—which he called "actual entities." This was a significant departure, though not entirely without antecedents in the history of philosophy, as we saw in the previous chapter. Even as far back as the fifth or sixth century BCE, Heraclitus (ca. 540–480 BCE) in Presocratic Greece put forward the notion that "all is change"; and dialectical change was central to Hegel's metaphysics in the early nineteenth century. But what was radical in Whitehead's proposal was the assertion that nature's fundamental "events" were experiencing subjects—"actual occasions of experience."*

In his major work of speculative philosophy, *Process and Reality,* Whitehead develops a highly detailed and original cosmology based on his ontology of experiencing events. His system makes such a radical break with modernist assumptions that he often found it necessary to coin new words and to introduce unfamiliar notions to explain his ideas. For this reason, reading Whitehead can sometimes be a little like learning a new dialect. But the effort is well worth the reward.

## Begin with Experience

For instance, one of his novel approaches to speculative philosophy and to laying a foundation for a new science was to begin with human experience as a way to understand the structure and operations of the natural world. Of course this may not seem so novel at all to anyone familiar with Descartes's method. For Descartes, human experience—in fact his own consciousness—was the starting point. But whereas Descartes went on from there to develop a philosophy in which human experience was fundamentally different from all other things in the natural world, Whitehead develops a cosmology in which all of nature is composed of experiencing entities. By extrapolating from human experiences as natural events, he drew analogies to explain even subatomic events as natural "occasions of experience."

I will introduce some of Whitehead's key ideas (and also give a flavor of some of his unusual phraseology) in this chapter and develop their implications further in the next two chapters.

---

*And even here, Whitehead was clearly impressed by the emphasis on fundamental process and experience in Henri Bergson and William James. In fact, the list of philosophers, scientists, and other scholars prior to Whitehead for whom the notion of evolution—sometimes extended to evolutionary cosmologies—was a central feature of their work includes such obvious names as Charles Darwin, Herbert Spencer, T. H. Huxley, Bergson, and Samuel Alexander and their predecessors Maupertuis, Diderot, Lamark, and Goethe (see Glass, Temkin, and Strauss, *Forerunners of Darwin: 1745–1859,* 1959, pp. 265–91). Whitehead's significant contribution to speculative cosmology was his rigorous, detailed, and systematic working out of the implications of a fundamental ontology of "experiential process," his "occasions of experience."

## Understanding Whitehead

Understanding Whitehead is both very simple and very challenging. It is simple because the essence of his cosmology can be summed up in a few straightforward sentences:

- **"Events" not "things."** The essential nature of reality is not material substance—it is organisms in process. Very simply: *process,* not substance, is fundamental.
- **Nature feels all the way down.** Universal process is necessarily sentient—it unfolds by *feeling.* Thus what we call "matter" and "mind" (both abstractions) are derived from fundamental actual events that are inherently experiential.
- **Fundamental interrelatedness.** All events are mutually co-creating. They interfuse and interpenetrate each other so that it is a fallacy to speak of the reality of any actuality as an isolated, self-contained entity.

Whitehead is very challenging because he works out these three core ideas in great detail in a number of books—including *Science and the Modern World, Modes of Thought, Adventure of Ideas,* and, particularly, *Process and Reality*—often using new language to explain complex concepts. Part of the difficulty is because his core ideas run counter to the cosmology and metaphysical worldview that have prevailed in Western thought for nearly four centuries. In fact, one element of this worldview—the notion of *substance*—has dominated Western thinking since the time of the Presocratics. We are born into certain habitual grooves of thought that no longer work for the postmodern cosmology offered by Whitehead. The whole thrust of our thinking needs to radically shift if we are to successfully work with Whitehead's ideas.

In short, then, Whitehead's worldview can be difficult to grasp because it requires a new way of thinking about the universe and its contents. Our language is dominated by spatial metaphors—even our attempts to talk of time are often phrased in spatial terms. Yet it is precisely the *temporal* aspect of reality that is central to Whitehead's philosophy, and that we need to focus on. Our language is noun-oriented, whereas the world that Whitehead describes is verb-oriented. For instance, instead of cosmos—understood as a vast, perhaps infinite, expansion of space populated by innumerable galaxies, stars, and planets, and all the objects they contain—we would begin thinking in terms of "cosmosing"—a vast, perhaps infinite, network and hierarchy of interrelated events, where all "objects" are in reality the coming into being and fading away of energetic patterns-within-patterns, self-organizing cascades of creativity, converging pulses of *sentient energy*.

Whitehead challenges the notion that the world is divided up into two kinds of substances: those that are sentient, that feel, that have subjectivity or consciousness and those that are insentient, are unfeeling, are wholly objective and are without consciousness or experience. As we've seen, this dichotomy is modernism's legacy from Descartes who, in separating mind from matter, said that only minds can feel and think and know and that matter is wholly devoid of feeling or capacity for knowing. By separating mind and body, Descartes set in place a couple of dualisms: (1) the basic dualism of mind and matter, and (2) the derivative dualism of sentient matter and insentient matter. Since according to (1), only minds can feel, any instances of bodies that feel (such as humans) must therefore have an additional mind or soul that animates them. Whitehead's second core idea rejects both of these dualisms.

On its own, the idea that all matter—that nature through and through—is blessed with feeling, with a capacity for experience, is not at all difficult to grasp. We may or may not accept such a view, but either way it is easy enough to understand. It is the other core idea—of fundamental process—that begins to make Whitehead's philosophy such a challenge. The challenge deepens even more when we realize that Whitehead's metaphysics is based on a profound insight that the three core ideas are deeply and intimately interwoven: Not only is the world composed of interdependent events, Whitehead is telling us, but these events are themselves intrinsically experiential. How can an *event* be a locus of experience? Or, put another way: How are feelings connected with process?

Whitehead's philosophy is an attempt to work out a solution to this question. A fourth core idea, then, and the most challenging of all to the modernist paradigm, is:

- **Fundamental process is inherently experiential.** Process and feeling are connected because in order for one moment, *now,* to be related to the immediately previous moment, *past,* and to the immediately subsequent moment, *future,* the "now" moment must feel (or "prehend") aspects of the past by including them as *constituents* of its own actuality; and to give something of itself to the next, future, moment.

This is the essence of Whitehead. The connection between process and experience, between events and feeling, is his alternative to what he terms the "fallacy of simple location." The phrase "simple location" is an example of what is both easy and challenging about reading Whitehead. On its own, we probably have little difficulty grasping what the phrase means: A thing is simply located where (and when) it is, and not somewhere else. This desk, for example, is in this room and not partially upstairs. This cup is on this table, and not in the dishwasher. My body is sitting in my chair, and not in yours. But behind the simplicity of the phrase "simple location," and Whitehead's critique of it, lies a profound and revolutionary philosophy. Unpacking this, and many other apparently innocent phrases, such as "actual entity" or "eternal object," opens a metaphysical Pandora's box— and in Whitehead's hands out flies a virtual lexicon of neologisms.

A good place to start with Whitehead, therefore, is to identify some of his more unusual concepts and begin to unpack them. This is not always an easy task, because as Whitehead wrote he did not take the time to clearly explain his new terminology, and because any single new term often presumes many of his other new terms. However, we can make a start. The following is a list of ideas taken from *Science and the Modern World* (*SMW*) and *Process and Philosophy* (*PR*) that are crucial to even a basic understanding of Whitehead's philosophy.*

**Substance:** That which exists by itself.
**Simple Location:** A thing just is where it is, and nowhere else.

---

*Many of these concepts appear in pages 103–5 of *Science and the Modern World*. The core of Whitehead's metaphysics is right there in those three pages.

**Fallacy of Misplaced Concreteness:** Confusing abstractions with concrete actuality.

**Prehension:** "Taking account" of at-a-distance.

**Events:** Happenings over time—embracing past, present, future.

**Fundamental interrelatedness:** Every event is related to every other event.

**Actual entity:** *That* which is. What actually exists. What is really real.

**Eternal objects:** Changeless forms, the ultimate ingredients of all events.

**Internal relations:** Each relationship enters into the essence of the event. Apart from that relationship, the event would not be itself.

**Epochal process:** Processes come in whole units—pulses of self-creation and perishing.

**Organicism:** All concrete enduring entities are organisms: the *whole* influences its parts (its various suborganisms) that come together to form it. Part-whole relationships are mutually determining; an alternative to mechanism.

In clarifying what Whitehead meant by these terms, I will use his words where I think they are clear, and where not, I will offer my own clarifications. I'll begin, not with a Whiteheadian neologism, but with a word that figures centrally in his work because he is committed to providing an alternative.

## SUBSTANCE

*Substance is that which exists by itself.* In ordinary talk, we use "substance" usually to mean "solid stuff"—and if not solid, then definitely "stuff" of some sort. We mean it much the way we use the word "material." It is what the world or its contents are made of. Substance, then, tends to mean "matter" or "energy"—the fundamental *substrate* of real forms and qualities.

But this is not the formal meaning of substance in philosophy, as described by Descartes in his *Principles of Philosophy,* for instance: "By substance we can conceive nothing else than a thing which exists in such a way as to stand in need of nothing beyond itself in order to its existence."[3]

Technically, substance refers to that which can subsist by itself and needs nothing else to sustain its existence. For example, left to itself, a lump of matter such as a stone, would continue to exist for all eternity. The stone is an instance of substance. But substance need not refer to solid or spatial "stuff" like stones, or even to less dense "stuff" such as energy. As Descartes argued: Nonspatial mind, or "thinking stuff," can exist on its own; it does not depend on a body for its existence. Thus, for Descartes, both matter and mind were substances.

Whitehead not only objects to the notion of substance as material substrate, he argues against the notion of substance in its strict philosophical sense. Commonsense would seem to suggest that the ultimate nature of the universe must be self-sufficient—it must be self-sustaining, it must be substantial. Otherwise, it would depend on something else, and so would not in fact be ultimate. This line of reasoning leads quickly to an infinite regress—"turtles all the way down." So, it would seem, there *must* be substance of some sort at the bottom (or highest), ultimate, level of reality.

Whitehead disagrees—and he does so for two reasons. First, he says that there can be no such thing as a wholly self-sustaining ultimate. There may be an ultimate—in fact, he insists *there must be an ultimate* to avoid infinite regress—but this ultimate is not self-sustaining. The ultimate is not a substance. And this is because of his second reason: By itself, the ultimate is an abstraction, it can have no meaning apart from its particular instantiations. *Actual reality* is a process of interchange between what Whitehead calls "eternal objects" (see below) and "actual entities" (see below). Eternal objects may exist at the level of ultimate reality, but this is not *actual existence*—it is "existence" only in the form of pure potentiality. Eternal objects can be expressed only as ingredients of some (or many) actual entities.

Thus the ultimate is *interdependent* with some, many, or all of its *actual* manifestations. Neither ultimate eternal objects, nor limited and determined actual entities, are self-sufficient. They are wholly dependent on each other, and so are not substances. They are, instead, *processes* because the relationship between eternal objects and actual entities is one of *act* or *acting*. The eternal objects "ingress" into (become ingredients of) actual entities that come into being through the "coming together" (or "concrescence") of eternal objects passed on from previous, completed actual occasions.

There is no substance because *nothing exists by itself.* The world is a network in time and space of interconnected and interpenetrating processes. Whitehead: "There are no single occasions, in the sense of isolated occasions. Actuality is through and through togetherness."[5] And, "Each volume of space, or each lapse of time, includes in its essence aspects of all volumes of space, or of all lapses of time."[6]

## SIMPLE LOCATION

*A thing just is where it is, and nowhere else.* Closely interwoven with the notion of substance is the "common sense" belief in simple location. It follows that if something can exist wholly by itself, then at *any time* and at *any place* that object remains *wholly itself* in that place, at that time. In other words, it is simply located (in time and space).

According to this view, real objects are extended in space *by necessity*— for if they did not occupy space (e.g., numbers) they would be abstractions. But, from this perspective, real objects need not be extended in time. The passage of time for any object is an *accident.* It is something that happens to the object but is not an integral part of its essence the way space or volume is.

Thus, according to this notion of simple location, an object can be wholly itself at any instant of time (where "instant" means without duration). It doesn't *need* time to exist. Take any slice of time, no matter how small, and the object is still *there* wholly itself. On the face of it this seems to make sense. If I watch my cup for a minute, it is still exactly and wholly the same cup as it was an hour ago. If I watch it for a minute, or a second, or a nanosecond, the cup doesn't change.

Whitehead disagrees with all of this. First, that any object is simply located in space, and second, that it is simply located in time. He says that every object is the result of a process whereby aspects of the universe converge ("concresce") to *become* that object. Thus, the "object" is really a process extended over distances that involve the entire universe.

Furthermore, it also has to be extended over time. If it were possible for an object to exist wholly as itself at any instant, then the question arises: How could it be the *same* object the next instant? If it is *wholly* itself at an instant, then *no part* of it can extend to either the previous instant or to the subsequent instant. It would be wholly a *different* object from instant to instant. So what would account for the apparent continuity from instant to instant of what we take to be a self-identical object? How, for instance, could you be the same person that woke up this morning as the one who went to sleep in your bed last night? Without some connection between instants—that is, without some extension from moment to moment—you could have no memory of what happened even a split-second ago. Without extension in time there could be no self-identity. According to Whitehead:

> To say that a bit of matter has *simple location* means that, in expressing its spatio-temporal relations, it is adequate to state that it is where it is, in a definite region of space, and throughout a definite finite duration of time, apart from any essential reference to the relations of that bit of matter to other regions of space and to other durations of time.[7]
>
> . . . the concept of simple location is going to make great difficulties for induction. For, if in the location of configurations of matter throughout a stretch of time there is no inherent reference to any other times, past or future, it immediately follows that nature within any period does not refer to nature at any other period. . . . For there is nothing in the present fact which inherently refers either to the past or to the future. It looks, therefore, as though memory, as well as induction, would fail to find any justification within nature itself.[8]

## FALLACY OF MISPLACED CONCRETENESS

*Confusing abstractions with concrete reality.* According to Whitehead, both the notions of substance and of simple location are examples of "misplaced concreteness." To account for the idea of substance or of simple location, we need to abstract the object from its embeddedness in the process matrix of space-time. It is not wholly untrue to say that an object exists at a particular place—and for practical purposes we can (and do) behave this way. But the full truth of the situation is that the "object" is embedded in a flux—a flux of events that are *creating* that "object" at that location, for that duration. Beyond that, the "object" has no real existence. It is merely an abstraction from the flow of the whole.* A helpful way to picture this is the way a tornado forms. It is nothing more than a concrescence of meteorological events, swirling cones of wind. Yet we even give it a name. The tornado looks like a thing—we can point to it, measure it, and see its devastating effects—but in essence it is just rapid, patterned movements of air. It emerges from the flux of weather events, has its own particular form, moves across the landscape, and eventually releases its energy and dissolves back into the flux from which it arose.

## PREHENSION/CONCRESCENCE

*"Taking account" of at-a-distance.* What we call "objects" are really the focal points—or "gatherings together" of events—of processes streaming in from the universe. Whitehead calls this streaming together the act of "concrescence." But this coming together is not merely a receptive, passive affair. The focal entity *actively selects* from the innumerable, if not infinite, possibilities streaming its way—otherwise, there would be no way of explaining why one "object" or event should differ from any other. Yet all actual entities are individuals, they are distinct.

This act of selection is what we call "perception" at the level of human organisms. It is a "reaching out" and "taking account" of what is distant in space (and time) from the actual entity occupying this point *here* in space at this moment *now*. This "reaching out" is not unique to humans, nor even to animals. Whitehead extends the concept, calling it *prehension,* to

---

*Whitehead describes, in somewhat technical language, this interpenetration of processes or "prehensions": "[If *A* is a 'prehensive unity' of an actual occasion which prehends an aspect of *B* ] I will say that the aspect of *B* from *A* is the *mode* in which *B* enters into the composition of *A*. This is the modal character of space, that the prehensive unity of *A* is the prehension into unity of the aspects of all other volumes from the standpoint of *A*. . . . I can use Leibniz' language, and say that every volume mirrors in itself every other volume in space."

And he goes on to say that temporal durations are "exactly analogous": "Each duration of time mirrors itself in all temporal durations. . . . An instant in time, without duration, is an imaginative logical construction [i.e., an abstraction]" (*Science and the Modern World*, p. 65).

*all* actual entities all the way down. He quotes Francis Bacon to clarify his point:

> [Francis Bacon said] "It is certain that all bodies whatsoever, though they have no sense [i.e., cognition] yet they have perception [uncognitive apprehension]." I construed *perception* (as used by Bacon) as meaning *taking account of* the essential character of the thing perceived, and I construed *sense* as meaning *cognition*. We certainly do take account of things of which we have no explicit cognition. . . . I will use the word *prehension* for *uncognitive apprehension*. . . . Accordingly, there is a prehension, *here* in this place, of things which have a reference to *other* places.[9]

And he continues:

> This unity of a prehension defines itself as a *here* and a *now,* and the things so gathered into the grasped unity have essential reference to other places and other times. For Berkeley's *mind,* I substitute a process of prehensive unification. . . . Note that the idea of simple location has gone. The things which are grasped into a realized unity, here and now, are not the castle, the cloud, and the planet simply in themselves; but they are the castle, the cloud, and the planet from the standpoint, in space and time, of the prehensive unification. . . . It is, therefore, aspects of the castle, the cloud, and the planet which are grasped into unity here.[10]

With this understanding, Whitehead introduces his notion of "sense-object": "An entity of which we become aware in sense perception is the terminus of our act of perception. I will call such an entity a *sense-object.* . . . I will say that a sense-object has *ingression* into space-time."[11]

Whitehead here is proposing an epistemology that avoids the lurking skepticism in Galileo and Locke's distinction between *primary* and *secondary* qualities. Whitehead makes no such distinction; instead, he embeds *sense objects* in the domain of space-time. The prehension of a particular sense-object (e.g., color green, or sound of a note—previously, a "secondary" quality)—follows the "ingression" (the becoming an ingredient of) into space-time of that sense-object (making it what previously would have been called a "primary quality").*

---

*Whitehead: "Thus, the sense-object is present in A [prehensive unity of an actual occasion, i.e., an "event"] with the mode of location in *B*. Thus, if green be the sense-object in question, green is not simply at *A* where it is being perceived, nor is it simply at *B* where it is perceived as located; but it is present at *A* with the mode of location in *B*. [*Science and the Modern World,* p. 70.]

"I am merely describing what we do perceive: We are aware of green as being one element in a prehensive unification of sense-objects [p. 71]. . . . Perception is simply the cognition of prehensive unification . . . perception is cognition of prehension. The actual world is a manifold of prehensions; and a 'prehension' is a 'prehensive occasion'; and a prehensive occasion is the most concrete finite entity, conceived as what it is in itself and for itself, and not as from its aspect in the essence of another such occasion [p. 71].

"Space and time exhibit the general scheme of interlocked relations of these prehensions. You cannot tear any one of them out of its context. Yet each one of them within its context has all the reality that attaches to the whole complex. Conversely, the totality has the same reality as each prehension; for each prehension unifies the modalities to be ascribed, from its standpoint, to every part of the whole. A prehension is a process of unifying. Accordingly, nature is a process of expansive development, necessarily transitional from prehension to prehension. What is achieved is thereby passed beyond, but it is also retained as having aspects of itself present to prehensions which lie beyond it" (p. 72).

And later he says: "This concrete prehension, from within, of the life-history of an enduring fact is analyzable into two abstractions, of which one is the enduring entity which has emerged as a real matter of fact to be taken account of by other things, and the other is the individualized embodiment of the underlying energy of realization" (p. 105).

But this is confusing. It seems to contradict itself. On the one hand, Whitehead says the "concrete prehension" of "an enduring fact" is "analyzable into two abstractions." He goes on to identify one of these "abstractions" as "an enduring entity." He seems to be making a distinction between (a) "concrete prehension," (b) "enduring fact," and (c) "enduring entity." (a) and (b) qualify as "actual entities," (c) is an "abstraction." But then, on the other hand, he goes on to say that the "enduring entity" (an abstraction) "emerges as a real matter of fact to be taken account of by other things," and this would qualify (c) as an actual entity. So which is it? Is an enduring entity an abstraction or a concrete actual entity? The distinction is not trivial because it involves Whitehead's important notion of the "fallacy of misplaced concreteness"—which is mistakenly talking of abstractions as though they were concrete, actual entities.

It is clear from the rest of his work that the second term, "individualized embodiment," *is* an abstraction from the matrix of embedded internal and external relations. So this is not a problem.

## EVENTS

*Events are happenings over time and space—embracing past, present, future.*
They enfold the past, mirror the present, and anticipate the future. Whatever
is prehended (or perceived) is always an event. According to Whitehead:

> An event is the grasping into unity of a pattern of aspects. The effec-
> tiveness of an event beyond itself arises from the aspects of itself which
> go to form the prehended unities of other events.[12]
>
> The word *event* just means one of these spatio-temporal unities.
> Accordingly, it may be used instead of the term "prehension" as mean-
> ing the thing prehended.[13]

## FUNDAMENTAL INTERRELATEDNESS (NEXUS)

*Everything (every event) is related to everything else (every other event):*

> My theory involves the entire abandonment of the notion that simple
> location is the primary way in which things are involved in space-time.
> In a certain sense, everything is everywhere at all times. For every loca-
> tion involves an aspect of itself in every other location. Thus every spatio-
> temporal standpoint mirrors the world.[14]

The holographic character of Whitehead's organicist worldview
echoes Buddhist descriptions of the fundamental interrelatedness of all
beings. In both, the overall impression is of a cosmos mirroring itself in
all its parts, a hierarchic cosmos in which every entity is partly created
and sustained by every other. Compare this quote from Whitehead,

> A nonmaterialistic philosophy of nature will identify a primary organism
> as being the emergence of some particular pattern as grasped in the unity
> of a real event. Such a pattern will include the aspects of the event in ques-
> tion as grasped in other events, whereby those other events receive a modi-
> fication, or partial determination. There is thus an intrinsic and an extrin-
> sic reality of an event, namely, the event as in its own prehension, and the
> event as in the prehension of other events. The concept of an organism
> includes, therefore, the concept of the interaction of organisms.[15]

with the following, where the cosmic ecological balance is caught, for example, in the *atvatamsakka sutra* in the imagery of Indra's net and in the *jijimurge* doctrine in Zen Buddhism:

> In the heaven of Indra, there is said to be a network of pearls, so arranged that if you look at one you see all the others reflected in it. In the same way, each object in the world is not merely itself but involves every other object and in fact *is* everything else.[16]
>
> All things are One and have no life apart from it; the One is all things and is incomplete without the least of them. Yet the parts are parts within the whole, not merged in it; they are interfused with Reality while retaining the full identity of the part, and the One is no less One for the fact that it is a million-million parts.[17]

In both Whitehead's philosophy and in Eastern mysticism the "parts" of the cosmos are not independent bits of matter, they are organisms creating and being created by their environment. In a purely mechanical universe, where all things happen due to outside disturbances, the only reality is extrinsic—where all things are related externally as configurations of independent substances. All *internal relations* (see below)—interiority, experience, or consciousness—are squeezed out of existence.

In *Process and Reality,* Whitehead uses the term "nexus" to point to a distinctive node in the network of universal relationships streaming and interpenetrating into each other: "[A] nexus is a set of actual entities in the unity of the relatedness constituted by their prehensions of each other."[18] Thus, what in normal language we might refer to as an "individual" (you or me, for instance), Whitehead describes technically as a "nexus" of unified dynamic relationships.

## ACTUAL ENTITY

*That which is. What actually exists. What is really real.* It is not sufficient, metaphysically, to simply say that an actual entity is what actually is, for although that defines it, it does not begin to identify it. To know *that* something is, is one thing; it is something else to know *what* that thing is—i.e., "*what* that is which is."[19] According to Whitehead:

"Actual entities"—also termed "actual occasions"—are the final real things of which the world is made up. There is no going behind actual entities to find anything more real. They differ among themselves: God is an actual entity, and so is the most trivial puff of existence in far-off empty space. But, though there are gradations of importance, and diversities of function, yet in the principles which actuality exemplifies all are on the same level. The final facts are, all alike, actual entities; and these actual entities are drops of experience, complex and interdependent.[20]

Although Whitehead here says that *what is* ("the world") is "made up" of actual entities, seemingly implying that it is made up of some underlying substance, later, he is quite explicit that "an actual entity is a process, and is not describable in terms of the morphology of a 'stuff.'"[21] The very being of an actual entity is that it *acts,* it "becomes itself," its becoming *constitutes* what it is. In short, an actual entity is wholly a process of coming into being—an actual entity is the *act of existing.* Beyond the process of coming into existence, there is no actual existence. Thus, the world is "made up" of actualities in the sense that they are its dynamic ingredients. Its own *process* is what creates the world from moment to moment to moment; universal process is the fundamental constituency of all reality. Without act, no actuality; without process, no actual existence. And this underlies Whitehead's famous ontological principle: "Actual entities are the only *reasons;* so that to search for a *reason* is to search for one or more actual entities."[22]

## ETERNAL OBJECTS
*Changeless forms, the ultimate ingredients of all events.* In the discussion of actual entities the emphasis is on *actual* existence—implying that there may be some other kind of existence that is not actual, that does not involve change, or process. And, according to Whitehead, this is the case. Some objects exist but do not have actual existence; they exist *potentially.* But their being potential does not diminish their importance in the scheme of things, for without them no actual entities could exist. The reverse is also true: No eternal objects could exist in the absence of actual entities.

But what exactly is an "eternal object"? What are examples of something that is "eternal" and in what way are they "objects"? Whitehead gives as examples of eternal objects: "colors, sounds, scents, geometrical characters." They are what in classical and medieval metaphysics were called "universals."* Where an actual entity is a particular, an eternal object is a universal. Socrates is an example of a particular human; humanity as such is an example of a universal. Each human is a *particular* exemplar or

---

*On eternal objects as transcendental, Whitehead says: "The foundation of the metaphysical position which I am maintaining [is] that the understanding of actuality requires a reference to ideality. The two realms are intrinsically inherent in the total metaphysical situation" (*Science and the Modern World*, p. 158).

And on universals: "These transcendent entities have been termed 'universals'. I prefer to use the term 'eternal objects'. . . . Eternal objects are, thus, in their nature, abstract. By 'abstract' I mean that what an eternal object is in itself—that is to say, its essence—is comprehensible without reference to some one particular occasion of experience. . . . But to transcend an actual occasion does not mean being disconnected from it. On the contrary, I hold that each eternal object has its own proper connection with each such occasion, I term its mode of ingression into that occasion" (*Science and the Modern World*, p. 159).

However, later in *Process and Reality* (ironically, again on p. 158), Whitehead flatly contradicts his earlier equivalence of actual entities with particulars, and of eternal objects with universals: "The philosophy of organism . . . admits two ultimate classes of entities, mutually exclusive. One class consists of 'actual entities,' which in the philosophical tradition are mis-described as 'particulars'; and the other class consists of forms of definiteness, here named 'eternal objects,' which in comparison with actual entities are mis-described as 'universals'."

The resolution of this apparent (if it is only apparent) contradiction, perhaps, is that Whitehead is taking issue in *Process and Reality* with the medieval or "traditional" treatment of particulars and universals as though they were (or could be) "disconnected." For Whitehead (as for Aristotle's hylomorphism in classical philosophy), there could be no separation between immanent particulars and transcendent universals. In *Science and the Modern World,* Whitehead is quite explicit there is not (nor could there be) any immanent-transcendent or particular-universal disconnection. In Whitehead's philosophy, actual entities and eternal objects necessarily implicate each other all the way down—and all the way up.

So, even though Whitehead very clearly states in *PR* that actual entities are "misdescribed" as particulars, and that eternal objects are "misdescribed" as universals, it is the traditional *disconnection* between particulars and universals that Whitehead is rejecting in *PR,* and not so much the equivalence of particulars and actual entities or of universals and eternal objects. As long as we realize that particulars and universals (actual entities and eternal objects) are inescapably mutually implicated, the equivalence is unproblematic.

instantiation (or manifestation) of *universal* humanity. Without humanity, there could be no individual humans; without individual humans, there could be no humanity. Particulars *participate* in universals.

Whitehead's eternal objects, therefore, are akin to Plato's Forms, in that all mundane things—actual entities—derive their reality or actuality from participating in universal forms. But unlike Plato, and like Aristotle, Whitehead's "forms" (eternal objects) cannot exist independently of, and transcendentally to, *at least one* (and probably numerous) instance(s) of particular actualities. Actual entities and eternal objects require each other for their existence. Whitehead says:

> This interfusion of events is effected by the aspects of those eternal objects, such as colors, sounds, scents, geometrical characters, which are required for nature and are not emergent from it. Such an eternal object will be an ingredient of one event under the guise, or aspect, of qualifying another event. There is a reciprocity of aspects, and there are patterns of pattern of aspects. Each event corresponds to two such patterns; namely, the pattern of aspects of other events which it grasps into its own unity, and the pattern of its aspects which other events severally grasp into their unities.[23]

And later:

> We conceive actuality as in essential relation to an unfathomable possibility. Eternal objects inform actual occasions with hierarchic patterns. . . . Every actual occasion is a limitation imposed on possibility, and . . . by virtue of this limitation the particular value of that shaped togetherness of things emerges.[24]

### INTERNAL RELATIONS AND VALUE

*"Each relationship enters into the essence of the event."* For Whitehead, every actual entity is constituted by a set of internal relations—meaning it derives its very being, its essence, and its value from the relationships between the various prior actual entities and eternal objects that stream

into it from the past in each moment. Without these *constitutive* internal relations, *nothing actual would exist.* Reality, therefore, is essentially both relational and interior. Furthermore, these relationships are *felt* or prehended. The only way for a set of internal relationships to endure from one moment to the next is for interiority to be experiential—to literally *feel the presence of the past.* Internal relations, then, account for the experiential interiority, or subjectivity—the "whatitfeelslike from within"—of every actual entity or event all the way down. According to Whitehead:

> *Each relationship enters into the essence of the event;* so that, apart from that relationship, the event would not be itself. This is what is meant by the very notion of internal relations. It has been usual, indeed universal, to hold that spatio-temporal relationships are external. This doctrine is what is here denied.[25]

All entities are not of equal value. The hierarchical depth of internal relations experienced by any particular entity (from humans and dolphins, to amoeba and bacteria, to electrons and photons) *is* the relative value of that entity within its hierarchical network. For instance, a cell is more valuable than a molecule or an atom, and a dog or fish more valuable than a single cell, because it literally incorporates more reality, more complex nesting of levels of internal relations. Quite simply, because the fish and the dog *unifies* its multiplicity of constituent cells, molecules, and atoms (exemplifying downward causation), whereas the reverse is not true, they have, or *are,* greater value. On this analysis, downward causation (e.g., instances of creativity from mind to brain) is more valuable than upward causation (e.g., instances of mental activity determined by events in the brain). Again, Whitehead says:

> An actual event is an achievement for its own sake, a grasping of diverse entities into a value by reason of their real togetherness in that pattern, to the exclusion of other entities. . . .[26]
>
> This really means that each intrinsic essence, that is to say, what each eternal object is in itself, becomes relevant to the one limited value emergent in the guise of the event. But values differ in importance. Thus,

though each event is necessary for the community of events, the weight of its contribution is determined by something intrinsic in itself.[27]

Whitehead identifies this "something intrinsic" as a property he calls "retention," or "endurance," or "reiteration." Value, therefore, is graded, hierarchical. It depends on the hierarchical depth of self-identity. Value is the "recovery" in a later entity of the self-identity from a prior entity. The more of the layered spatio-temporal hierarchy of organisms that contributes to this self-identity, the more value that organism-as-a-whole has. Value, then, is the mirroring of internal relations. It is the mirroring of the self-identity of the whole in its parts, and of the parts in the whole:

> There is the same thing-for-its-own-sake standing before you. Thus the event, in its own intrinsic reality, mirrors itself, as derived from its own parts, aspects of the same patterned value as it realizes in its complete self. It thus realizes itself under the guise of an enduring individual entity, with a life history contained within itself.[28]

## EPOCHAL PROCESS

*Processes come in whole units—pulses of self-creation and perishing.* Reality consists of pulses or vibrations of patterns of process that transition from one event to the next.

> No duration can become until a smaller duration (part of the former) has antecedently come into being . . . [leading to] the Aristotelian view there is no first moment . . . an irrational notion. . . . [This] difficulty is met by conceiving temporalization as the realization of a complete organism. This organism is an event holding in its essence its spatio-temporal relationships (both within itself, and beyond itself) throughout the spatio-temporal continuum.[29]

Whitehead is proposing an alternative to both the notions of time or process as atomic and time or process as continuous. If time is atomic—i.e., composed of self-contained instants or moments—it raises the difficult problem of accounting for duration and self-identity, for the experienced fact that something gets carried over from one moment to the next (e.g., the sense of self). If time is continuous, an equally difficult problem arises, as Zeno's paradoxes demonstrate: If moment **A** is continuous with a subsequent moment **B**, then one part of **B** ($B_a$) must be closer to **A** than another part of **B** ($B_c$), which is closer to the next moment **C**. But this must also be true of $B_a$ (and of $B_c$): A part of $B_a$, call it $B_1$, will be closer to $B_a$ than to $B_c$. Continuity of process leads to an infinite regress, which logically prohibits any process from ever occurring. There could be no transition from one moment to the next.

Whitehead recognized the difficulties with both the atomic and continuity notions of process. Unwilling to accept the alternative of Parmenidean static changelessness, he proposed a version of process that combines both atomicity and continuity. He said that as soon as an event comes into being (as a concrescence of eternal objects), it *completes* itself—it *perishes*. Process, therefore, is *epochal*—i.e., it is an "epoch" with a beginning and an end. But before it perishes, it passes on its essential actuality to a subsequent event. Process, therefore, is also a *succession* of epochs. Actuality, in Whitehead's view, is more like the process of a movie which is a sequence of individual frames—except for a fundamentally important difference: Unlike movie frames, epochs interpenetrate and pass on part of themselves (their "form" or "eternal objects") to the next epoch.*

## ORGANICISM

*All concrete enduring entities are organisms:* The *whole* influences its parts (downward causation of its various suborganisms) that come together to form it. Part-whole relationships are mutually determining. Parts determine the whole, but not completely—for *wholes inject novelty or creativity* into the system of parts. The whole always *adds something* to the sum of its parts. Mechanism cannot account for creativity in relationships, and thus organicism offers a more comprehensive, postmodern, alternative to the mechanistic materialism of modernism.

---

*I will return to the crucial importance of this idea of "epochal process" in chapter 9, "Integrating Worldviews: Past Matter, Present Mind," when unfolding Whitehead's solution to the mind-body problem.

The doctrine which I am maintaining is that the whole concept of materialism only applies to very abstract entities, the products of logical discernment. The concrete enduring entities are organisms, so that the plan of the *whole* influences the very characters of the various subordinate organisms which enter into it. In the case of an animal, the mental states enter into the plan of the total organism and thus modify the plans of the successive subordinate organisms until the ultimate smallest organisms, such as electrons, are reached. Thus an electron within a living body is different from an electron outside it, by reason of the plan of the body.[30]

But where does consciousness come in?

Whitehead then goes on to make a very curious statement: "The electron *blindly runs* either within or without the body;"[31] (emphasis added). This seems to exclude electrons from the community of purposeful, experiential entities, thus contradicting the panpsychist position of experience all the way down; even though in the next sentence he says: "But it runs within the body in accordance with its character within the body; that is to say, in accordance with the general plan of the body, and this plan includes the mental state."

This last statement acknowledges that the "mental state" is intrinsic to the organism of the body, but, it seems, not to the electron. The electron's character is affected only by the *body's* mental state, not by any mentality intrinsic to the electron itself. Whitehead, here in *Science and the Modern World,* seems to be offering *organicism* as a more cautious alternative or preliminary model to the more explicit panpsychism in his later work, notably *Process and Reality.* In *Science and the Modern World,* there still seems to be some ambiguity or hesitancy on Whitehead's part regarding mentality or experience as intrinsic to prehension *all* the way down. If electrons "blindly run," it is hard to square this with their engaging in prehension that includes sentience and volition.

In fact, on the next page, Whitehead says that his lectures amount to "the theory of *organic mechanism.* In this theory, the molecules may blindly run in accordance with the general laws, but the molecules differ in their intrinsic characters according to the general organic plans of the situations in which they find themselves."[32] Although the theory of "organic mechanism" is a significant advance on mechanistic materialism (based on the notion of simple location), because it can account for the "presence of the past" and an "orientation toward the future" in the present actual occasion, it is still a "flatland" theory.

Like contemporary systems theory, the "organic mechanism" of *Science and the Modern World* cannot account for the depth or *interior* dimension of experience or subjectivity in the world. Unless the fundamental constituents of organic systems—let's say electrons or quanta—are themselves intrinsically experiential, then any theory of "organic mechanism" or systems theory can account for mentality (i.e., subjectivity, experience, sentience, volition) only as an *emergent* property. But, as we've seen, such "emergence" of an ontologically novel phenomenon requires a miracle that begets the "wine of consciousness" from the "water of the brain" (as Colin McGinn put it). Any explanation in which "a miracle then occurs" fails as an explanation. Like systems theory, organic mechanism seems to call for a miracle to account for consciousness.

## THE STRUCTURE OF EXPERIENCE

But by the time Whitehead produces his magnum opus *Process and Reality,* he has developed an ontology in which each "occasion of experience" is a momentary unit of subjectivity—and although indivisible, it has an internal dynamic structure or process. This structure results from the fundamentally time-based nature of experience. Every experience always occurs "now"; in fact, our only direct experience of time is through moment-by-moment experience (we have no sense organ for time, we are aware of it extrasensorily).

Each "occasion of experience" is a dipolar unity, or a nondual duality, that enfolds, or prehends, the past (objects) into the present (subject) and orients the organism toward the future in a "creative advance." Each "occasion of experience," therefore, consists of past moments flowing into the present. That is, the present experience feels the past experience through "physical prehension," for example, through somatic cellular activity (Whitehead calls this "perception in the mode of causal efficacy").

Some occasions of experience, those with sense organs—such as eyes, ears, noses, taste buds, touch receptors, sonar, and radiation receptors—also receive information from objects in the world through the mode of "perception in the mode of presentational immediacy." Whatever the source of its prehensions, each "occasion of experience" synthesizes the feelings of the world out of which it arises, *and unifies them in a "creative advance"*—a subjective orientation or projection toward the future.

One of the most significant consequences of Whitehead's ontology—his transcending the Cartesian split—is that experience, our entire epistemology, is rooted in the matter of our body. We know the world (and ourselves) by *feeling* how it impresses itself upon our bodies. What we ordinarily call "sense data" are not the beginning of our knowledge. They are, rather, the end products of "long and highly complex selection and amplification, by the particular physiology of the human body, of elements of the external world entertained in the mode of 'causal efficacy.'"[33] Feeling in the mode of causal efficacy corresponds with unconscious somatic experiences of the world as it literally *enters into* us. Perception in the mode of presentational immediacy corresponds with knowledge of the world as it is filtered through our sensory-cognitive systems. In this sense, perception in the mode of causal efficacy is extrasensory and, though intuitional, is still necessarily bodily based.

One consequence of Whitehead's worldview is that in his epistemology familiar sensory perception (presentational immediacy) is derivative of a more fundamental *extrasensory* perception or feeling (causal efficacy). Whitehead says:

> The irresistible causal efficacy of nature presses itself upon us . . . and we are left with the vague feelings of influences from vague things around us. . . . Our bodily experience is primarily an experience of the dependence of presentational immediacy upon causal efficacy.[34]

## PSI PHENOMENA

Among the events that a human occasion of experience prehends are the constituent events of its body's cells, molecules, atoms, and elementary particles. In other words, even subatomic events enter into the flow of momentary experiences unconsciously felt by the person (and may conceivably rise to conscious awareness). Even quantum events can influence the "subjective form" of our moment-by-moment experience. And given the nonlocal nature of quantum events, what is prehended need not be located within the person's own body. Therefore, given Whitehead's naturalistic view of experience, extrasensory phenomena involving action-at-a-distance, such as telepathy and clairvoyance, are no longer problematic.[35]

Furthermore, just as human experience may prehend quantum events, it is equally consistent to suppose that subatomic events may include among their prehended internal relations the influence of human experiences. In other words, physical events "external" to the body of the experiencing human may prehend or feel and respond to human experiences in ways consistent with the data of psychokinesis.

Data supporting psi phenomena pose some of the most troubling challenges to modern science rooted in the metaphysical assumptions of objectivity, sensory empiricism, reductionism, determinism, and mechanism.[36] Psi phenomena simply do not fit into the conceptual and theoretical boxes shaped by modernism. The result: typically, the modern scientific mind refuses to accept psi data (or even to seriously look at the evidence), dismissing all such claims as "irrational" and either methodologically flawed or fraudulent. But such blanket rejection is itself a symptom of irrationalism and scientism.

Entrenched scientific irrationalism should not surprise us, however, if Whitehead's radical analysis of the roots of modernism is correct.

## Whitehead's Reassessment of Modernism

Whitehead takes issue with the idea that modernism is distinctive by its emphasis on rationality, as a move away from the supposed irrationalism and superstition of the premodern medieval "Age of Faith." In stark contrast to, even in contradiction of, the orthodox view, Whitehead argues that modernism is characterized by a move toward irrationalism—hence the characterization of deconstructionism as a brand of "late-late modernism" and not true postmodernism. How can we account for two such opposing views?

From the orthodox perspective, as we have seen, modernist rationalism begins with Descartes's philosophical method as a reaction to the authoritarian medieval paradigm. Whitehead, on the other hand, sees the origins of modernism from the perspective of the scientific emphasis on empirical method. According to Whitehead, by focusing so diligently on the observed and measured particularities of nature—the reductionist program—science broke with the previous premodern scholastic preoccupation with the application of intellect and reason for thoroughgoing study of scripture and theological exegesis. To support this view, he cites, for example, Father Paul Sarpi's *History of the Council of Trent* where in 1551 the Papal Legates decreed that the Italian School of Divinity ought to use the "authorities of the Holy Fathers" and not to "useth reason."[37] This decree was described as a "novity," as a novel introduction that ran counter to the prevailing rationalism of Thomas Aquinas, St. Bonaventure, and other Scholastics. In other words, the use of reason had long been a tradition within the medieval community.

Whitehead, then, is telling us that the break with medieval Scholasticism, which the birth of modernism represents, is a move away from rationalism. This move, as already noted, was toward Baconian empiricism and the consequent reductive methodology of determining the causal relations between parts. Modernism, then, as characterized by Whitehead, is a program of empirical investigation of efficient causality; and this emphasis, in turn, gave rise to the modernist paradigm of mechanism. But mechanism claims far more than it can justify either empirically or rationally (as we will soon see). The move toward empiricism characteristic of modern science is, in fact, a move away from rationalism.

Whitehead acknowledges that this move toward empiricism, reductionism, and mechanism was necessary for modern science to make the immense progress it has. But it did so at a cost—by ignoring or dismissing the possibility and actuality of self-causation (Aristotle's final causation), of the entire domain of subjectivity, and the causal efficacy of experiencing subjects.

Despite Descartes's championing of rationalism and modernism's rejection of rationalism in favor of Baconian empiricism, Whitehead still recognized Descartes's major role in the origin of modernism. But Descartes's major influence on science was not his rational methodology, as is usually supposed. It was his *mind-matter dualism* that resulted from the application of this method. The focus within science was on the *consequence* of Cartesian rationalism, not on the rational method itself.

Fledgling modern science took up the Cartesian split, the fragmentation of mind and matter, and applied this program of fragmentation and separation first by focusing exclusively on just one component of the Cartesian split—matter—and second by further fragmenting and separating the domain of matter into constituent parts. This move represented the Newtonian extension of Cartesianism and Baconianism: the reduction and fragmentation of the world machine (without mind) to its mechanical parts (Cartesianism) by rigorous empirical observation and inferred causal relations between the parts (post-Baconianism).

The move away from rationalism, according to Whitehead, was propelled further by David Hume and Immanuel Kant. First, Hume, through his defense of empiricism in *An Inquiry Concerning Human Understanding*,[38] demonstrated that causality could never be an object of empirical observation. He argued, rightly, that if empiricism depends on data detected by the senses, then since we have no sense for detecting causal relations (all we can observe are successions of "conjoined events"), we cannot build a science or philosophy on an understanding of the world as a system of causal relations. Understanding is limited to the data of sense perceptions, and causal mechanisms do not qualify as such.

Hume, thus, presented a devastating critique of the notion of causality by demonstrating that if all our knowledge is gained through our senses, then since we have no sense organ for detecting causality, all notions of causality are merely inferences, not true empirical knowledge. Causality, therefore, should have no place in an empirically based science. All our senses can give us are regular sequences or succession of events. We can know that one thing comes after another, but not that one thing "causes" another. We never actually see that happening.

This was a major problem for the modernist worldview that assumed science could and should be wholly empirical (meaning based on sense perception), a view that assumed data gained by this method could, and had, revealed the universe as a network of (efficient) causal relationships. This was Newton's and Laplace's basis for the idea of the world as a machine.

Hume's critique undermined that notion: If science was empirical (which it was), then it could give us no knowledge of causality and therefore of mechanism. Without mechanism, no explanation. Without explanation, no science.

Second, Kant attempted to rescue philosophy and Newtonian science from Hume's critique of rational understanding in his masterful *Critique of Pure Reason*.[39] In the *Critique,* Kant argued that the ultimate task of philosophy was to turn the function of reason onto the structure and operations of the rational instrument itself. The purpose of this project was to discover the outer limits of reason. Kant concluded, in the final analysis, that is all that reason, philosophy, or science could do: to know the instrument of knowing, not the world as it is itself.

Kant's extreme irrationalism, according to Whitehead, was to propose that reason could never tell us anything about the real nature of the world. In this way, Kant may be regarded as the arch idealist or antirationalist. However, Kant's major project following Descartes, Berkeley, and Hume, was to overcome the dichotomy between idealism and realism. His compromise solution was to propose that there is a real world in-itself, distinct from our perceiving, categorizing, rational minds (Kant's extreme Cartesianism)—but that we can never know it as it is in itself. All we can know, said Kant, are our empirical *a posteriori* constructions that are shaped by our innate *a priori* mental categories, such as space, time, quantity, quality, and relation. Reason gives us these "constructions" as the data by which we know the phenomenal world. The world behind these phenomenal appearances, the transcendent noumenal world, is forever beyond us. Reason, in other words, is not adequate to the task of giving us true knowledge of the real world.

This extreme antirationalism of Kant and Hume persuaded the academic world of philosophy and science that the business of the human mind was not to understand the nature of the real world as such (metaphysics and ontology), but rather to be content with epistemology and with describing the world of appearances as detected by our senses and instrumentation. In other words, the business of philosophy was to become, eventually, analytical philosophy and linguistic analysis, not metaphysics, while the business of science was empirical observation, precise mathematical description, and empirical testing of hypotheses based on these descriptions. This, according to Whitehead, was the essence of the modernist move. And this is what he challenged.*

Not surprisingly, Whitehead regarded Kant's *Critique* as the major culprit in the modernist's recoil from rationalism and metaphysics. The task of philosophy and science after Kantian modernism ("postmodernism" is not a term used by Whitehead) is to restore rationalism so that we can have a meaningful metaphysics and cosmology. In the postmodern world envisioned by Whitehead, reason would be able to connect us with an accurate (if necessarily always incomplete and provisional) understanding of the world as it is in its concrete relations, not simply mere descriptions of appearances.

## Causality as Feeling

Whitehead argued that the problems of Kantian-inspired modernism were derived from the Cartesian error and could be resolved by a combination of unorthodox moves—including a redefinition of "matter" or of the so-called objective world, and by an expansion of the notion of causality.

First, objects are—by conventional definition—"not subjects." According to Descartes, human beings are the only experiencing subjects in the natural world. And, as Hume demonstrated, relations between objects are only ever perceived as a succession of before and after. There can be no observation of influence of one object acting on another. All notions of causality are, instead, derived from our own experience of actually *felt* influences—Whitehead's "perception in the mode of causal efficacy." The only actual instance of influence or causality is what we experience in our bodies or through the effect of our past experience on our present experience.[40]

This is a crucial insight. It means, as John B. Cobb observed:

---

*See Cobb, "Alfred North Whitehead," in *Founders of Constructive Postmodern Philosophy: Peirce, James, Bergson, Whitehead, and Hartshorne*, 1993, for a more detailed analysis of Whitehead's critique of modernism.

All other meanings of causality are derivative from this experience or else vacuous. Either the relation between successive events in the subatomic world is analogous to the relations we experience, or we have no way of thinking of them at all. Whitehead proposes that before we lapse into total silence we try out the hypothesis that there are analogies among all events.[41]

And not just in the subatomic world: Wherever we assume causation, we can understand it only if we assume that there is some analogous experience taking place whereby at least one of the entities involved feels the influence of one or more other objects. For causality to be real anywhere in the world, then, subjectivity must exist there, too. This is just one example of how Whitehead applies rational analysis within his complex speculative cosmological system to support his initial ontological assumption of panpsychism. The internal coherence of his metaphysics is itself a demonstration of the usefulness of reason that he advocates.

By making a case for panpsychism—or panexperientialism (see next chapter)—Whitehead has offered a postmodern resolution to the major issues in the philosophy of mind inherited from the modernist paradigm. Specifically, his panpsychist ontology opens the way for a resolution of the perennial mind-body problem by proposing a relationship between psyche and physis as two *temporally ordered* poles of the one experiencing individual entity. The interaction of mind and matter become a relationship between events, or "occasions of experience," where through the natural process of the flow of time, subjects (minds) become objects (physical matter). The missing link in the perennial mind-body problem, it turns out, is time.

# 8

# CONSCIOUSNESS ALL
# THE WAY DOWN?*

A true meeting of minds is a transformative event. Participants shift and change internally, and subsequently experience the world from a different perspective. Even a clash of minds may leave the combatants different in some significant way. If, however, neither side shifts or is moved from its starting position we may wonder what potential insights or creative progeny might have been stillborn.

When philosophers engaged each other at a conference on consciousness in 1994, sponsored by the Center for Process Studies, in Claremont, California, it was a rare opportunity for a meeting of minds between representatives of the academic mainstream and a marginalized minority of process philosophers.

"Consciousness in Humans, Animals, and Computers," the theme of the conference, raised intriguing questions: Is it possible? How could we know? Underlying each presentation were ontological and epistemological issues regarding the relationship between mind and matter. Before we could have any clear scientific or philosophical position on the question of consciousness in machines or animals, we would first of all need to know how consciousness is possible in ourselves—and this, of course, implies

---

*A shorter version of this chapter previously appeared in the *Journal of Consciousness Studies* 1, no. 2 (1994): 217–29, under the title "Consciousness All the Way Down? An Analysis of McGinn's Critique of Panexperientialism."

the broader question of how mind and matter could interact in any case.

As we have seen, the "problem of consciousness" in philosophy has, typically, involved three major approaches: dualism, materialism, and idealism. Given the Whiteheadian background of the organizers, the central focus of the conference was on the fourth option: panpsychism (or, as they prefer to call it, panexperientialism) and its merits or demerits vis-à-vis the two positions of dualism and materialism. (Idealism was sidelined because it denies the reality of a world external to mind. This did not fit the process philosophers' "realist" agenda. Realism—the assertion that there *really is* a world "out there" external to the mind—was assumed by these philosophers to be a precondition for any adequate theoretical position on the nature of mind and matter and their relationship.)

And as we have also seen, both dualism and materialism appear to involve insuperable difficulties when faced with the problem of mind-matter relation. To repeat: for dualism, the difficulty is accounting for interaction of these two radically distinct kinds of "substances," and for materialism the difficulty is in accounting for the emergence of sentience and subjectivity from otherwise wholly insentient and objective matter. Therefore, the implicit theme of the conference was whether panexperientialism could fare any better. Panexperientialism takes the position that *all* individual instances of reality are intrinsically *experiential*. That is, anywhere an individual unit of matter exists—from quanta and quarks to human beings—there is also at least some trace of experience or mind.

The central tenet of panexperientialism, then, is that experience goes "all the way down." "Pan" means "all of," "the whole," or "universal"—therefore "panexperience" means experience as an ingredient all through the universe, permeating all levels of being. Not just human brains, but individual cells, individual molecules, individual atoms, and even individual subatomic particles incorporate a capacity for "feeling," a degree of subjective interiority.

However, although *experience* may go all the way down, according to philosopher David Ray Griffin, one of the organizers of the conference, it is inaccurate to say that *consciousness* goes all the way down. Griffin, along with other process philosophers, such as John B. Cobb, distinguishes between experience and consciousness. According to this view, experience precedes consciousness—not the reverse. Consciousness is a derivative characteristic of a more primary experience, and emerges at a certain threshold of neuronal complexity. Individual neurons may have experience, but they are not conscious. According to Griffin, only at the higher level of individual brains does conscious experience emerge.

The viability of the panexperientialist worldview appears crucial to the mind-body debate because, as we have seen, it is the only realist option that does not get bogged down in the difficulties of interaction and emergence. The "Consciousness Conference," therefore, was an exceptional (perhaps even historic) opportunity to have some of the leading proponents of panexperientialism present a case for critique by skeptical philosophers from the mainstream analytical tradition, which is fundamentally physicalist (or crypto-dualist).

Given my thesis of radical naturalism—that resolving the mind-body problem will involve a radical revisioning of fundamental ontology and epistemology, and that such a solution will have profound implications not just for philosophy and science but for overcoming many of the pathologies afflicting society in general as well as our personal lives—I was particularly interested in observing how panexperientialism would withstand the criticisms of the skeptics. The viability of panexperientialism—and, therefore, the possibility of a resolution of the pathological epistemology and ontology of the modernist mind-body schism—goes far beyond mere academic interest for me. As I have argued here, it is not extravagant to assert that healing this split may be a fundamental requirement for the viability of humanity in a global environment subjected to pervasive Western technology and "corporatization," which is the fruit of materialist-mechanistic science, which is in turn grounded in a metaphysic that takes as its basic assumption the primacy of "dead" matter or physical energy.

From this context, then, I eagerly anticipated the interchange between the skeptic Colin McGinn (Rutgers University) and the Whiteheadian panexperientialist David Ray Griffin (Claremont School of Theology and Center for Process Studies). Although their dialogue ran aground almost as soon as it began, their exchange was nevertheless enlightening. It highlighted strengths and weaknesses of both the analytical and the panexperientialist positions and helped clarify my own position, which in some ways is a synthesis transcending these opposing views. I will, therefore, take some time here to discuss and critique the key arguments from both sides.

## The Mysterious Flame

On the one hand, McGinn argues from a background in analytical philosophy that the "problem of consciousness" is closed to human understanding.[1] Essentially, his view (echoing, though hardly advocating, Henri Bergson) is that we know the world of matter empirically through our senses—a world of spatial objects and spatial relationships. On the other hand, we know consciousness only through introspection—a domain of nonspatial phenomena* (a form of "hyperdimensional dualism"). We cannot know how these two domains could interact. McGinn does not deny that they do in fact interact—it is eminently clear that consciousness and matter do in our own human lives. What he forcefully denies is that we have the *cognitive capacity* for understanding the nature of this interaction.

We simply need to face it, he says, that we have not evolved as creatures for whom the mind-body problem has any survival significance. We have no more reason to expect that the human mind should be able to solve this problem than a dog's mind should be able to solve a problem in

---

*McGinn's position, of course, is much more sophisticated than this caricature. For example, he argues (1994 and 1997) that the problem of consciousness has more to do with the problematic nature of matter or space itself than with consciousness *per se*. According to McGinn, consciousness is not some mysterious force or principle additional to matter, but is in some way a property of space that naturally emerges when matter reaches a certain level of evolutionary complexity. So, McGinn proposes, consciousness is not *really* nonspatial, it just happens to "inhabit" a kind of space radically different from that familiar to our empirical senses (and our sensory-derived rational understanding), and therefore is beyond our ken. Ultimately, it is this "radical space" that is a mystery to us, much as ordinary three-dimensional space is constitutionally a mystery to Flatlanders. Consciousness as such is not a mystery—after all, we know it directly in our experience; it is the relationship or interaction between consciousness and matter that is mysterious because this involves the "hidden" parameters (whatever they may be) of the putative, unknowable space.

algebra.* According to McGinn, therefore, the "problem of consciousness" is, and will remain, a mystery to the human mind. He emphasizes, however, that the "mystery of consciousness" is not inherent in the mind-body relation itself. To some other being evolved for negotiating different evolutionary challenges, the problem may be clearly graspable. The "problem of consciousness" just happens to be insuperable for human minds. By implication, then, we should not waste time in philosophy or in science attempting to solve this problem. We should acknowledge the mystery— the unknowableness of mind-body interaction—in much the same spirit as Kant when he proclaimed the unknowableness of the noumenal world of things-in-themselves.

In both cases—in Kant's critique of reason, and McGinn's critique of consciousness—the mystery results from limitations inherent in our instrument of knowing. And in both cases this instrument has been identified as reason.

## Faith in Rationalism

Griffin takes an opposing view. He argues that the mind-body problem *is* amenable to rational analysis. And this is most explicitly worked out in the details of the process philosophies of Alfred North Whitehead and Charles Hartshorne.[2, 3] Griffin points to a categorical distinction between what he calls "artificial mysteries" created by human minds and "natural mysteries" that inhere in nature itself. Artificial mysteries, such as the mind-body problem, he maintains, are open to reason, while natural mysteries (such

---

*McGinn is not proposing that "algebra" (or any other capacity for abstract reasoning) evolved because it has survival significance for humans. However, among the capacities that we have developed in the course of evolution as part of our survival package as human beings have been certain powers for abstract reasoning (forming strategies for hunting or for avoiding becoming prey, for example). These capacities have incidentally produced ancillary nonsurvival capacities such as our faculties for doing mathematics or making art. But all such spin-off capacities, like the survival capacities themselves, arose as a result of evolutionary selective pressures for surviving among the contingencies of a *spatial* world. Our biological survival has not depended on a similar pressure for evolving capacities that enable us to negotiate a domain of nonspatial mental or imaginal dangers and opportunities.

as the origin of the universe, or what came "before" the big-bang) may be closed.[4]

The position I take is sympathetic to the Griffin-Whiteheadian view; nevertheless, at the same time it acknowledges the force and validity of McGinn's critique of human understanding. If McGinn and Griffin are so fundamentally opposite in their views, how, then, is the compromise position taken here to be supported? As we shall see, this apparent paradox is deeply related to the paradox of consciousness itself.

On the one hand, I think that McGinn is probably correct when he says that the problem of consciousness is beyond rational human understanding; yet, I hold, with Griffin, that the mind-body problem is amenable to a process solution. On the other hand, I differ with McGinn's claim that the mystery of consciousness is ultimately beyond the capacities of human beings to penetrate, and with Griffin's that the problem is amenable to rational understanding.

Human beings have other capacities for knowing beyond reason—extrarational capacities such as emotion and intuition that could be adequate to the mind-body task. Whereas the problem of consciousness may be "cognitively closed" to human understanding (McGinn's position), it may not be intuitively or somatically closed to us. For instance, the intimate nature of the psychosomatic relationship is directly and immediately available in emotional experience. A simple example may help: Just remember the last time you blushed with embarrassment. It would be hard to deny that in the heat of that moment you knew, without a shadow of doubt, the intimate connection between mind and body. Just because we may not be capable of translating this form of knowing into unambiguous rational concepts does not invalidate emotion as a mode of knowledge.

Such knowing, undoubtedly, differs in kind from knowledge as conceptual-rational understanding. Taking a cue from Michael Polanyi, I distinguish between two types of epistemology: *knowing that* and *knowing how.*[5] "Knowing that" is what I refer to as "participatory epistemology," involving the direct immersion or blending of subjectivity with the phenomenon being investigated. "Knowing how" is the objectifying epistemology familiar to modern science, where the phenomenon is abstracted for measurement and causal analysis. The first kind of epistemology involves knowing as *meaning,* the second involves knowing through *mechanism.**

I argue that in order to know consciousness, and to know the relation between consciousness and the physical world, we will need to cultivate an alternative epistemology beyond the faculties of rational analysis and conceptual understanding.[6] Other extrarational forms of knowing have been systematically developed in many non-Western traditions, such as Taoism, Buddhism, Hinduism, and Shamanism.

The spiritual or mystical practices of such traditions employ nonrational participatory epistemologies that enable them to make contact with "alternative realities" (perhaps even McGinn's "radical spaces") and to develop worldviews based on ontologies radically different from the modern Western paradigm of materialism and mechanism.[7] I mention here these alternative epistemologies and ontologies, not to defend or challenge their empirical adequacy, but simply to emphasize that other epistemologies and ontologies do exist, and have existed for many thousands of years in various cultures, and that these may serve as models and sources of inspiration for developing an adequate postmodern Western epistemology and ontology that can account for consciousness and the relationship between *psyche* and *physis*—between mind and nature.

A new epistemology of consciousness may incorporate different modalities—for instance a combination of rationality and a radical empiricism that includes meditation and a variety of psychosomatic techniques for inducing altered states of consciousness. Given that what is at issue is the mind-*body* relationship, it makes sense to use the body as an instrument of knowing as well as using the rational capacities. For if we accept panexperientialism, then one consequence is that consciousness-experience pervades the entire body, and may even in some sense extend beyond it.[8] The psyche may be, therefore, in some sense spatial (as McGinn said). Phenomenologically, we may discover that consciousness can be quasi-localized in different regions of the body. For example, some traditions identify distinct modes of knowing with distinctive bodily locations or "centers"—for example, reason (head), emotion (heart), and will (solar-plexus).

---

*I develop further the distinction between participatory knowing and mechanistic knowing in the forthcoming companion volume *Radical Knowing.*

In a telling moment during the conference when McGinn pressed Griffin on whether his consciousness was localized and therefore spatial, Griffin indicated that for him consciousness was localized "somewhere in here," as he pointed to his head. This is significant in view of Griffin's stated commitment to a rational explication of panexperientialism. For him, therefore, even experience might be something of an intellectual affair (at least philosophically), passing through the filter of rationality and thus conceptually objectified.

Another approach to consciousness, however, might focus attention on experience *without losing the subjective "feel,"* by using some other epistemological mode and its associated somatic center—for example, apprehending the world from the heart (emotion/compassion) or from the gut (will). Of these, the first epistemological modality may be characterized as receptive or subjective (emotion/compassion), the other as projective (will). Reason, by contrast, is analytical, dialectical, reductive, and objective.

In other traditions, different emphases are placed on different epistemological centers or modalities; and in some philosophical-spiritual disciplines practitioners are trained for flexibility and facility to move from one modality to another as well as to integrate them. Such an approach to the mind-body relation, of course, implies a way of doing philosophy radically different from the traditionally accepted rationality of Greco-Western systems.

## Talking Past Each Other

Griffin's and McGinn's positions seem irreconcilable, I suspect, because they are talking past each other from radically different metaphysical perspectives; and here we encounter another aspect of the paradox. On the one hand, Griffin, who holds that reason is up to the task of solving the consciousness problem, builds a case from an essentially extrarational metaphysic; while McGinn argues for the limits of human rationality wholly from within that limited rationality.

Although Griffin explicitly builds his case for a *rational* approach to the mind-body problem, his metaphysics is ultimately founded on *extrarational* premises. And ironically, herein lies the power of Griffin's position.

We can perhaps gain a little more clarity on this paradox by teasing open the dichotomy of Griffin's and McGinn's positions. Although I agree with Griffin that Whitehead's process philosophy is a well-worked-out rational speculative system, it is nevertheless *ultimately* an extra-rational metaphysics. This is because Whitehead's process philosophy is based on the metaphysical assumption that the fundamental ontology is not substance but events with *experience*. At the deepest levels of reality, according to this version of process philosophy, the ultimate entities are essentially *feelings,* and we know about feelings at this level through extrapolation from our own felt experience as human beings. In other words, prerational experience or feelings, not reason, constitute the primary epistemology.

It should not be surprising, therefore, that McGinn's analytical critique of the mind-body problem should miss the mark of Griffin's position: One is talking from a rationalist-rationalist perspective, the other is talking from an experientialist-rationalist perspective. We may approach this dichotomy from another angle, one that will help clarify the labels "rationalist-rationalist" and "experientialist-rationalist."

McGinn's critique, both of the mind-body problem specifically, and of panexperientialism in general, is based on purely logical arguments. His arguments are *spatial*—in two senses. On the one hand, as we saw earlier, he maintains that whereas reason deals with matter via concepts derived from objects and events in ordinary three-dimensional space, it attempts to deal with consciousness via concepts derived from nonspatial or nonordinary spatial objects and events. On the other hand, as mathematician-process philosopher Arthur M. Young pointed out, reason itself analogically requires at least two spatial dimensions.[9] Reason, or rationality, comes from the Latin *ratio,* which requires in some sense the ability to compare two objects by placing them alongside each other. At the very least, this requires an analog of a geometric plane—even if it is a conceptual plane.

We may gain a clue to the nature of the fundamental incompatibility—ontological, epistemological, and even psychological—between Griffin's and McGinn's perspectives from Young's analysis of the "geometry of meaning." According to Young's ontology as developed in his Theory of Process,[10] reality is structured dynamically on four levels: (1) the dimensionless level of photons, of light or spirit; (2) the one-dimensional level of time and nuclear particles; (3) the two-dimensional level of planar space (breadth and width), and atoms; and (4) the three-dimensional level of time-plus-space, of "molar matter," of molecules and familiar space-time objects.

As well as its distinct ontological nature, each level also requires its distinctive epistemology—we can access the different levels only through appropriate modes of knowing. For instance, level 2, the dimension of time, involves knowing through feeling or emotion—it is the level of "soul." By contrast, level 3, the planar dimension, involves knowing through concepts and comparison—it is the level of the rational mind. Level 4 involves a combination of time and space, of emotion and reason. Level 1, the dimensionless level of spirit, transcends all distinctions between knower and known.[11]

As a gross generality, then, we might say that everyday knowing involves a mixing of emotion and reason. It is the knowledge we call "common sense"—a biasing of objectifying rationality and empiricism with the subjective or "projective" force of emotion. Scientific knowing is typically "planar"—it is *spatial* knowledge—acquired through manipulation of rational concepts based on empirical measurements. Artistic or empathetic knowing, by contrast, is essentially obtained through the force of feeling or emotion; it is *temporal,* as in music (though may often be expressed spatially, as in a painting or a written poem). Mystical knowing, or spiritual/religious experience, may involve elements of all other forms of knowing, but it also transcends them. The *experience as such,* as reported by mystics, saints, and sages in the perennial philosophy, embraces all time and all space (or, more accurately, is "nondurational" and "nonlocal").

Scientific—or spatial—knowing objectifies; it works by standing back from nature, by separating the observer from the phenomenon, and searches for descriptive laws. Artistic-empathetic—or temporal—knowing is participatory; it engages subjectivity in the ongoing flow of events, feeling for "tones" and "patterns" in the flux of process. Mystical knowing may be characterized as "fusion epistemology," a mode of "knowing" or "no-knowledge" in which the subjective and objective poles of being are wholly and completely merged.

In modern Western philosophy, knowledge typically relies on the spatial form of epistemology—on objectification—and thus has great difficulty accounting for subjectivity. Feelings and emotions are not considered valid modes of knowing for approaching truth. In fact, scientific empiricism-rationalism prefers to eliminate all emotionality as though it were a subjective distortion and impediment to truth. (It is interesting to note that even in the one Western philosophical system that takes feeling-events as the fundamental ontology—Whitehead's process metaphysic—great efforts are made to build a *rational* foundation and edifice for the system.)

Here we come to the underlying incompatibility snarling the Griffin-McGinn debate. Griffin's Whiteheadian process critique of the mind-body problem, and his response to McGinn, are based on one-dimensional *temporal* distinctions of events or "moments of experience." Feelings and experience are nonspatial, they require only time (though they may, of course, contingently occur in space)—with a geometrical analog of a single-dimensional line. This single-dimensionality of temporal experiences (the line from past through present to future) is the foundation for Whiteheadian process philosophy, in contrast to the spatial paradigm characteristic of McGinn's logico-analytical mode of discourse.

The difficulty of a satisfactory "hearing" between Griffin's and McGinn's critiques of the mind-body problem, I suggest, is due to their differing modes of discourse: Whereas Griffin speaks, ultimately, from a one-dimensional temporal domain, McGinn speaks from a planar-dimensional domain. The mystery each encounters in hearing the other's arguments is a form of the Flatlander paradox. We might say that the clash of critiques is due to mutually incompatible "geometries of discourse" (at least metaphorically, but perhaps also literally)—of *epistemologies.*

Griffin defends a philosophy infused with an epistemology rooted in a temporal-experiential (one-dimensional) domain, whereas McGinn's philosophy is exclusively based on spatial-conceptual arguments. To the extent that Griffin's argument is also spatial and rational, there remains a possibility for a meeting of minds between him and McGinn. However, to the extent that Griffin's argument is grounded in his experience or issues forth from analogies with his own feelings, it cannot be accommodated within McGinn's conceptual framework (which requires spatiality and reasoning, not temporality and experience). To McGinn, Griffin's position is ultimately paradoxical or absurd, while to Griffin, McGinn seems to stubbornly miss the point. They are speaking to each other from radically different epistemologies.

Each, however, would be capable of understanding the other if they both recognized the nature of their epistemological incompatibility. McGinn is no less capable of experience or feeling than Griffin is of rational analysis. However, whereas Griffin demonstrates a great deal of rational argumentation, McGinn does not admit his philosophy to be informed by the temporal-experiential dimension fundamental to process philosophy. There is a fundamental asymmetry in their positions.

We could say that Griffin argues from within three dimensions—the single temporal-experiential dimension plus the two spatial-rational dimensions (hence "experientialist-rationalist")—while McGinn sticks to the latter two spatial dimensions (hence "rationalist-rationalist"). The ultimate force of Griffin's argument, therefore, would require a "conversion" of McGinn to augment his rationalist epistemology with an experientialist one. Without this experientialist ingredient, Griffin's position will necessarily remain at least partially mysterious, paradoxical, or absurd to McGinn, and McGinn will always seem to Griffin to stubbornly miss the fundamental point.

Whereas the process philosophy of Griffin and Whitehead aims to be thoroughly rationalist, it paradoxically goes beyond reason in asserting the ontological primacy of experience or feelings. I am proposing here that process philosophy in general, and panexperientialism in particular, needs to go further than the rationalist paradigm, to acknowledge the radical basis of its metaphysics and to make explicit the implicit epistemology of paradox, of experience beyond rational belief.

## Consciousness All the Way Down?

Keeping in mind the epistemological divide separating Griffin and McGinn, let's look now more closely at the details of their philosophical differences on the mind-body problem.

Recall Griffin's distinction between "consciousness" and "experience"— he says that experience goes all the way down but consciousness doesn't. This raises a difficult problem, says McGinn. He argues that this distinction between experience and consciousness involves the same old problems of dualism and emergentism that panexperientialists attempted to avoid in the first place. The strong panexperientialist position states it is inconceivable that sentient, experiencing entities could evolve or emerge out of wholly insentient, nonexperiencing substance or events. If experience wasn't there to begin with, it couldn't emerge *ex nihilo*. This is the bottom-line rationale for panexperientialism: Experience can only come from what has experience to begin with.

However, McGinn points out, we have precisely the same problem if we say that consciousness emerges from wholly nonconscious experience. To McGinn, the notion of "wholly nonconscious experience" is absurd. He questions: What could "experience" possibly mean devoid of all traces of consciousness? According to McGinn, if panexperientialism is correct, then we must also accept that consciousness—in some form, or to some elemental degree—must also be a property of matter all the way down. Of course, McGinn *denies* the panexperientialist hypothesis, so that neither experience nor consciousness are to be found below a certain level of physical complexity.

Even if we accept panexperientialism, however, McGinn's criticism of the experience-consciousness split must be addressed. Griffin's response is that this distinction does not, in fact, invoke the old problems associated with dualism and emergentism because there is no *ontological* distinction implied. In Griffin's view, experience and consciousness are the same kind of "stuff." They partake of the same reality—unlike Descartes's ontological distinction between extended and nonextended (two different *kinds* of) substance. Since there is no ontological distinction between experience and consciousness, there is no mystery about how one could derive from the other, nor how they could interact.

But this defense doesn't satisfactorily address McGinn's criticism. As he emphasizes, the panexperientialist position is that consciousness emerges from *wholly* nonconscious events, and therefore an ontological distinction is implied. If the complete reality of primitive or elemental experience can be accounted for without any trace of consciousness (that is, if it is *wholly* nonconscious), then this reality is substantially and constitutively different from some event or substance that does possess the quality of consciousness. It seems to me that if we are to hold the pan-experientialist view then we must acknowledge that both experience and consciousness do go all the way down.

As I understand Griffin, his reason for employing the distinction between "experience" and "consciousness" is the same as his reason for coining the term "panexperientialism" as distinct from "panpsychism." He rightly felt it was important to avoid any implication that the experience of, say, an electron possessed anything like the qualities of consciousness we know human psyches to possess. Too often, the knee-jerk response to panpsychism has been the retort that it implies atoms, molecules, or cells, as well as plants and rocks, experience an interior psychic life with all the conscious richness of human desires, fears, evaluations, thoughts, emotions, choices, and dreams. Such a vision of nature would indeed be exaggerated projection and absurd anthropomorphism. But just as a dog or chimpanzee can have experiences that differ from human conscious-ness, so too lizards, worms, bacteria, molecules, atoms, and electrons may each have their own characteristic, species-specific forms of experience—primitive *feelings* that respond to their particular environmental stimuli.

Griffin's emphasis on *experience* rather than consciousness is an attempt to get away from projections of human mentation onto non-human entities. But it is one thing to distinguish between wide-awake human conscious awareness (with all its thoughts and self-reflective men-tation) and nonawake experience; it is something different to distinguish between consciousness-as-such and experience-as-such.

The problem is partly one of terminology and definition. As we have seen in chapter 4, "consciousness" can have at least two quite different meanings. Its narrow meaning is the psychoanalytic sense of the "conscious" as distinct from the "unconscious"; its wider meaning is ontological, a qual-ity of being, or, more fundamentally, the "ground or context of being."

If we use "consciousness" in the psychoanalytic sense, meaning "the conscious," then the distinction between "consciousness" and "experi-ence" can hold. We may, by definition, say that "consciousness" is always conscious (i.e., awake), while experience may be either conscious or unconscious. But in this scheme, even the "unconscious" is part of the psyche—and, therefore, is a manifestation of consciousness using the wider meaning of the term. According to this wider meaning, "consciousness" is less a thing (such as "the conscious") and is better thought of as an ontological state or a quality.

As a quality of being, consciousness, like experience, may be either conscious or unconscious. And in this sense, the two terms—"consciousness" and "experience"—are virtually synonymous. But what can it mean to talk of "unconscious consciousness" or "unconscious experience"? These notions are extremely difficult to express verbally, mainly because language has evolved to express the contents of conscious states. By definition, we are unaware of what is unconscious; and without awareness of something we cannot identify it; and without identification we cannot name it or talk about it. We only know of unconscious contents or forces either by inference, for instance when they influence emotions, cognition, or behavior we are aware of; or when they surface into conscious awareness, for instance, in creativity—although by then, of course, they are no longer unconscious.

In speaking of unconscious processes, the best we can do, it seems, is to resort to poetic images and metaphors. Hence, the profound importance and significance of symbols in Jungian psychology. We can talk of "blind urges" and "longings," of "drives," "passions," "purposes," and "entelechies" without self-reflection or thought. We may have a vague sense of something groping—a primitive lamprey in a dark, watery cave—impelled by some interior urge to explore its surroundings, to probe a matrix of possibilities, and then through some dim unconscious choice, selecting its way forward. Here, we have an image of what it would be like to possess unconscious experience.

And this, I believe, is the sense in which Griffin uses the term. But this usage employs the (narrow) psychoanalytic distinction between "conscious" and "unconscious," and does not fit the wider metaphysical sense of consciousness as a quality of being. In the psychoanalytic sense, "the conscious" does not emerge from a wholly nonconscious unconscious. Even the unconscious partakes of consciousness and experience—which crosses a threshold from the "shadows" into the light of conscious awareness. There is no discontinuity between unconscious experience and conscious experience.

Even more so, as McGinn has argued, there cannot be a discontinuity between conscious and unconscious experience in the metaphysical

sense—consciousness cannot emerge from wholly nonconscious experience. Yet, although McGinn's critique is valid, Griffin's distinction
between experience and consciousness may also be meaningful.

To strike a compromise between these opposing views, at the conference I suggested the image of a line. Picture experience as a line starting
out with infinitesimal curvature, and gradually curving more and more
as the line extends. In this analogy, consciousness is the increase in the
line's curvature; it is the line's "purpose" or "blind urge"—its teleology.
Beginning with almost zero curvature (a virtual straight line), experience
imperceptibly curves through evolution until it creates a sort of "hook"—
which we might correlate with the first stirrings of "the conscious" from
the unconscious. As the line curves even more, at some point it bends
back on itself and connects with its own sense of purpose. We could call
this: "self-awareness" or "self-consciousness."

I agree with McGinn that some such model of experience/conscious-
ness seems to be necessary if panexperientialism is to avoid getting tangled
up in the old problem of emergence.

An alternative would be to say that there is no ontological problem
in the emergence of consciousness from wholly nonconscious events in a
way analogous to saying there is no ontological problem in the emergence
of "wetness" from nonwet molecules of hydrogen and oxygen. There is no
"proto-wetness" in the molecules. Wetness is truly an emergent quality of
matter as a result of the laminar flow of the molecules. Consciousness, in
this analogy, would be an emergent *property* of experience. However, if we
follow this analogy, we would still be left with a problem: Consciousness
would be an epiphenomenon, wholly determined by or supervenient on
experience. It would then be difficult to imagine how to account for consciousness (as distinct from experience) as a causal agent without slipping
into the sort of dualism that is implicit in Roger Sperry's notion of emergent "downward causation."[12]

Yet one of the challenges for any metaphysic—idealist, dualist, materialist, or panexperientialist—is how to account for the apparent causality of consciousness. We are all familiar with our own sense of freedom
to choose, to decide on a course of action that affects some part of the
world—lifting a coffee cup or building a dam, for example. If, as panex-

perientialism proposes, experience and self-agency are integral elements of the world at all levels, then the problem of human choice and freedom would be a matter of explaining it in terms of the elemental freedom-of-choice of nature's ultimate entities or events.

Although McGinn's critique of the distinction between experience and consciousness may be satisfactorily addressed by the metaphor of the curved line, he has a more forceful argument against panexperientialism: If experience/consciousness goes all the way down, then we still need to account for the conflict between the purported self-agency of, say, electrons and protons, and the apparent stability of gross matter. Simply stated: If all elementary particles are constantly exercising some degree of choice, how do they ever manage to avoid complete anarchy, and instead cooperate to form stable "societies" of atoms, molecules, cells, and higher organisms? There appears to be no evidence in physics for the self-determinism of elementary particles, and plenty of evidence for their determined, law-like behavior. How can panexperientialism account for this?

## MCGINN'S CRITIQUE OF PANEXPERIENTIALISM

McGinn didn't simply pick on some vulnerable semantic difficulties in the panexperientialist position—posing specific challenges that could be countered through careful clarification of terms. He attempted a simple, but potentially damning, *reductio ad absurdum* of the entire panexperientialist metaphysic.

Essentially, McGinn's strategy was to impale panexperientialism on the horns of one of two fatal options: Either panexperientialism presupposes the supervenience of consciousness on a physical substrate* or it contradicts

---

*Supervenience is an awkward concept adopted from ethics into the philosophy of mind in an attempt to present a mind-body solution compatible with materialism, yet which avoids the problems of reductionism. The idea, essentially, is that although mental events may not be *reducible* to neurophysiological events, they are nonetheless wholly dependent on or determined by such neurophysiological events. The implication of supervenience (following the use of the term in ethics) is that the mind-body relation need not be causal—consciousness may be supervenient on (i.e., dependent on) the brain, but not necessarily caused by the brain (in the way that a person's goodness may be dependent on his or her having a physical body, but is not caused by merely having that body). Consciousness, therefore, would be a *property* of (certain types of) matter.

the adequacy of modern quantum-relativistic physics. In the first case, if the supervenience argument holds, then consciousness is merely epiphenomenal and could not be causally efficacious (which undermines the panexperientialist ontology). In the second case, if the supervenience argument does not hold, then the causal agency of some nonphysical property (e.g., experience) is affirmed and consequently panexperientialism automatically entails the inadequacy or incompleteness of modern physics. And this second option, according to McGinn, is patently absurd, given the immense demonstrable predictive success of quantum-relativistic physics. For panexperientialism to be true, therefore, it would have to provide a radically different alternative to modern physics with at least as much predictive success. The bottom line of McGinn's critique poses a dilemma for panexperientialism. However, it is not insuperable—and, ironically, it may even support Griffin's position.

If McGinn is correct in his syllogism that *panexperientialism implies a radical revision of physics,* I think it is entirely appropriate for process philosophers to face this implication head-on and affirm that this is indeed the case. For example, Marilyn Schlitz, director of research at the Institute of Noetic Sciences, presented a paper* at the 1994 Claremont Consciousness Conference outlining evidence for psi—statistically significant yet highly anomalous data that the current science of physics is incapable of explaining.[13] McGinn's critique depended on the notion that if panexperientialism were correct the fundamental entities of physics such as electrons and protons would also possess nonphysical (e.g., subjective) properties. If so, then a complete or adequate physics should be able to account for the apparent *lack* of any self-determination in electrons and protons. The question then is, "Would a panexperientialist-based physics be able to explain why individual electrons do *not* behave as if they had subjectivity?"

To see how panexperientialism as developed by Griffin based on

---

*Schlitz's paper, "Direct Mental Influence on Living Systems: A Review of Data and Implications for Consciousness Studies," summarized the scientific data from remote electrodermal experiments. For example, data from remote staring studies supported the hypothesis that, in the absence of all known sensory and subliminal cues, staring at someone from a distance could measurably influence that person's autonomic functioning. Such "psychokinetic" effects confound the contemporary sciences of physics and molecular biology.

the philosophies of Alfred North Whitehead and Charles Hartshorne responds to this challenge, we need to revisit a couple of key terms in process philosophy.

## COMPOUND INDIVIDUALS AND AGGREGATES

The notions of "compound individuals" and "regnant monads of experience"—which are essential to an understanding of Whiteheadian process philosophy—can provide a coherent panexperientialist explanation for the nonself-motion of electrons *within* any organism—be it an atom, a cell, or a human body. A "compound individual" is a hierarchical society of suborganisms, each of which has its own level of experience and capacity for self-determination (for instance, an animal compounded of living cells, or a cell composed of organic molecules). However, because of the overpowering influence of the regnant monad's dominant experience, the self-action of the lower "organisms" is held in check. Thus, electrons within the molecules of a living cell will have their degree of self-motion constrained by the superordinate influences of the intervening levels of molecules (such as DNA, RNA, or proteins), and by the dominant experience of the cell or whole organism itself.

Compared with a "compound individual," an aggregate society of experiential events—such as a rock, a pool of water, a chair, or a computer—have no dominant monad of experience. The rock, chair, or computer is a nonholistic *aggregate* of constituent molecules, atoms, and subatomic particles. Now, according to panexperientialism, each of these constituent lower-level "organisms" is an individual with its own low-level form of experience and capacity for self-action. However, in aggregates the self-motions of the innumerable individual organisms cancel each other out. Consequently, the rock, pool, chair, or computer does not possess experience or self-motion of its own (just as we see in the world, and just as normal physics predicts). Therefore, in compound individuals and aggregates, there is no fundamental conflict between panexperientialism and modern physics regarding constituent "particles."

But what about *isolated* electrons, remote from any (higher-level) compound organism? This was the question that McGinn forcefully tried to pose. Given panexperientialism, how can any physics account for the apparent absence of self-determination as a property of individual electrons or protons? There are at least two responses to this.

1.  The indeterminateness of individual subatomic particles, their unpredictable behavior, could actually be interpreted as supporting evidence for the hypothesis of "choice" or "self-action" just as easily as for the alternative interpretation of acausal "randomness." Perhaps radioactive decay or double-slit experiments are, after all, instances of "quantum choice"?

2.  If current theories of physics are founded on laboratory data derived from experiments on *individual* particles, this, surely, is a gross abstraction and distortion from what actually occurs most of the time in nature (certainly in our corner of the cosmos). How many naturally "free-floating" isolated electrons and protons are there compared with electrons incorporated in atoms, molecules, and cells? A complete and adequate physics should be able to account for the behavior of elementary particles within living systems as well as for the behavior of each system as a whole. I think it is clear that current physics does not meet these criteria.

Panexperientialists, therefore, need not be troubled by the implications of McGinn's critique: *Current physics is incomplete in the strong qualitative sense* (not simply in the trivial quantitative sense of needing to do more work of the same kind). I believe we do need a radically different physics. This is not to say that current physics is all wrong—that, indeed, would be absurd, as McGinn argued. It may be, however, a *limit* case of a more complete physics, analogous to Newtonian physics being a limit case of relativistic physics. The new physics hinted at here would include not only the four currently known forces (electromagnetism, strong and weak nuclear, and gravitation) but also data and theories that account for the panpsychist notion of inherently sentient, subjective, and self-agented matter-energy. It would be a physics compatible with true psychology because it would include both matter and mind.

McGinn's critique, then, to be a satisfactory refutation of panexperientialism, depends on empirical evidence, not simply on syllogistic traps. And this empirical component in his argument provides a way out for defenders of panexperientialism. If panexperientialists can show that this metaphysic can be supported by an empirical science of matter in which self-causation is operable all the way down, McGinn's "supervenience-reductio" would be invalid. Furthermore, as Griffin might have argued, even the empirical tests required to demonstrate the adequacy of physics (whether materialist or panexperientialist) are theory-laden, and therefore the question is ultimately inextricably tied into the underlying metaphysical assumptions, and requires an evaluation and choice between competing epistemologies—between ways of knowing based on reason or feeling. And this, I've attempted to show, is precisely the difference between McGinn and Griffin, and why they inevitably talked past each other.

## Consciousness All the Way Up

I want now to make a shift in direction, and to pick up on a theme introduced earlier.* Back there, in the context of Plotinus and Neoplatonism, I discussed the relationship between emanationist idealism and consequent panpsychism, emphasizing in particular their compatibility and shared conception of a material world suffused with consciousness. I also introduced a critique of panpsychism where I argued that, under analysis, this position turns out to be either a form of covert dualism or a form of idealism. I then went on to present a strong critique of idealism where, having challenged the "maya hypothesis" as untenable for empirical science or rational philosophy, we were left with two options: Either idealism is a covert materialism or a covert dualism.

After introducing the "Ep-On bootstrap principle," stating that epistemology and ontology are tangled in an eternal loop, I took an "epistemological leap of faith"—supported by somatic *feeling* as a way of knowing—to break this charmed circle, and decided that my best choice for an ontology would be what I called "radical naturalism." Radical naturalism, I went on to explain, makes the assumption that matter is intrinsically experiential. I thus decided on an ontology compatible with emanationist idealism and consequent panpsychism.

---

*In chapter 6, "Panpsychism: A Long Lineage of Mind-in-Matter."

However, I also indicated a residual, but fundamental, problem in any attempt to reconcile these two cosmology stories. Emanationist idealism is ultimately an atemporal ontology, while panexperientialism is a thoroughly process metaphysic. The problem, then, is how do we reconcile the timeless with process?

I will now revisit the discussion of Neoplatonic-inspired emanationist idealism and its notion of timeless evolution, and see how this might be squared with panexperientialist process philosophy—both of which use "evolution" as a key concept. This will throw us headlong into the controversial topic of emergence and hierarchy. The concept of emergence is pivotal in understanding the mind-body problem, and it is inevitably tied in with the concept of hierarchy. I'll begin by restating the core of the idealist-panexperientialist problem.

Strictly speaking, evolution takes place in time—it is a *process*—a rolling out (*e-volvere*) of potentials into actuality in temporal sequence. What comes into being is nascent in germ or potential before it emerges. Neoplatonic and other emanationist ontologies describe the One becoming the many and the many returning to the One as an involutionary-evolutionary relationship. But it happens outside time. It is "timeless evolution," a notion that immediately appears paradoxical, if not contradictory.

However, the apparent contradiction vanishes once we realize that what is being described is a *logical,* not a chronological, relationship. We could, therefore, speak of "logovolution," an unfolding, manifesting, or self-expression of unitary logos into multiplicity, an unfolding of logical relationships from potential into actuality. However, it is more than a mere logical relationship. It is an *onto*-logical relationship—a relationship through *being,* not through *time.* Therefore, a more appropriate, and more elegant, term to describe this rolling out of being is "onvolution" (in Greek *"on"* is a prefix indicating "being"). Onvolution encompasses both involution and evolution, and happens out of time.

This notion of unfolding outside time may be easier to grasp if we remember that a similar atemporal relationship exists in the world of mathematics. Numbers generate each other outside time and space. One becomes two, which becomes three, and so on into infinite multiplicity *at every instant.* The "journey" from one to any number greater than one, takes no time. It is a timeless series, and at every moment we have access to any point in the sequence. Similarly, at every moment any stage in the ontological sequence One ——→ many ——→ One is available—if our consciousness is suitably prepared.

If onvolution is the timeless generation of the many from the One and the return of the many to the One, how do time and evolution result from this? How does the timeless generate time? How does onvolution beget evolution? How does structure yield process? These questions involve the same kind of logical difficulties we encounter in emergentist materialism where insentient matter is claimed to produce consciousness. But, as argued by many critics of materialism, getting mind from matter is much like getting wine from water—it requires a miracle. The great British geneticist C. H. Waddington objected that it is inconceivable that consciousness or self-awareness could have "originated from anything which did not share something in common with it and possessed only those qualities which can be objectively observed from outside."[14]

However, the notion of emergence is clearly central to the emanationist model of stages of involution-evolution through the "great chain of being."[15] That is precisely the implication in the idealist continuum ontology with its emerging levels of matter, body, mind, soul, and spirit. But if we accept one form of emergentism (spiritual onvolution), why not the other, where mind is supposed to emerge from matter (material evolution)? To explore this question, we need to understand something of the nature of hierarchies and the concept of "holon."

In *Sex, Ecology, Spirituality* Ken Wilber proposes a novel ontology, compatible with ancient spiritual cosmologies—such as Neoplatonism and those of Sri Aurobindo, Hegel, Schelling, Shankara, and the *Lankavatara Sutra*—on the one hand, and with modern systems theories, including the sciences of chaos and complexity, on the other. The depth and the scope of Wilber's panoramic synthesis is so comprehensive that it would be foolhardy to attempt to do it justice in a few pages here.* But I will try

---

*Elsewhere, I have written a detailed critique of Ken Wilber's collected works. See "The Promise of Integralism," *Journal of Consciousness Studies* 7, no. 11/12 (2000), and "A Theory of Everything?"*IONS Review* 55 (2001).

to extract the essence of his position on hierarchy, to help get a handle on the problem of emergence.

Basically, Wilber says the fundamental unit of all reality is not a material or physical thing, such as an atom, elementary particle, quark, or quantum. It is, rather, a set or structure of relationships that he calls a "holon" (a word borrowed from Arthur Koestler and created from a combination of the Greek *holos*, meaning "whole," and *on*, meaning "being"). A holon has two fundamental, characteristic relationships: It is always, simultaneously, both a whole and a part. It is a whole made up of lesser, constituent holons, while itself being a part of an even greater whole. Thus, holons necessarily occur in a relational hierarchy, which may be pictured as concentric, or nested circles within circles within circles of being. The hierarchy of holons is open-ended: There is no smallest holon, and no upper limit to the hierarchy. The entire infinity of holons constitutes the Kosmos.*

Thus, according to Wilber's model, reality has an essential and fundamental *structure* of graded or nested levels of being—of holons within holons within holons ad infinitum. That is to say, reality is hierarchically graded with some levels possessing more being or reality than others. The deeper the nested circles of holons, the more reality that particular structure of holons has. Each level of the hierarchy encompasses or embraces all the levels below it. Each holon includes everything, every quality and property, of its constituent holons, but because it is a whole in its own right, it *adds something extra*. Thus, at each new level, some new quality or capacity emerges, something that is not available to its constituents. Holarchy (another Koestler term for hierarchy), thus, automatically entails emergence. Because reality is structured as a hierarchy of holons, emergence is integral to Kosmos, like a natural and universal law. Novelty or "creative advance," as Whitehead calls it, is built right into the Kosmic system.

If emergence is so ubiquitous, then, why should we think that the emergentist solution proposed by absolute materialism, for mind emerging from matter, is such a problem? After all, if mind can emerge from body

---

*Instead of "cosmos," Ken Wilber, in *Sex, Ecology, Spirituality: The Spirit of Evolution*, 1995, prefers "Kosmos," to distinguish between the single-level ontology of mere physical reality and the multileveled ontology of Plotinus's Kosmos, which includes living body, mind, soul, and spirit, as well as matter.

and matter in the emanationist's Kosmic scheme, why not in the material-ist's cosmic scheme?

The problem of emergence has a long history in philosophy, and is particularly relevant to philosophy of mind. Whenever we encounter a clash of ontologies attempting to explain the mind-body relationship, the issue of emergence is always in the background, if not actually the cen-tral issue of the debate. For example, materialists claim that consciousness emerges through evolution from insentient matter; emanationist idealists say that multiplicity of forms emerge from the onvolution of spirit; and panexperientialists say that different qualities of experience and conscious-ness evolve and emerge at different levels of complexity. Only dualists can avoid the issue of emergence altogether because for them mind belongs in a completely different ontological domain.

Of the various positions, only idealism makes a claim for emergence of different *ontological* levels, or distinct *types* of being. Materialists claim that the physical properties of matter are sufficient, given evolution, to account for the emergence of mind from matter. However, the claim remains promissory because no satisfactory account of how this *could* occur has yet been provided.

Panexperientialists and panpsychists, on the other hand, reject materi-alism on metaphysical grounds, claiming that the notion of emergence (as true ontological novelty) is logically absurd. The gist of the anti-emergentist argument is that "something cannot come from nothing," or, more accu-rately, "something cannot *emerge* if it wasn't already there to begin with" (even if just to an infinitesimal degree, or as a faint potential).

The critique of emergence is critical to the panexperientialist position, so it is important to spend some time exploring its ramifications more closely. If the logic of the discussion is demanding, following it through will be rewarding in advancing our grasp of the mind-body problem as treated in materialism, idealism, and panexperientialism. It will, I believe, allow us to arrive at an ontology that, if not synthesizing the three posi-tions, at least promises to transcend their fundamental differences.

To repeat the question posed earlier: If we accept emergence in ema-nationist idealism, why not also in materialism? Or, to approach it from a different perspective: Ignoring idealism, if there are good independent arguments in favor of evolutionary emergence (in biological evolution), thus undermining the key objection by panexperientialists to materialism, are we compelled to conclude that materialism is at least plausible, if not true?

## AN ARGUMENT AGAINST EMERGENCE

Let's begin with the argument *against* emergence. I see two fundamental options for materialism: Either (1) the mental is part of the physical, intrinsically and always; or (2) the mental is in some way distinct from the physical and came into being at some moment in time. (A third option, of course, is to deny mind or the mental any distinctive ontological status, and claim that it is merely a *function* of particular arrangements of matter—or, more extremely, to deny *any* reality to mind whatsoever, as extreme eliminativists do. But neither functionalism nor eliminativism can account for the fact of subjectivity.)

If (1), we have, in fact, the "radical naturalism" characteristic of panexperientialism, then mind or consciousness ceases to be a problem. It was there all along. (However, we still would have the secondary problem of accounting for how mind and matter are related and could interact. This problem is addressed in chapters 9, "Past Matter, Present Mind," and 10, "Stories Matter, Matter Stories.")

If (2), then we have the following logical (and chronological) situation: At some time, $T_1$, in evolution all that existed was matter-energy (and corresponding physical laws). Then at some later time, $T_2$, there was matter plus something that wasn't there before: namely, mind or consciousness. At $T_2$, therefore, something absolutely new, which didn't previously exist *even minimally*, came into being. This, as German panpsychist Friedrich Paulsen pointed out, is a possibility that flies in the face of science:

> Is the first feeling in the first protoplasmic particle something absolutely new, something that did not exist before in any form, of which not the slightest trace was to be found previously?[16]

This amounts to "creation out of nothing," which is not only unscientific, it is logically absurd. Impossibility of "creation out of nothing" means that something must come from something.

But this, as Paul Edwards replied, can mean two things: (1) Everything that happens or comes to be must have a cause (that is, every effect has a cause); or (2) Any property that exists in an effect must also reside in the cause (a proposition dating from the scholastic philosophers in the Middle Ages).[17]

However, scientific adequacy requires only (1), says Edwards: that everything has a cause. Proposition (2) is not unscientific, he says, citing the plentiful evidence from evolution where "there are any number of effects possessing new properties—properties not present in the cause"[18]— the property "wetness" would be one example. Although (2) contradicts a point of scholastic logic, it does not contradict science.

So, the argument goes, the materialist position does not violate the scientific principle of conservation (of energy, mass, force, momentum, and so forth): It does not claim creation out of nothing when it says that at $T_1$, only matter, then at $T_2$, matter plus mind.

This defense of materialism in effect says (1) mind did not emerge mysteriously *ex nihilo* into the material world at $T_2$, it was caused by matter that previously existed at $T_1$. So, mind was not uncaused, was not a creation out of nothing. Mind was, as both science and logic require, a creation of something—namely, matter.

But this causal defense of materialism involves a deceptive sleight of hand. For by asserting that matter is the cause of mind, that matter is the "something" from which mind emerged, we are really restating the original problem, without resolving it. The defense merely begs the question which (to remind you) is: If we reject panpsychism, then materialism tells us that at time $T_1$, only matter, but at time $T_2$, matter plus mind, which is to say that at $T_2$, *something absolutely new* entered the world. How? And this, as always, has been the Achilles' heel of materialism. Its best response, which in fact is very weak, is promissory empiricism—that *someday* science will develop to the point of experimental and observational sophistication to be able to provide the missing data.

Meanwhile, we still wait for a scientific answer to the "scholastic" challenge of "how can something that was not present in the cause possibly emerge in the effect?" The usual materialist defense of pointing to numerous instances in chemistry or evolution (as Edward does), where something novel emerged, does not hold up. Typically, such a defense will point to the phenomenon of wetness or liquidity emerging when molecules of nonwet gases, hydrogen and oxygen, combine to form water. At $T_1$, only nonwet H and O molecules, at $T_2$, water and wetness. Or from biology, the claim that organs such as stomachs, eyes, or wings or functions such as digestion or flight, which emerged as purely novel features in evolution, are examples of biological emergence. But such a defense fails because the analogies are false.

What is at issue here is not the emergence of something merely new (novelty is a precondition for evolutionary advance), it is the emergence of an *entirely new ontological type* of phenomenon (consciousness) and an *entirely new epistemological* phenomenon (subjectivity). Evolutionary novelty, whether in physics, chemistry, or biology, is altogether different from ontological or epistemological novelty. In other words, the emergence of mind is a problem *sui generis* because it entails the emergence of an absolutely new ontological and epistemological *kind*.

Wetness, eyes, wings, stomachs, digestion, and flight may have been novel, even radically novel, when they first appeared, but they are not ontologically and epistemologically different in kind. They are still physical and still objective.

It may be objected that claiming mind is ontologically different in kind—nonphysical as opposed to physical—just begs the question: "Is mind physical or something else?" But if it is not different in kind, then it must be physical. And if mind is physical, it would then be just another (very) interesting emergent property of matter, much like wetness, digestion, or flight.

However, this last objection is not valid because mind is also *epistemologically* different in kind from anything else in the universe of objective matter. For the most distinguishing mark of the mental, its definitive characteristic in fact, is its *subjectivity*.* No purely objective, physical entity (if there were such) would, by definition, possess a subjective point of view. And this means that any entity possessing this unique epistemo-

---

*I examine subjectivity and intersubjectivity in greater detail in *Radical Knowing,* 2005.

logical difference in kind qualifies *by that very fact* as an ontological difference in kind. Any phenomenon possessing subjectivity is ontologically different in kind from any merely purely objective entity.

If, however, as a last line of defense, a materialist claims that the notion of "purely objective physical kind" is too extreme (and it is this extreme that makes the critique so decisive), then the materialist is forced to conclude that there is no such thing as a "purely objective physical kind" of thing, and this is the same as admitting that something like subjectivity and consciousness is intrinsic to the material world. In other words, subjectivity/consciousness all the way down—which is precisely the position of panexperientialism and radical naturalism.

To recap, then: The panexperientialist's argument against the materialist's explanation of mind as an emergent phenomenon of physical-biological evolution holds.

However, we still have the issue of emergence in emanationist idealism. As I asked earlier, if emergence works here, why not in materialism, too?

As we have just seen, even if we admit the possibility and actuality of evolutionary emergence, we cannot make the jump to absolute *ontological* emergence. Something of the emergent ontological kind had to be there, at least in potentia.

Nevertheless, given the impossibility of pure ontological emergence, we may still admit the possibility of both evolutionary and onvolutionary emergence of mind from matter if we assume either a panexperientialist or an idealist ontology. On the one hand, panexperientialism does not require ontological emergence because it *starts* with the assumption that both mental and physical reality were always there. Any new emergence is due to evolutionary novelty.

On the other hand, idealist emergence differs from materialist emergence in at least one very important respect. Materialism allows only for *evolution*—a one-way track of hierarchical progression from less complex to more complex material relationships, the claim being that at some point in evolution matter became complex enough to produce minds.

This characterization of materialism as a one-way track does not ignore entropy, the process whereby more complex and ordered configurations of matter decay into less complex and disordered systems. In fact, according to the second law of thermodynamics, a keystone of materialist modern science, entropy is the rule—order, organization, life, and mind are the great exceptions. But the point is that nowhere in materialism is it ever suggested that the devolution of matter due to entropy would, or could, lead to mind or consciousness—in fact just the opposite: mind/brain are the epitome of order and organization.

In materialism, minds evolve along the upward track of evolution. The downward track of entropy is inimical to mind. Thus, with only evolution as an explanatory mechanism, materialism is forced to choose between two equally problematical positions:

1. Mind is an emergent *physical* phenomenon, requiring no ontological jump. All there is is physical matter-energy, and mind is just a rather difficult-to-understand physical by-product of exclusively physical processes. Mind is merely a physical property of matter squeezed out at certain levels of physical complexity.
2. Mind is an emergent nonphysical property, a truly novel production that results in an entirely new ontological state.

If (2), not only does materialism become a form of "neo-dualism," with all its attendant interactionist problems, it also encounters the problem of the mysterious ontological jump—of getting one kind of reality from another. And as we have just seen, this is both scientifically implausible and logically inconceivable.

However, if we examine (1), we find we are in exactly the same boat with regard to the ontological jump. For the claim that mind is physical (meaning derived from wholly insentient matter) still leaves unanswered the problem of how sentience could emerge from insentient matter, and how *subjectivity* could possibly emerge from pure objectivity. Option (1), therefore, presents far more than promissory materialism could resolve. It involves an ontological jump (sentience from insentience) and an epistemological jump (subjectivity from objectivity). Emergence, thus, remains problematic for materialism.

However, the situation is fundamentally different for idealism. First of all, here, the phenomenon of emergence does not rely on the one-way track of evolution—from less complex to more complex. In its emanationist form, as expounded, for example, in Neoplatonism, idealism explicitly asserts a *two-way onvolution*—with a "downward" track of involution in addition to an "upward" track of evolution. No ontological jump is required, because the "downward" track *begins* with consciousness or spirit—with the infinitely all-encompassing Kosmic holon, Plotinus's unimaginable, utterly uncharacterizable, ineffable One. Thus, all that emerges on each level through evolution is *already there*—a plenum of potential in spirit—because of the timeless involution of consciousness through all levels of the holarchy, including matter.

There is no absolute ontological discontinuity. Instead, there is a gradation of ontological levels—a continuum ontology—composed of a hierarchy of nested holons. Consciousness is present throughout the entire holarchy, throughout the entire onvolutionary "process": spirit $\longrightarrow$ matter $\longrightarrow$ spirit (and all levels in between). And this is necessarily so, because, as Wilber defines it, consciousness is the hierarchical *depth*. Each level of the Kosmic hierarchy has its own particular depth of nested circles of holons (holons within holons within holons, and so forth). And, on this model, the depth of relationships between the levels of holons *is* consciousness.

At different hierarchical levels, different levels of reality emerge: At one level, for instance, the nested system of holons will result in the ontological level of souls (archetypes, forms), at another less deep level, the nested holons will result in minds (thoughts, desires, beliefs, egos, and so forth), at a still lower level we get bodies (living animals and plants), and yet lower still we get matter (inorganic physical objects). Further down, again, we move into the submaterial realms of atoms, particles, quanta, and, perhaps, "superstrings," and beyond that science has yet to reach.

We see here, again, that Wilber's grand synthesis of Neoplatonic idealism and contemporary systems theory shows that emanationist idealism (Wilber would prefer to call it "spiritual holism") is fully compatible with the essential panexperientialist tenet of "consciousness all the way down"—and up.

Evolutionary—or, better, *onvolutionary*—emergence of mind (emanationist idealism), then, is not a problem for science or philosophy; but *ontological* emergence (materialism) is. In ontological emergence, mind is supposed to leap into existence from nothing, something utterly new—from matter that did not possess even the slightest trace of it up to that point. In onvolutionary emergence, mind evolves through different *levels* or *depths* of holons-within-holons—consciousness or spirit is present at *all* levels because, according to this view, "depth" is consciousness. The reach, or hierarchy, of holons is infinite in both directions, and there is, therefore, depth at all levels.

"Depth" here, clearly, must have two related meanings: On the one hand, depth alone—that is physical, spatial, hierarchical relationship—by itself cannot account for subjectivity. If depth equals consciousness, then depth must have an intrinsic *interiority*—and this is a point that Wilber skillfully elaborates in his four-quadrants model in *Sex, Ecology, Spirituality.*

"Depth," therefore means levels of subjective interiority—gradations of the what-it-feels-like of being (Wilber's left quadrants)—as well as levels of objective, external relationship (right quadrants). In Wilber's model, both interiority and exteriority also have individual and relational aspects: individual interiority the domain of the subjective "I," relational interiority the domain of intersubjective "we," exterior individuals the domain of objective, autonomous "its," and exterior relations the domain of objective interrelated systems (more complex "its").

Taken as a whole, these four aspects or domains of being account for

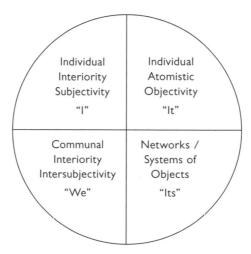

*Ken Wilber's four-quandrant Model of Reality.*

all possible variations of ontology and epistemology, which Wilber refers to as the "Big Three" of "I," "we," and "its"—that is, the epistemological domains of subjectivity, intersubjectivity, and objectivity, and the ontological domains of subjects, intersubjects, and objects.

The above explains why emanationist idealism can account for the "emergence" of mind from matter through levels of onvolution—but we still need to explain how/if idealism can account for the emergence or emanation of *matter from mind*. This is the crux of the "problem of idealism" discussed in chapter 6, "Panpsychism: A Long Lineage of Mind-in-Matter," in the section "Problem with The Perennial Philosophy?" The resolution to this problem of "downward" emergence of matter from mind is a topic for the next chapter, where panpsychism or radical naturalism is shown to reconcile the competing worldviews of idealism, materialism, and dualism.

# 9

Integrating Worldviews

# PAST MATTER, PRESENT MIND*

Every worldview expresses some deep truth—and is in error only if it claims possession of the whole truth. The most compelling attraction of the worldview of panpsychism is that it makes so much sense—*hard-core common sense.* It is inclusive of matter and mind, of determinism and freedom, of mechanism and creativity, and it offers a way of reconciling the apparently conflicting worldviews of materialism, dualism, and idealism.

In this chapter, I will focus on the work of one of the most perceptive theorists in contemporary philosophy of mind, David Ray Griffin, the philosopher who, as we saw in the previous chapter, champions panexperientialism. Building on Griffin's work, I will argue that panpsychism presents the most coherent and plausible resolution to the mind-body problem, and thus opens the way toward a comprehensive science of consciousness.

Even more than David Chalmers's attention-grabber *The Conscious Mind*, Griffin's *Unsnarling the World-Knot* deserves to be carefully studied by any serious and honest explorer of the mind-body problem.[1, 2] And for a very important reason: Although Chalmers presents one of the best analyses of the deepest issue in philosophy of mind, he does not offer a solution to the "hard problem"—How can conscious experience be

---

*An earlier version of this chapter previously appeared in the *Journal of Consciousness Studies* 6, no. 1 (1999): 91–106, under the title "Past Matter, Present Mind: A Convergence of Worldviews."

explained as a result of the purely physical processes of the brain? (This is the "world-knot" of Griffin's title, a phrase first used by Schopenhauer.) Chalmers does outline a direction for a possible solution: a form of dual-aspectism that posits information as (perhaps) ontologically fundamental to both the physical and the phenomenological. But, he admits, the full working out of this Janus-faced ontology will require elucidation of new, fundamental "psychophysical bridging laws" to account for the existence of, and relations between, the subjective and the objective.

It is precisely such a bridge between the subjective mental and the objective physical that Griffin provides (or at least promises)—based on the panexperientialist ontology of Alfred North Whitehead and Charles Hartshorne.[3, 4] Griffin offers a way to "unsnarl" the world-knot, Chalmers is still fingering it.

## Criteria for an Adequate Worldview

From the start, Griffin lets us know where he stands. The mind-body problem has seemed so intractable, he says, because philosophers have been confused about common sense. Many have mistaken socially constructed— and therefore optional—"soft-core common sense" for unavoidable "hard-core common sense." The latter are unavoidable notions because, as Griffin says, they are those that *all human beings inevitably presuppose in practice* . . . even if we deny them verbally . . . [and therefore] they should be taken as the ultimate criteria for judging a theory's adequacy." He gives as examples of hard-core common sense: the fact that we have conscious experience; that we always presuppose we have a degree of freedom; and that we presuppose the reality of some normative ideals. Any ontological theory, any worldview, that does not meet such hard-core criteria automatically fails the test of adequacy.

Griffin, then, makes clear what he believes are the conditions to which any theory must conform. He sets a high standard for intellectual responsibility by declaring the ground rules or "regulative principles" he presupposes when discussing the mind-body problem. Some of these regulative principles are formal, such as "a theory should be self-consistent"; "that in a conflict between hard-core common sense and soft-core common sense, the latter must submit"; and, when evaluating competing worldviews, "*all* realistic theories must be examined," and furthermore, "the strongest versions of each . . . should be compared" (this last is crucially important for critiques of panpsychism, as we shall see). Some are substantive, such as "we should accept only a *realistic* theory about the 'physical world,'" or "all actualities should be assumed to exert efficient causation"—i.e., there should be an "unbroken causal nexus," no inexplicable ontological leaps.

Having declared these regulative principles (sixteen in all), Griffin sets out to evaluate the major competing worldviews—dualism, materialism, idealism, and panpsychism.

## Lurking Idealism?

I became a confirmed panpsychist when I first read Whitehead in the early seventies, and a reconfirmed panpsychist when I read Griffin's Whitehead-Hartshorne inspired panexperientialism a decade or so later. I have always felt uneasy, however, about this version of panpsychism. My concern was double-edged: On one hand, Griffin explicitly rejects idealism as a candidate ontology for solving the mind-body problem because it does not satisfy his regulative principle of realism—a necessary condition for "fully naturalizing the mind," which is his stated intention.

On the other hand, it seemed to me that panexperientialism (the Griffin-Whitehead-Hartshorne version of panpsychism), despite its advocates' claims to the contrary, did not do full justice to "matter," running the risk of minimizing its fundamental ontological significance. At the root of this concern was the suspicion that, when all is said and done, panexperientialism is itself a form of idealism. Even after reading *Unsnarling the World-Knot,* I still suspected panexperientialism to be a form of idealism—but idealism with a difference. And because of this difference, my concern about panexperientialism's treatment of matter has been allayed—as I will explain.

The thesis I've been building toward in this book is that the preferred resolution to the mind-body problem is a form of panpsychism I've called "radical naturalism," where matter-energy is considered to be fundamental and real, but to its roots *sentient*. Intrinsically sentient matter offers a solution to the mind-body problem without the pitfalls of interactionist substance dualism or of materialist or idealist identism.

Now, this is precisely Griffin's claim for panexperientialism. But in Griffin's case, idealism becomes an issue because the fundamental units of reality are taken to be what Whitehead called "occasions of experience." If experience alone is fundamental or primary (and Griffin is quite clear that his ontology is a monism), then logically matter-energy must be secondary—at best derivatively real. A sort of reverse emergentism, characteristic of emanationist forms of idealism.

However, to suggest that panexperientialism may be a form of idealism is not by any means to dismiss Griffin's detailed working out of this ontology. In fact, his work is one of the most persuasive attempts to solve the mind-body problem around today. I mention this possible idealist reduction because Griffin, by dismissing idealism, leaves his position open to a charge of self-refutation. And that's one of my few qualms about Griffin: He does not acknowledge panexperientialism's idealist leanings. This is especially unfortunate because I think panexperientialism can serve as a bridge between materialism and idealism—a bridge that allows for a version of idealism compatible with realism. One of the greatest services this ontology offers philosophy of mind is that it can play the unlikely role of reconciling (some versions of) the otherwise apparently incompatible ontologies of dualism, materialism, and idealism.

Griffin does argue that panexperientialism not only resolves the major problems dogging both dualism and materialism, but that it also *shares* with dualism the position of *mind-body interaction* and with materialism the ontological *primacy of physicalism.*

Griffin's panexperientialism achieves these reconciliations, however, by redefining the meaning of "physical." As I hope to show, it is Griffin's implicit idealism and his redefinition of "physical" that could leave panexperientialism most vulnerable to materialist critics—assuming they share his rejection of idealism as a nonstarter for realism, and if they fail to carefully study and understand panexperientialism's process-based worldview (including a process view of "physical").

This shift in thinking from substance to process is by no means easy, as Whitehead's highly innovative, and often difficult, terminology in

*Process and Reality* underscored. Nevertheless, that kind of conceptual shift seems to be what a resolution to the mind-body problem demands. *We need to think differently about the nature of matter and the nature of mind.* And Griffin shows us how to do this by reinterpreting Whitehead without so many of the latter's difficult neologisms.

## Matter, Mind, and Mystery

Where Griffin offers a way to "unsnarl" the world-knot, Colin McGinn, as we saw in the previous chapter, has declared the task hopeless—a permanent mystery.[5] Human reason, McGinn says, cannot comprehend how sentience could emerge from insentient matter; indeed, the possibility of understanding any causal relationship between matter and mind is forever closed to us. *Unsnarling* is Griffin's robust response to such pessimism. He agrees with McGinn and other mysterians on the first point—the permanent inconceivability of mind emerging from mindless matter—but disagrees on the second point. We *can* come to a rational understanding of the mind-body relationship, says Griffin, and he presents an incisive critique of McGinn's analysis of the hopelessness of the mind-body problem.

He takes McGinn to task for rejecting panpsychism, arguing that this is the only reasonable way out of the impasse of materialism. (McGinn believes materialism must be true, even if he cannot understand *how* it could be true.) Griffin points out, rightly, that most critics of panpsychism do not distinguish between various presentations of this ontology. Usually, moreover, the critics focus on the weakest presentation of the case, not on its strongest (contravening one of Griffin's regulative principles).

Attacking a weaker version, McGinn on more than one occasion has tried to reduce panpsychism to absurdity—without addressing the distinction between compound individuals and aggregates that is central to Whitehead and Hartshorne.[6*] However, given the challenge of Griffin's meticulous defense of panexperientialism, McGinn can no longer simply fall back on a questionable reductio—otherwise he (or any other critic of

---

*See previous chapter.

panpsychism) cannot seriously claim to have understood this ontology or to have offered an adequate critique.

As Griffin notes, Galen Strawson, by contrast, does grapple with a more mature conceptualization of panpsychism—and consequently comes to a very different conclusion from McGinn's.[7] Strawson, like McGinn, is agnostic about the mind-body issue having a solution. But whereas McGinn lays the lion's share of the blame on our inadequate notions about mind, Strawson lays it on our flawed conceptions of matter.

And it is precisely our inadequate conception of matter—the inherited flawed Cartesian intuition that matter is insentient—Griffin says we need to overcome if we are to move in the direction of a mind-body solution.

## EMERGENCE REVISITED

As noted in the previous chapter, Griffin emphasizes a distinction between "experience" and "consciousness" (the latter he identifies with "*conscious experience*")—mainly as a tactic to ward off the kinds of silly critiques often leveled at panpsychism.* But McGinn accuses Griffin's distinction of exactly the same kind of miraculous emergentism (consciousness from wholly nonconscious experience) that panexperientialists accuse materialism of (sentience from wholly insentient matter). What kind of *experience* could be *wholly* devoid of something of the nature of consciousness?

Griffin's response, as we've seen, is that the two claims for emergence are not similar in kind. The latter claim (sentience or mind from insentient matter) requires an ontological leap (the emergence of an entity with an interior, subjective viewpoint from *wholly* objective entities); and this is not so in the former case (where primordial experience already is subjective, and so the emergence of consciousness, or conscious experience, does not require an ontological objective-to-subjective leap).

---

*Typically, the critique goes something like: "If mentality goes all the way down, then not only brain cells and bacteria would be 'conscious,' but rocks, tables, telephones, and thermostats would be, too. How absurd to think that rocks or thermostats have thoughts and feelings!" Griffin is right: This is a silly and irresponsible mischaracterization of panpsychism. In order to avoid leaving the mature version of this ontology open to such lazy rebuke, Griffin prefers to talk not of "consciousness" all the way down, but of *experience* all the way down—hence, panexperientialism.

Because the problem of emergence is central to the mind-body issue, it is important to take another look and expand on a point noted in the previous chapter: We should make a critical distinction between *ontological* or *type* emergence and *evolutionary* or *token* emergence. What is at issue in the mind-body problem is *ontological* emergence: how one ontological type or kind (e.g., subjective experience/consciousness) could emerge from a wholly different ontological kind (e.g., objective matter/energy). This kind of emergence is at the heart of the hard problem. It seems unresolvable, and it is what fuels the agnosticism of philosophers such as Thomas Nagel, Colin McGinn, and Galen Strawson.

But ontological emergence of unique types, of different kinds, is not the same as evolutionary emergence of different properties or tokens of the same ontological type. Evolutionary emergence—new tokens of the same type—is not uncommon. It is the familiar process of speciation, whether in chemical or biological evolution. No two species, no matter how remote and different from each other (an amoeba and a human, for instance), are ontologically distinct. They are all organisms composed of variations of the same atomic elements. They are all of the same ontological *type*—i.e., (sentient) matter-energy. Yet they differ enormously as tokens of that type.

A paradigm case of token emergence is the transition from gas to liquid when molecules of hydrogen and oxygen combine. Here is a case where the liquidity of water emerges as a new property from wholly nonliquid gases. But what is wholly new is a property, a *token,* of an *already* existing type (objective matter-energy). Nothing new ontologically, no new *kind* or *type,* has emerged. It is, furthermore, unsurprising that the physical properties of these two gases would undergo a state shift—from gas to liquid—given what we know about the structure and dynamics of molecular bonding and laminar flow. It is not a mystery how a recombination of physical properties could result in entirely unprecedented physical states.

But it would be completely surprising—indeed, an unsolvable riddle—how one ontological kind could give rise to an entirely different ontological kind. For materialists, this leaves two options, as we saw in the previous chapter: (1) Deny that consciousness or experience is ontologically a different kind from matter-energy; or (2) Explain how ontological emergence could occur.

If (1), the materialists need to explain how subjectivity and objectivity (a *pour-soi* and an *en-soi*) could be identical in kind. This has been the project attempted, and failed, by mind-brain identists. (When all the physical facts of the brain are accounted for, something—qualia, raw feels, subjectivity—is still left out. Ergo, brain cannot equal mind.) Recognizing this ontological impasse, some materialists claim that consciousness is either merely a property or a function of matter,[8] or that it is merely a "folk fiction" that should be eliminated from our scientific-philosophical vocabulary.[9] But functionalists have notoriously failed to show how subjectivity could be a function of wholly objective matter, and eliminativists, in denying consciousness, fall into a performative contradiction (it takes consciousness to deny consciousness).

If (2), materialists need to explain how subjectivity could emerge from objectivity, how qualia could arise *ex nihilo*—how, in short, an entirely new ontological kind could emerge. Both of these conundrums, as Nagel has eloquently argued, confound materialism.[10]

Griffin, McGinn, and Strawson agree with Nagel: Ontological emergence of mind from matter, of the phenomenological from the physical, has materialism stumped. But McGinn and Strawson part company with Griffin on the notion of emergence of consciousness from experience. Griffin denies this is a case of ontological emergence and would like us to accept it as a case of evolutionary emergence—that is, emergence of a new token, not of a new type. (He doesn't use these terms, nevertheless this is his position.)

This distinction between experience and consciousness is very important to Griffin—he comes back to it again and again. However, from what he says, it is clear that he is using "consciousness" in a sense different from McGinn and Strawson, and other philosophers of mind. Griffin, in fact, is not using "consciousness" philosophically or ontologically, but *psychologically*. Whereas McGinn uses "consciousness" to distinguish it from "nonconsciousness" (i.e., wholly objective, insentient matter), Griffin contrasts it with the psychoanalytic notion of the "unconscious."*

---

*For example, see his reference to Freud in *Unsnarling the World-Knot,* where he discusses "consciousness" (p. 107).

Once this difference in use is understood, the whole debate over whether consciousness is the same as experience, or whether it emerges from experience, becomes moot. In this argument between McGinn and Griffin, I think responsibility for the confusion rests on Griffin's shoulders: He does not make it clear that he is using "consciousness" with a psychological rather than an ontological meaning.* Griffin is by no means alone among philosophers of mind in this omission. Failure to make this distinction between psychological and philosophical meanings of "consciousness" is a major reason for breakdown in communication between various positions on the mind-body problem.†

## The Panexperientialist Solution

It is now time to look in some detail at panexperientialism's resolution of the mind-body problem—and address the assertion that panexperientialism is a form of idealism.

Ironically, Griffin claims that panexperientialism actually provides a solution to (1) above—the identist proposition that mind and matter are of the same ontological kind. Materialists fail in solving (1), Griffin forcefully argues, because of their flawed definition of matter as insentient, and their flawed understanding of it as substance. By changing some basic metaphysical assumptions—from insentient to sentient matter, from

---

*Griffin's omission is all the more surprising because on a couple of occasions he even says that these other philosophers (McGinn and Strawson) must be using "consciousness" in a different way. In a footnote in his "Introduction: The Reenchantment of Science," 1998, p. 127, Griffin says, in response to McGinn, Strawson, and William Seager—who (either rhetorically or literally) "attribute consciousness to amoebas let alone atoms and electrons"—that they "must be presupposing some very different notion of consciousness." Precisely. This "very different notion of consciousness" is the difference between Griffin's psychological interpretation of consciousness (distinct from the Freudian or Jungian unconscious), and McGinn, Strawson, and Seager's using "consciousness" in its ontological meaning (distinct from wholly nonconscious experience, sentience, subjectivity—absent *all* traces of mentality whatsoever). It is this distinction that Griffin seems to miss or ignore. For him, consciousness is synonymous with cognitive discrimination or intellectual knowing ("Introduction: The Reenchantment of Science," 1998, pp. 126–27, 130–31).

†See chapter 4, "Language, Energy, and Consciousness."

ontological substance to ontological process—panexperientialism can provide a coherent (nonreductive) explanation for how experience (and/ or consciousness, i.e., subjective actuality) and matter-energy are identical in kind (type-identical), yet remain *numerically* distinct. Process, unlike substance, can account for this seemingly paradoxical "difference-yet-sameness" of matter and mind. In process ontology (as we shall see), nothing ontologically new comes into being when subjective reality becomes objective, or vice versa. This is Griffin's (following Whitehead) great contribution to philosophy of mind.

Panexperientialism's identity of mind and matter amounts to the claim that *experience or mind is the same ontological type as body or matter.* This assertion is the core of Griffin's thesis. How, then, can mind and body have the same nature? In a phrase, the answer is what Whitehead called "occasions of experience," or what I prefer to call "moments of experience" (MoE). And positing MoE as the fundamental ontology underlying both mind and body is what makes it difficult for panexperientialism to avoid the accusation that it is a form of idealism.

Perhaps one of the most difficult shifts in thinking required by panexperientialism—besides substituting process for substance, verbs for nouns—is grasping the relationship between time, or duration, and spatial extension. A few moments of introspection and self-observation will reveal the intimate and obvious relationship between time and experience. Clearly, one of the main characteristics of mind or consciousness is *flow*—experience endures. Similarly, we can easily observe the intimate and obvious relationship between body and space. What is not so clear is how, on the one hand, consciousness may be related to space, and, on the other, how body may be related to time. In fact, these relationships are so unobvious that Descartes's famous intuition about the mind-body distinction was that mind is utterly nonspatial, and body is defined as *res extensa*—things that occupy space.

Panexperientialism, switching from substance to process thinking, radically questions this Cartesian intuition. If panexperientialism is to succeed in its identity of experience and body, then, it must do so by explaining how experiences have spatial extension and how bodies endure through time. Griffin takes on both of these issues, and he succeeds by showing how panexperientialism explains the mutual co-arising of the physical and the mental. His explication of panexperientialism is so persuasive it is difficult to imagine other philosophers of mind not seriously engaging with his thesis.

Following Whitehead, Griffin introduces the notion of "physical prehensions" or "physical feelings" as the ground phase in a MoE. A prehension is defined as a "taking account of" (i.e., intentionality) some other occasion(s) of experience—some other actuality—*not* the subject having the prehension of feeling. That is, prehension is of some object distinct from the experiencing subject. A "physical prehension," therefore, is of an actual object. By "physical prehension" Griffin and Whitehead mean those events or phases of events that involve *efficient causation*—that is, exchange of energy. Whitehead calls this the "physical pole" of an event.

Again following Whitehead, Griffin goes on to distinguish physical prehensions from mental prehensions, where the object is not actual but an abstraction or a possibility. This is the "mental pole" of a MoE, the creative experience of an event exercising its own ability to act spontaneously, to choose, to be a self-determining agent. In short, the physical pole corresponds to Aristotelian efficient causation, the mental pole to *final* causation, teleology, purpose, aim. Since both physical prehensions and mental prehensions are merely distinct phases in a unitary MoE, they thus share the same temporal and experiential nature.

Griffin sums up his panexperientialist solution to the mind-body problem by indicating how this ontology may be considered a form of physicalism: "[M]ental experience which in its most sophisticated forms may *seem* to be completely detached from the actual world, always in fact arises out of a physical experience, with the body being the most powerful source of physical experience." And in a footnote he adds: "This point is the basis for calling panexperientialism of this sort a species of 'physicalism'."

But, critics may object, this move merely renames one experiential event (or phase) "physical" to distinguish it from a "mental" phase without giving a satisfactory explanation for calling it "physical" in the first place. Thus, the physical aspect of a panexperientialist moment of experience may seem arbitrary, ad hoc. This move does not explain how a *temporal* extension (momentary duration of a physical prehension) becomes a *spatial* extension. How does duration account for, or transition to, extension in space?* Again, it seems only one half of the Cartesian dualism of temporal mind and spatial matter is to account for both. And since this half is experiential, we are left with idealism, not physicalism as Griffin claims.

But now let's see how Griffin/Whitehead explain how a MoE becomes physical, and how physical gives rise to mind.

## MIND FROM "PHYSICAL" EVENTS—AND VICE VERSA?

For Griffin and Whitehead, mind is a "temporal society of occasions of experience," that is, it is inevitably spread out over time. It is the *process* by which completed, or past, experiences pass on (via causal efficacy) some aspect or aspects of that experience to a subsequent moment of experience that prehends, or takes into itself, those aspects. It then adds its own spontaneous, creative experience to integrate new inputs (mostly from the host body, but also some from beyond in the wider environment). Mind, then, is not a thing with some constant essence that remains the same through time.

But if all experiences are rooted in efficient causation of prior actualities—the *physical* pole—from whence does the mental pole arise to step in and "unify the various elements imposed on it by its past?"[11]

It is one thing to *state* that the physical pole gives rise to (or gives way

---

*I should admit that after reading *Unsnarling* and rereading Whitehead's *Process and Reality* it is still not clear to me how *spatial extension* is accounted for in an ontology that takes *process,* or duration, as ontologically fundamental. On the one hand, to merely stipulate that processes or events must take place in time and space does not explain why or how this is so. On the other hand, if space is somehow derivative of process, or time, this smacks of yet another instance of problematic ontological emergence—or else poses another problematic identity, of time and space.

Griffin, via Whitehead, does present a strong case for the *type*-identity of the physical and the mental, of body and mind, but does not clearly do the same for the relationship of time and space. In what way could time (as duration) and space be tokens of the same ontological type? In the later chapters of *Process and Reality,* Whitehead seems to indicate that the type identity of time and space is somehow embedded in a deeper ontology of *geometrical* extension. How "geometrical" extension (which seems a paradigm case of abstraction) could count as the ground for *actuality,* for actual entities, escapes me. Is Whitehead here intimating a kind of neo-Pythagoreanism (which, once again, pushes his ontology toward idealism)?

to) the mental pole, but this does not explain how such a transition could occur. If there is an ontological jump from "physical" to "mental," this would be merely a restatement (albeit in panexperientialist terms) of the old mind-from-matter emergentist puzzle facing materialism.

Griffin is emphatic, however, that the transition from physical pole to mental pole is *not* an ontological leap. It is a continuous process within a MoE. But this takes us back to idealism—renaming one phase of the process "physical," when in fact it is just as experiential as the mental pole. The crux of Griffin's resolution of the ontological dilemma of getting either mind from matter (experience from energy—materialism) or of getting matter from mind (physical actualities from experience—idealism) is the crucial shift from a substance interpretation of ontology (being made of "stuff") to a process ontology (where being, or rather becoming, is constituted by *events*). Thus, if we consider the present MoE as "mind" (subject), then as soon as it completes itself and perishes, and slips into the past, it becomes "matter" (object). It is no longer an experiencing entity (with the quality of a "mental pole") because experience is always *now*. The completed moment—"matter"—thus is devoid of experience because it is *expired experience*.

But—and this is crucial, too—no sooner has one MoE expired, than it is replaced by a new MoE; and, through physical prehension or causal efficacy, *this subsequent MoE is constituted by past, completed MoEs.* So, current actualities incorporate the past (body) and endure into the present *only because they are prehended by current MoEs.* Thus we have a resolution to a seeming "paradox of matter": If we artificially slice up time by an act of abstraction (into a series of discrete, self-contained instants isolating past from present) we can see that in one sense "matter" is devoid of experience (as materialists and dualists have claimed). But this is an *abstraction* not an actuality, and when we take this nontemporal-instantaneous (i.e., *substance*) view of "matter" to be actual we commit what Whitehead called the "fallacy of misplaced concreteness."

If, however, we deal not with abstractions (abstract substances), but with actualities and their inevitable duration, we see that what we call "matter" is actually a phase in a process. It exists only because it endures, and it endures—continues from the past into the present—only because it is prehended *in the present* by some current subject of experience. On this more holistic-process view, the abstraction "matter" is replaced by a concrete actuality, an experiential, creative embodiment of former actualities.

Thus, what is actual—reality—consists of both objects and subjects in a dance, or flow. Each new subject is constituted in part by antecedent actualities (physical objects), but each new MoE, in addition to its physical constituents, is also a *creative subject* that exercises its freedom and creativity to unify *in the moment* its constituent completed MoE. Each object is an expired experience (mentality providing the raw ingredients for physicality—idealism); *and then* these objects provide the raw material for subsequent subjects (physicality providing a ground for mentality—materialism). And so the cycle proceeds: subject to object to subject to object . . . probably without beginning or end.

In Griffin's worldview, then, mind and body are *numerically* distinct. But they are not different in kind, not *ontologically* different. The numerical distinction is wholly a consequence of the process nature of reality, as just outlined. Mind and body arc both made of the same kind, or *type,* of reality (experience-in-process), and their distinction is wholly a consequence of their intrinsic *temporal* reality—the inevitable arising and perishing of experience.

Griffin, thus, redefines "physical" as the prehension (or causal efficacy) of past actualities—and the "physicalism" of panexperientialism differs from the physicalism of materialism inherited from Cartesian dualism by being defined more in terms of time than of extension in space. As Griffin emphasizes, this is not to deny the role of space in actualities. All actualities are events, and all events, by definition, take place in time and space—they must occur *somewhere* and *somewhen.*

One consequence of the spatio-temporal nature of all actualities is that panexperientialism rules out the possibility of disembodied souls. All actualities are embodied. There are no mere ghosts. Similarly, it rules out the possibility of "vacuous" matter, of independent, raw, dead stuff. All actualities are experiential. There are no mere machines. Thus pure idealism ("nothing but ghosts or spirit"), and pure materialism ("nothing but mechanical matter"), and pure Cartesian dualism ("the ghost in the machine") are equally rejected in panexperientialism. Instead, this ontology reconciles their deeper intuitive insights in the concept of "experiencing organisms all the way down."

## Reconciling Materialism and Idealism

But what about the issue of that "lurking idealism"? How can panexperientialism be a form of idealism when Griffin explicitly rejects idealism as a contender in the ontological stakes? Does Griffin, then, contravene his own regulative principle of "realism"—requiring any acceptable ontology to acknowledge the actuality of matter-energy?

Idealism is typically understood to mean a worldview that denies the reality of matter independent of mind. And to this extent, panexperientialism accords with idealism: No "physical pole" of an MoE exists independently of the "mental pole." The reverse is equally true (which seems to support materialism). However, since the common factor in both poles is *experience,* idealism appears to win out.

Yet Griffin is emphatic that the "physical pole" (matter) is just as real as the "mental pole" (mind). Panexperientialism, as developed by Whitehead and Griffin, is a detailed, rational, and *empirical*—in the broadest sense of being based on experiential data—working out of what we could call "idealist realism." It is idealism, as already suggested, because its ultimate ontology is experiential—moments of experience—and it is realism because these ultimate units are the paradigm actualities.

Panexperientialism, thus, achieves the impressive function of providing a bridge or tunnel between the apparently opposing ontologies of materialism and idealism. It does so by showing that "matter" (physical actuality) is fundamentally real, as materialists insist, but that this matter/energy is essentially constituted by experiential occasions, as idealists insist.

The apparent contradiction or paradox of a mutuality of materialism and idealism is resolved by recognizing the fundamentality of process, of time: This moment's unit experience is completed as soon as its brief duration is over; at that "instant" it is no longer "now," and becomes part of the past. It ceases being an experiencing subject and becomes an object experienced by the subsequent MoE—the subject occupying the next "now."

Process, thus, involves an alternation or spiral of phases—from experiencing subject (the unifying agent of past objective moments) to a completed subject-as-object (physical), which becomes "raw material" for the next moment of experience (mental). The slogan "now subject, then object" sums up the panexperientialist solution to the mind-body problem. (Perhaps every philosopher concerned with the mind-body problem should use this slogan as a bumper sticker, or alternatively: "past matter, present mind.")

Griffin is a little more explicit about the points of commonality between materialism and panexperientialism than between panexperientialism and idealism. In fact, he gives ten reasons why panexperientialism may be considered a form of physicalism: These ten points "may be helpful in showing how much more materialism and panexperientialism have in common than might otherwise be apparent."[12]

With a comparable openness to idealism, I'm sure Griffin could come up with an equal number of points to show commonality here, too. However, unlike materialism, idealism is not a dominant philosophical position these days, and so Griffin is not at pains to win the favor of idealists in supporting his panexperientialist cause.

Toward the end of *Unsnarling*, Griffin does come around to acknowledging that panexperientialism can serve as a bridge between materialism and idealism: "Panexperientialism in effect combines [materialism and idealism] into a more inclusive stuff, Whitehead's 'creativity'."[13] It is here that we need to look for the psychophysical bridging principles that Chalmers seeks. For Griffin, the link is Whitehead's "creativity" or creative experience. The inherent creative power of the universe is Whitehead's ultimate category of actuality/reality—it is what manifests in the physical pole of an event as energy, and in the mental pole as self-action, freedom, choice, and intentionality. The "laws," or "habits," of creativity detailed in the philosophies of Whitehead and Hartshorne provide Chalmers's sought-for "bridging laws"—for example, the "laws" or "habits" of nature (we might call them "principles of actuality") that determine the physical-biological-psychological distinction between "mere aggregates" of matter and "compound individuals."* The former

---

*See footnote 2, previous chapter.

do not have the unifying power to possess unit-experience or action (e.g., sand castles, rocks, computers, thermostats). The latter can and do have the kind of unity of experience required to solve the binding problem.

## The Binding Problem:
## A Solution

A standard critique of any form of panpsychism is that if it is a true worldview, it is confronted by a seemingly insuperable "binding problem," expressed by William James: "How can many consciousnesses be at the same time one consciousness?"[14] James was referring to the fact of a multiplicity of sensations, coursing through his body at any given moment, that are *somehow* experienced in the singular as *his* consciousness.

The modern psychological version of James's "compounding of consciousness" is: How can those brain cells that process colors, say, combine their consciousness with those that process shapes, or tastes, or textures, so that when we bite into an apple it is a unified experience? The philosophical panpsychist version of this conundrum is this: The body or brain is composed of billions of units—cells, molecules, atoms, elementary particles—and each unit has its own complement of consciousness, so how do we account for the fact that in our own case we don't experience consciousness as a thing or a process composed of innumerable "little consciousnesses"?

Here's the problem: If we ignore the relativity of time in Einsteinian physics, then it is plausible to imagine billions of tiny events in the brain or body all occurring at the same moment we identify as "now." In panpsychism/panexperientialism each of these events has its own micro-consciousness. So at the moment "now" there are billions of little "consciousnesses" (this was James's point). But somehow, in addition to all these micro-consciousnesses there is also the dominant, *unitary* consciousness of the host organism composed of those billions of consciousness-events. *How?*

Panpsychism offers a "bottom-up" solution: At "bottom" we have innumerable cells (or microtubules, or quanta, or whatever), and each of these is sentient—each has its own "little consciousness." Each "bottom-level" entity is an event—it is fundamentally a process. That is, it comes into being as a result of the "causal efficacy" (i.e., prehension) of prior completed subjects. As completed subjects (units of expired experience), they play the role of "objects." These objects are the raw material for subsequent subjects. Thus objects exist in the past, and subjects exist in the present, in the "now." And since each now-subject is *constituted* by antecedent objects (via prehension—the taking account of prior actualities), each subject is composed of "many."

But this is only part of the story. Each subject is not exhaustively constituted by past actualities (call them cells or microtubules), it is intrinsically a *creative* entity. It is not wholly determined. It has freedom, self-agency, an ability to choose. It chooses or "reaches out to" or "prehends" those aspects of past actualities it will incorporate. It is selective. It is this creative agency that draws together into a unity the various past actualities that constitute it. Picture a number of small bubbles being incorporated into a single, larger, dominant bubble; or picture a number of small ripples on a pond conjoining to form a larger ripple. The "many become the one." Except in this case, the one is not merely a passive recipient of its constituent members; it actively selects them.

Even more important for process philosophy, as Whitehead said, "the many become the one *and are increased by one*." The "one" now adds to the multiplicity by becoming itself an object for subsequent subject(s). And so on for different levels in the hierarchy of an organism. At each level, the "now-subject" is the dominant creative agent, drawing into a unity all its constituent member-events. A cell is the dominant subject for its constituent object-organelles; an organism as a whole is the dominant subject for all its constituent organs, and their constituents all the way down.

## PROCESS, HIERARCHY, AND CREATIVITY

This is a "bottom-up" solution par excellence to the binding problem. The "creative" aspect of the solution is the subject's injection of novelty into the process by unifying aspects of the past (via prehension/causal efficacy, i.e., efficient causation) in the present (via self-agency, i.e., first cause or final cause), and thereby adding something new to the process (the many becoming the one and being increased by one).*

And in response to James's question, Griffin points out: "The fatal assumption was that [consciousness has] to be both 'many' and 'one' *at the same time.*"

Let's sum up the steps in the panpsychist solution to the binding problem:

1. **Unit Binding** (*successive—like beads on a string*).
Billions of sentient events are happening in an organism's hierarchy of cells, molecules, atoms, and subatomic particles. And at each level, each unit (or "monad") endures through the process of subject-becoming-object for the next subject (e.g., a neuron prehends its own past "neuronic occasions" and unites them; it is constituted by them). This is *"unit* binding," where *successive* moments or occasions of experience are formed into a new unity at each new moment. Each event or monad, then, is unified in each new moment of experience (its subjective pole) and includes all relevant past or expired moments of experience (the event-monad's objective pole). Each event-trajectory or serial time-line is unified as a phased moment of experience (MoE).

2. **Horizontal Binding** (*simultaneous—like strings in a net*).
No unit monad exists in isolation. Not only does it contain or unify its own past history, it is also simultaneously in relationship with innumerable other monads. Again, through acts of *prehension,* each monad draws into itself aspects of many other monads (which includes their histories). Each monad, then, is potentially infinitely complex.

---

*Griffin expresses the panexperientialist solution to the binding problem thus: The brain at any moment is composed of billions of neuronic occasions of experience, whereas our conscious experience at any moment belongs to a "dominant" occasion of experience, which is a new, higher-level "one" that is created out of the "many" neuronic experiences (being partly created by them—by their efficient causation on it—and then partly self-created). . . . The many neuronic occasions of experience exist first for themselves, as subjects of their own experience. It is only after their own moment of subjective immediacy has perished that they enter into, as objectified experiences, the dominant occasion of experience (1998, p. 179).

Monads connect with other monads (e.g., atoms and molecules connect with other atoms and molecules) to form networks on the same hierarchical level. When multiple units or monads on the same hierarchical level prehend each other (e.g., billions of neurons in a human brain), "*horizontal* binding" occurs.

### 3. Hierarchical Binding (*asynchronous—like layered nets*).

When multiple units from one level are prehended as objects by a subject on the next higher level they contribute to the physical constitution of the monad at that higher level.

But because, as objects, the prehended monads are in the past, they no longer have *at that moment, for that subject,* any experience/subjectivity (it has expired).

Thus, the actualities that inform and contribute to the subject at the next level up are *not* "little consciousnesses" any longer. Therefore, there is no problem of many little consciousnesses becoming one consciousness/subject *in the same moment,* as Griffin says in response to James. This is "*hierarchical* binding"—between different levels in the hierarchy of the organism.

### 4. Object Binding (*unifying embodiment*).

Now, it is also true that at that "same time" lower-level cells and molecules are in continual process and possess their own "now-subjectivity" (on the unit level [1] and the horizontal level—[2]). *But it is not the **contemporary** subjectivity of the cells that the organism as a whole is prehending. It is their previous "incarnations" from just a moment ago* (which in this moment "now" is expired experience). In short, hierarchical prehension binds together, or unifies, *objects*—the physical constituents of the higher-level monad.

It might help to think of each lower level of the organismic hierarchy being just a slight moment in the past with respect to the next level above it. So that at the level of the dominant monad (say, the human self), "binding" of little consciousnesses is not a problem because what is being "bound" are just-past objects (expired subjects), not billions of contemporaneous little subjects. Horizontal binding is going on "down below," while hierarchical binding is going on "up here."

5. **Dominant Monad** (*the coordinating subject*).

Hierarchical binding between different levels of an organism—cells, molecules, atoms, subatomic particles—accounts for the unity of the organism's *objective physical* body. Meanwhile, that organism as a whole constitutes a higher-level dominant monad with its own unit subjectivity (as a unified actual occasion it has its own "mental pole"). The subjectivity of the dominant monad coordinates the multifarious aims and trajectories of the multiplicity of components that constitute the monad.

At every moment, each monad at each level in the hierarchy has its own *unit consciousness* (as well as its own integrated unified physical embodiment). For example, while each molecule has its own present unit consciousness (its subjective pole), it contributes its physical pole (expired moments of experience) *as an object* to be experienced by the subjective pole of the unitary cell of which it is a part. Past objects are *passive* and *acted on* to form the body of the cell; but the present subjectivity or consciousness of the cell is *actively self-creative*—it unifies the physical poles of its constituents. It does not unify or bind the subjective poles or consciousness of its constituents. Consciousness (the subjective pole) of every monad at every level in the organism's hierarchy is *autonomous*.

Every monad has some degree of freedom to exercise choice or self-agency. Mental anarchy is avoided because each dominant monad coordinates or "persuades" the subjective poles in its constituent hierarchy of monads to cohere toward a collective, mutually shared purpose (e.g., biological survival).

A dominant monad coordinates and aligns the choices enacted by its constituent monads. This intersubjective alignment is achieved by *sharing intention* (where "intention" is defined as the creative, spontaneous expression of an aim or purpose) and by *sharing meaning* (where "meaning" is defined as *experienced fit between self and its environment*").

It's a two-way process. Lesser monads also relay their intentions and meaning up the hierarchy to inform the dominant monad. The higher a monad is on the organismic hierarchy, the more potent its self-agency is and the more influence it has over its constituents. For example, I can choose to walk across the room, and all my cells, molecules, and atoms cohere with this decision. However, none of my cells or molecules has sufficient agency to move my body.

Panpsychism, thus, aims to present a coherent account of how the multiplicity of consciousness that exists (per hypothesis) at low levels can result in the unity of consciousness we know empirically in our own case. Whitehead and Griffin describe the process nature of the relationship between objects (expired subjects) and "live" subjects, and how such process can account for the hierarchical constituency of subjective wholes from multiple object "parts" (especially when the part-whole relationship involves *internal* relatedness), and how the "wholeness" or unity is the result of the creative agency of the emergent whole.

The panpsychist solution involves both quantum-like "units" of duration and ongoing continuity. There are no discrete timeless "instants" in Whiteheadian process metaphysics. Everything endures for at least a minimal period, but almost as soon as a low-level unit comes into being, it perishes. (This is the "quantum-like" component.) And, as soon as an MoE has perished it is prehended by a subsequent subject and contributes to the constituency of the new monad with its own subject and its own moment of experience. (This is the process component.) In addition, this "epochal process," as Whitehead called it, is completed by the creative component—the subject, having experience, therefore has freedom and self-agency, and this creative agency is what draws into a unity the multiple objects from its immediate past. The hierarchical component is accounted for by the fact that larger entities, or wholes, are constituted by nested systems of lower-level wholes.

Now, all three of these—process, hierarchy, and creativity—are empirical phenomena. They are not merely theoretical or speculative. We know from our own experiences that duration is an inescapable fact of experience. There are no "frozen" experiences. (Mystical experience is a whole other discussion.) We know from both quantum and relativity physics that process-events are the "stuff" of the world. We know from biology that evolution (in some form) is also a fact. Process is empirical. And from basic physics, biology, and ecology we know that the "stuff" of the world is ordered hierarchically (electrons + protons within atoms; atoms within molecules; molecules within cells, and so forth). Hierarchy is empirical.

We know, too, from our own case that freedom is something we all (without exception) presuppose in practice (even if we verbally deny it—one of Griffin's hard-core common sense "regulative principles"). Freedom or creativity is empirical.

## Free Will All the Way Down

A standard, and expected, objection to this solution runs something like: "Free will even in humans is a difficult enough concept; attributing it to microtubules just compounds the difficulty." True, we cannot understand how even human freedom could exist in a world governed by the mechanical, deterministic laws of standard physics. Free will is difficult (if not impossible) if we assume materialism/mechanism. In fact, the emergence of free will from wholly mechanistic units is another aspect of the hard problem that requires a miracle for a solution. But it is precisely such a materialist worldview that is in question in panexperientialism. If free will exists in our own case, then just like experience, it must go all the way down. Griffin maintains that the only coherent way to account for the experience of freedom in our own case is to adopt the panexperientialist view that even microtubules and electrons have some degree of freedom. (The total, intrinsic, ontological indeterminacy of quantum events supports this possibility. To an observer, total randomness is indistinguishable from the exercise of free choice. But to an entity with self-agency, there is a world of difference between randomness and the experience of choice.)

The solution to the binding problem, then, according to panexperientialism, is to be found in a combination of three key concepts: *process, hierarchy,* and *creativity.* The body-brain is a hierarchy of events, each unit event with its own degree of subjectivity relative to its role in the hierarchy. Mind is that singular, momentary *now* event that creatively unifies aspects of brain events. Each unit event, through the process of experiencing-subject becoming experienced-object, contributes itself to the larger whole—the organism in which it is a constituent. Mind, then, is the unifying process of the whole hierarchy of events.

Through evolution and ontogenesis, occasions of experience group together and relate to each other to form hierarchies of experiencing individuals. Each community of individuals experiences itself as a unified entity, and derives this unified experience from the felt experiences of its multiple sub-individuals *by actively and spontaneously exercising a multi-tiered temporal "concrescence" of past objects constituting the present subject—a process involving unit, horizontal, and hierarchical binding.* Thus a human being can experience him- or herself as a whole individual, a "dominant occasion of experience," or "regnant monad," by feeling or prehending the component organs and cells, which themselves are experienced as individuals. At a higher level, the collective consciousness of a (suitably attuned) group can derive its "individuality" and character from the felt experiences shared by the individual members of the group.[15*]

## Challenge to Epistemology

One final criticism—by no means deserved by Griffin alone because it points to a failure common to many philosophers of mind—Griffin does not address Richard Rorty's seemingly devastating critique of the whole enterprise of epistemology and philosophy of mind.[16] Just as any comprehensive analysis of the mind-body problem, to deserve that name, must take up Griffin's challenge, any thoroughgoing mind-body thesis needs to respond to Rorty's critique.

Rorty's position is that the entire project of philosophy of mind-cum-epistemology is based on the Cartesian fallacy that the mind is a "glassy essence" that reflects the world, and that knowledge is the more or less accurate inner perception of the more or less accurate reflections in the mirror-mind. If no such "glassy essence" exists, as Rorty insists, how could we *justify* any knowledge claim—for without the reflections of the external world in the mind there could be no correspondence theory of truth?

However, if we take Whitehead's notion of causal efficacy, where a prior moment of experience, having completed its duration, becomes an object that literally *causes* (via physical prehension) the character of the

---

*See David Bohm's *Creating Consciousness* for a discussion of Bohmian dialogue as a process for creating and engaging the felt consciousness of a group. See also *Radical Knowing,* chapter 13, "Dialogue: Consciousness and Cosmology."

subsequent subjective moment of experience—then the experiencing subject *knows* the objective world, not through reflection, but through *constitution.* The knowing subject is literally constituted, at least in part, by nonsensory perceptions (i.e., prehensions or causal efficacy) of prior events that constitute its environment. It would be *participatory* epistemology, as distinct from the separate subject-object epistemology that Rorty critiques, and that requires something like the Cartesian "glassy essence" to account for correspondence between subjective perceptions and knowledge and objective fact.

Instead of a correspondence theory of truth, Whiteheadian epistemology could be taken to be a "constitutive theory of truth." This is not at all the same as so-called postmodern constructivism, with its attendant relativism. In the Whiteheadian cosmology, there really is an actual world "out there"—it is not wholly constructed by the mind or by social consensus. It is a world that literally constitutes us as knowers, thereby overcoming the Kantian dilemma of knowing the things in themselves. We know the "things in themselves" because we *are* them to a great degree. The body literally incorporates the world. It does so not mechanistically (as in standard biology), but *experientially,* through acts of physical prehension—acts that take into the moment of experience the completed forms of prior moments.

The "to a great degree" in the previous paragraph leaves room for the Whiteheadian subject to exercise voluntary, creative spontaneity—the creative act of unification of the multiplicity of prior, completed moments (i.e., objects). This process of creative unification *is* the mind—it is the whole that integrates all the parts of which it is constituted, with the addition of its own injected creativity. This process view of the mind, creatively integrating input from the body and brain through a hierarchy of levels, provides a solution to the long-standing "binding" problem in philosophy of mind (which has been one of David Chalmers's main critiques of Whiteheadian panexperientialism).*

---

*Personal conversation.

## Conclusion

Using Whitehead's "speculative cosmology," Griffin presents a highly coherent alternative to, and provocatively challenging critique of, both dualism and materialism. His work is powerful because it bravely tackles the definition of "physical" head on. Any subsequent account of the mind-body problem will have to address Griffin's bold thesis—if it is to claim a balanced analysis of competing worldviews.

The comprehensive integrative power of panexperientialism—bridging opposing worldviews—is one of its most compelling features. It fits one of my favorite paraphrasings of John Stuart Mill: "In any dispute between philosophers, they tend to be right in what they affirm, and tend to be wrong in what they deny," an insight echoed by Niels Bohr's "'deep truths' are statements in which the opposite also contains deep truth."

Taking a cue from such wisdom, my own guiding motto for philosophy is this: There is probably some deep kernel of uncommon truth in every worldview—whether scientific materialism, spiritual idealism, mind-body dualism, or panpsychism—and the task of honest philosophers is to uncover such truths. The task of great philosophers is to find how these uncommon truths cohere in a common reality. Such discoveries, almost certainly, will involve creative shifts in our ways of knowing.

I think Whitehead was one such great philosopher. And I think that fully grasping the implications of panexperientialism will involve a willingness to shift our epistemology—to switch from substance- to process-thinking, and to supplement both sensory empiricism and rationalism with nonsensory, extrarational ways of knowing.

# 10
## Conclusion

# STORIES MATTER, MATTER STORIES

If we are to feel at home in the cosmos, to be open to the full inflowing and outpouring of its profound creativity, if we are not to feel isolated and alienated from the full symphony of cosmic matter—both as distant as the far horizon of time and as near as the palpitating flesh of our own bodies—we need a new cosmology story. We need a new way to envision our relationship to the full panorama of the crawling, burrowing, swimming, gliding, flying, circulating, flowing, rooted, and embedded Earth. We need to be and to feel, as well as to think and believe, differently.

## Radical Naturalism

The direction philosophy and science will have to take to extricate us from the Cartesian mind-body split and its pathological consequences, I have been proposing, will involve a radical redefinition of both mind and matter.

Throughout this book the major focus has been the mind-body problem, and how both philosophy of mind and empirical science will have to change if we are ever to resolve this conundrum. Given that the central arguments revolved around issues in the philosophy of mind and what changes need to be made if we are to have a science of consciousness, it is understandable that much of this work has been concerned with mind or consciousness. However, another sub-theme running throughout this project has been that the major culprit in the mind-matter dilemma is not so much consciousness as matter itself.

## THE STORY OF MATTER

I will now focus on the matter half of the puzzle, beginning with a brief overview of its conceptual history in Western philosophy. I will conclude with a new proposal for how we may understand the long-standing mystery of mind-body relationship—a proposal that recognizes the ontological and epistemological primacy of embodied *feelings*.

To understand the notion of matter in the context of Western thought, we need to go back to the early days of Greek philosophy. Let's recap:

As far as we can read into the extant fragments from the Presocratics, it seems their cosmologies were stories about empirical nature. They wondered and wrote about the nature of the world, and it seems to have been a world in which the very consciousness that was involved in the contemplation was unnoticed or unremarkable. Prior to philosophy, Greek mythology showed a similar lack of interest in the phenomenon of thought itself. In the Homeric epics, for instance, the closest we come to evidence of awareness of psychic or spiritual phenomena are the forces of the gods that appear to have been experienced as "voices" in the heads of the mortals.[1]

Before Plato, the notion of distinct domains for matter and consciousness was alien to Greek thinkers. The Presocratics were monists—for example, Thales, generally regarded as the father of Western philosophy, said that the ultimate nature of the world was water, and Heraclitus said that it was fire. Thales's pupil, Anaximander of Miletus wrote a treatise, *On Nature,* that dealt with the origin and development of matter. As we saw, he called the ultimate, or first element, the *apeiron*—"the infinite and eternal, perfectly homogeneous but utterly structureless and amorphous primary substance constituting everything that exists in the universe."[2] According to Anaximander, who was an astronomer and an inventor of astronomical instruments, the universe evolved from the infinite *apeiron* by a process of rotation.

Beginning with Anaximander, then, near the dawn of Western philosophy, the story of "intelligent nature," of mind-in-matter, has a long history. He presents us with a universal primal substance, the *apeiron,* which, through spontaneous self-generated rotation, gives rise to the primordial patterns we recognize as matter. These spiraling patterns, or material forms, according to Pythagoras nearly one hundred years later, are manifestations of a deep geometry, which is the essence of matter itself. About a century and a half later, Plato takes the Pythagorean notion of perfect transcendental geometrical forms as the foundation of imperfect matter and turns it into a full-blown dualism of imperfect substance and perfect Forms. Critical of his teacher's metaphysical dualism, Aristotle, a generation after Plato, proposed a physical dualism of *hylomorphism,* a doctrine claiming that matter and form were wholly natural and inevitably linked together.

For the next twelve or thirteen hundred years, the Western notion of matter was either derived from Platonic dualism, where matter was imperfect and corrupt (common to mystical and religious traditions such as Neoplatonism, Gnosticism, and Christianity), or from Aristotelian hylomorphism, which described matter as intrinsically passive, wholly dependent on extrinsic form to give it shape and dynamic. Only with the sixteenth century arrival of Giordano Bruno do we get a view of matter that offers an alternative to the ontologies of Plato and Aristotle.

## Giordano Bruno: Revolutionary Cosmologist

In the late sixteenth century, about half a century before Descartes, Giordano Bruno, an excommunicated Dominican monk, took Aristotelian hylomorphism a radical step further. Bruno set himself up as Aristotle's nemesis by developing a complete cosmological system at odds with the great Greek philosopher's. For nearly two millennia the Western world, and for the most part this meant Christendom, had adhered to Aristotle's geocentric model of the cosmos. The Earth, and therefore humankind, was positioned at the center of the universe, and this was a picture that well suited Catholic dogma about the relationship between nature, humanity, and God.

Copernicus (1473–1543), a generation or so before Bruno, had shocked the Church establishment by challenging Aristotle's cosmological model and by proposing a heliocentric cosmology. But Bruno, as we have seen, was even more radical and declared that not even the sun was at the center of the universe. *"There is no center,"* he said, the universe is *acentric.*

Copernicus may have gained a place in history by removing humankind from the center of the universe, but it was Bruno, a comparatively unsung hero, who effectively removed the anthropocentric illusion that humanity was even remotely in a position of cosmic centrality or special importance. As one recent scholar put it, we should honor Bruno, and rehabilitate his image and historical stature, by talking not of the "Copernican Revolution" but more accurately of the "Brunian Revolution."[3]

Copernicus was severely reprimanded for daring to overturn Aristotle and the geocentric model. By withholding publication of his ideas Copernicus saved his skin from the horrors of the Holy Inquisition. However, Bruno, for his outrageous defiance of Church authority, was unceremoniously marched half-naked to the stake and burned alive in Rome, on February 17, 1600. Although Bruno's insistence on the truth of his acentric cosmology was most likely the main reason for the Church's extreme ire, his conception of the nature of matter was equally revolutionary, and equally subversive of Church authority.

Whereas Descartes may be considered the seventeenth-century philosopher who completed Plato's dualistic project, Bruno may be viewed as the sixteenth-century genius who completed Aristotle's hylomorphic project. As noted above, Bruno took Aristotle's ontology to the next step: Whereas Aristotle's matter was intrinsically passive and inert—*neque quale, neque quantum,* without quality or quantity—Bruno's matter was intrinsically active, it was self-informing. Form, the dynamic capacity for action and formation, was itself an intrinsic quality of matter.

Bruno's metaphysic, therefore, removed the last vestige of Platonic-Aristotelian dualism by proposing a thoroughly monistic view of the cosmos as composed of "intelligent matter," which he called *mater-materia* ("matter mattering," matter as the creative "womb" or "matrix" of all forms). Whereas Aristotle's hylomorphic matter-form could (with some distortion) be interpreted in support of the mechanical materialism of modern physical science, Bruno's "intelligent materialism" is radically at odds with the dominant modern conception of matter. Because his cosmology is based on a radical monism of matter, it could arguably be called a form of "materialism." But it is a materialism in which "intelligence" or "mind" or "consciousness" is a necessary and intrinsic essence of matter. It is, therefore, a *radical* materialism much more aligned with the radical naturalism or panpsychism of Whitehead than with mechanistic materialism.

Bruno's *mater-materia* represents the first time since Plato that Western philosophy returned to the monistic views of the Presocratics, and may be compared to Anaximander's infinite *apeiron*.* His radical conception of the ultimate cosmic substance influenced later great monists such as Spinoza and Leibniz; and, as just suggested, we can trace the lineage of Whitehead's panexperientialism back through Leibniz to Bruno.

But Bruno's philosophy is far from being an anachronistic throwback to the Presocratics; it is also arguably the first presentation of a truly modern scientific cosmology, accounting for the microcosm-macrocosm (Bruno's *minima-maxima*) relationship nowadays made explicit in quantum-relativistic cosmology.[4] However, unlike quantum-relativistic models of the universe, Bruno's cosmology has an intrinsic place for mind—not mind conceived as an emergent epiphenomenon, mind-out-of-matter, but *mind-within-matter*.

Bruno parted company with Aristotle also on the question of the fundamental structure of the universal *materia*. For Aristotle, the concept of a "void" was inconceivable, and therefore so was the notion of "atoms," indivisible, individual micropellets of matter. Action and interaction through a total void was considered impossible (*"actio in distans repugnat"*). As elsewhere, Aristotle here contradicted the earlier wisdom of Presocratic atomists such as Democritus (ca. 460–360 BCE), and later philosophers such as Epicurus (341–270 BCE) and Lucretius (98–55 BCE). Aristotle's was a continuum cosmology.

In sharp contrast, Bruno's cosmology was explicitly atomistic, and in some surprising ways a forerunner of modern quantum theory. For Bruno, matter could be broken down into its constituents until the ultimate unit, an indivisible physical minimum, was reached—the atom (read

---

*This statement holds, however, only if we are focused on a *natural* (matter-based) monism. For, as noted in earlier chapters, Plotinus and other Neoplatonists were very clearly radical monists—but squarely rooted in the idealist camp. Theirs is a *supernatural* monism of nonmaterial emanating spirit. Bruno, then, qualifies as the first philosopher in the Western tradition to rehabilitate the natural monism of *physis* (albeit a radically intelligent *physis*) that so ignited the imaginations of the Presocratics.

"quantum"). Again, this aspect of Bruno's contribution to the history and development of modern science is generally overlooked, as Ramon Mendoza[5] observed:

> Whereas Galileo and Gassendi are generally celebrated as the founders of modern atomism, the fact that Bruno developed the first modern coherent atomistic model to explain phenomena of physical reality remains widely ignored. . . .
>
> Galileo . . . viewed the atom as an unextended geometrical point, Bruno conceived of the atom as a three-dimensional physical particle *capable of spontaneously moving itself*. . . . [C]ontemporary nuclear physics informs us that the ultimate particles of matter are quanta, that is extended and measurable packets of mass/energy in spacetime.[6] [Emphasis added.]

Descartes, remember, conceived of matter as totally passive, inert, and devoid of all quality—except extension in space. Cartesian matter was, therefore, completely incapable of spontaneous, self-originated motion, and utterly without feeling. Unlike Descartes's mechanism, and the atomistic conceptions of Democritus, Epicurus, and Lucretius, to whom matter was simply inert compact stuff common to all atoms, Bruno believed that matter has

> the intrinsic power to generate all possible forms, and the immanent intelligence to direct and govern all organized complex forms that issue from it. . . . Bruno borrowed from Aristotle's concept of matter merely the aspect of real possibility, while rejecting the notion that matter was merely an empty receptacle of forms. Instead, he fancied matter as the perpetually pregnant mother of all forms. . . . Matter thus becomes for him "matrix" and "mater," the fecund womb of all forms.[7]

Bruno's "ultimate physical minima" were pictured as solid, impenetrable, compact "pellets" that he called "monads," a concept later taken up by Leibniz and developed into a detailed ontology in his *Monadology*. And although Bruno's atomism anticipates ideas in modern quantum theory, his solid soul-embodied monads are less like Planck's quanta than Leibniz's much more energetic monads. Leibniz, in fact, as Mendoza points out, was the first person in the history of Western thought to represent the ultimate physical minimum as pure force and energy, and may, therefore, be considered the forerunner of modern process philosophy where the ultimate constituents of the universe are events rather than things.

Where Bruno called the intrinsic self-motivation of matter "soul," Leibniz called it "force." In fact, Leibniz was the first to introduce the concept of "force" into the vocabulary of natural philosophy or science. But whether "soul" or "force," both Bruno and Leibniz were opposed to a purely mechanical understanding of matter, whose motions were governed entirely by external impacts. Both of these philosophers developed ontologies in which matter was intrinsically active and self-organizing. "Matter is already naturally and essentially disposed and prone to order and organization. Order, organization, and structure are matter's own peculiar forms of existence, intrinsic features of its facticity" as Mendoza expressed it.[8] This view of matter is sometimes referred to as "hylozoism," meaning that matter is intrinsically "alive," or active; a position supported by the German Idealist metaphysician Rudolf Hermann Lotze in his *Microcosmus,* in opposition to the idealist philosophies of Plato and Berkeley for whom matter was essentially inert and passive, or didn't really exist.[9]

Traditional dualism attributes the causes of order and organization to "spiritual" forms acting on passive matter from "beyond," from some domain transcendent to the physical world of space-time. By contrast, the basic monistic substance of Bruno and Leibniz is purposefully self-organizing mass/energy in space-time; it is, literally, the raw material of the world, "seeded" with implicate potential for realizing all explicate forms. It contains, as Mendoza puts it, "the virtuality and the actuality of everything that is or ever will be."[10] He sums up Bruno's radical reconceptualization of matter:

> The cornerstone of Bruno's ontology is his insight: *matter is intelligent and intelligence is material.* The dialectical élan is within matter itself, for it is of the essence of matter to be self-propelling, to evolve, and to bring forth from within itself all the forms it is capable of adopting. Matter is self-organizing and self-metamorphosing. . . . [emphasis added.]

According to Bruno, mind informs matter and is indeed necessary, not to create matter or to put order into it while remaining utterly alien to it, but rather to supply from within the patterns of all the forms capable of coming forth from the fecund womb of *mater-materia* (Matter, the universal Mother).[11]

With Bruno, therefore, we have a view of matter in which it is "animated" by its own intrinsic and essential soul. But Bruno's "soul of matter" is far from the dualist's "ghost in the machine," a "something added" to matter to make it alive, as we get from Descartes's account of the animation of biological matter in humans by God's injection of an alien soul substance. Bruno's matter is naturally organic, and is itself intrinsically intelligent. In modern jargon, we might say that Brunian matter is "autopoietic," or that it comes with its own internal algorithmic programming.

Although Bruno was adamantly opposed to the notion of number as the essence of matter, a view proposed by Pythagoras more than two thousand years earlier, this modern interpretation of Bruno's "intelligent matter," as matter essentially programmed with its own algorithms, does suggest a kind of "full circle" in the story of matter. For today, the notion of natural algorithms of matter is central to the new sciences of chaos and complexity, and fractal geometry.* According to these new sciences, left to its own natural processes, physical nature will spontaneously self-organize, that within the heart of chaos are "seeds" of implicate order. And this self-organization is manifested in the spontaneous formation of patterns of spiraling fractals that follow a mysterious geometry involving fractional dimensions. Thus not only does Brunian self-organizing *mater-materia* ironically lead us back to a view suggestive of Pythagorean number mysticism, where geometrical relationships are the very essence of matter, we also find the trail leading us back to Anaximander. For the spontaneous spiraling of fractal patterns in matter are reminiscent of Anaximander's *apeiron* that spontaneously generates the primal forms of the universe by means of rotation.

---

*See chapter 2, "A New Cosmology Story."

## "INTELLIGENT MATTER"

Bruno's ontology, then, borrowing from Aristotle's notion of inseparable matter-form, insists on a radical reconceptualization of matter. Similar to Anaximander's infinite *apeiron,* Bruno's infinite *mater-materia* is the "matrix" or womb of all forms. But it is "intelligent matter" in which the dynamics of material formation are essential to matter itself. Matter, in other words, relies on nothing external: It is self-organizing. Bruno's matter is also ultimately atomistic or quantized, consisting, fundamentally, of solid, impenetrable "monads."

Whereas Bruno's monads are animated by an intrinsic automotive "soul," Leibniz, a couple of generations after Bruno's death, proposed that the monads were ultimately impenetrable bundles of self-propelling "force," units of pure psychic dynamism. Nearly two hundred years later, Leibniz's philosophical monads, indivisible units of force, were given scientific expression when Planck discovered quanta. Although Planck attributed no psychic qualities to the quanta, as Leibniz had with his monads, later quantum theorists, following Schrödinger and Heisenberg, felt compelled to include consciousness in the complete description of quantum events. Inspired by Leibniz's monads and by the explanatory power of quantum mechanics, Whitehead in the 1920s developed a detailed cosmology based on the proposition that the ultimate constituents of the world are experiential events, which he called "occasions of experience." And finally, in the new sciences of chaos and complexity, and fractal geometry, we have an experimental and theoretical account of matter as intrinsically self-organizing, and self-propelled by internal programming or fractal algorithms.*

What this long historical lineage of experiential, intelligent matter†

---

*However, as developed in chaos and complexity theories, the notion of self-organizing matter does not include intrinsic interiority (psyche or consciousness). As developed, for example, by Kaufman (1993) at the Santa Fe Institute, self-organization is wholly a matter of external relations between objective entities. All self-organized complexity and order is to be accounted for wholly in terms of nonexperiential mathematical properties of matter. Such "self-organization" is, ultimately, blind—there is no purpose, no teleological impulse toward increasing order and self-transcendence. Bruno's "intelligent matter," on the other hand, is explicitly intelligent and purposeful.

†As we saw, chapter 6 presents a lineage of mind-in-matter all the way back to Thales, the founder of Western philosophy, and beyond to its prehistoric shamanic roots.

reveals is that for thousands of years our philosophy has contained an alternative ontology to the materialism of insentient, mechanical matter (à la Democritus), and to the dualism of separate domains of substance and Form, or of substantial matter and mind (à la Descartes). Building on the panpsychist lineage, therefore, I will conclude by drawing out some of the implications of the Whiteheadian solution to the perennial mind-body problem, the nature of the relationship between matter and mind, presented in the previous chapters.

## A New View of Mind and Matter

We need now to begin thinking of mind or consciousness as *process,* as philosopher-psychologist William James suggested when he spoke of the "stream of consciousness" and as Whitehead did when he spoke of "occasions of experience."[12] When we begin thinking of consciousness in this way, the mind-body problem disappears. The problem of interaction occurs only when we imagine mind and body to be two kinds of onto-logically distinct substances. When matter is the objective constituent ingredient of purposeful process, and mind is the creative self-agency that "scoops up" past matter into the present, then their interaction—their "action-between" each other—becomes a pseudo-problem. There is no "in between," no mysterious boundary or interface separating them and across which they must communicate.

There is no interaction between mind and matter because *mind is the action or process by which matter moves itself.* Note, I did not simply say that "mind is the action of matter"—that would be a restatement of func-tionalism. I am explicitly saying that mind is the intrinsic, purposeful self-motion of matter. I am making a clear distinction between *loco*-motion and *tele*-motion. Locomotion is what is expressed in Newton's laws of classical mechanics. It is motion that propels matter from one location to another by the action of an external force. Telemotion, by contrast, is the self-motion of an entity—it acts from within as a drive or urge.

Mind doesn't "do" something to matter, thereby interacting with it. It is not some external force or substance acting on a body. It is not even some internal force, if by "internal" we mean a spatial location within the boundary of a body—for instance, in the sense that nuclear forces are internal to the dynamics of an atom. Mind is neither outside nor inside matter, but is constituent of the very essence of matter—*interior* to its being.* It is part of the "isness" of matter, or, rather, is that which is responsible for matter's ability to *become* what it is. Mind is, shall we say, a "becoming" of matter, the intrinsic, interior, self-force of a body—what biologist Hans Dreisch after Aristotle called *entelechy.*

This idea is out of favor now in scientific and philosophical circles, where it is believed to be a throwback to prescientific cosmologies. However, I want to draw attention to entelechy because the idea fits so well with panpsychism or radical naturalism, especially when we begin to focus on the implications of this philosophy for practical human affairs—such as illness and health, and personal destiny. A worldview, such as radical naturalism, that acknowledges that meaning and purpose are intrinsic to the very fabric of nature inevitably confronts the question: "How do we fit in?" How do individual human purposes fit in with the consciousness and purpose of nature or the cosmos itself? If consciousness goes all the way down—if my consciousness is rooted ultimately in the deeper or higher consciousness of reality itself—what might be the relationship between my personal consciousness and the transpersonal Cosmic I? Can I reconcile my belief and experience of free will with the idea that some larger or deeper purpose is guiding or directing us? What meaning do we give to free will if human acts of volition are individualized expressions of some greater creative impulse?

---

*Ken Wilber distinguished between "internal," meaning spatially inside, and "interiority," meaning something like "experientially and essentially constituent of." In *Sex, Ecology, Spirituality,* Wilber notes the lineage of this concept: "Spinoza, Leibniz, Schopenhauer, Whitehead, Aurobindo, Schelling, and Radharkrishnan are just a few of the major theorists who have explicitly recognized that the within of things, the interiority of individual holons, is in essence the same as *consciousness,* though of course they use different names with slightly different meanings.

"Whitehead uses 'prehension' to describe the contact and thus 'feeling' of an object by any subject, no matter how 'primitive' . . . Spinoza uses 'cognition' for knowing an event 'from the inside' and 'extension' (or matter) for knowing the same event 'from the outside.' Leibniz uses 'perception' for the interior of his monads (holons) and 'matter' for the exterior. . . . As for Teilhard de Chardin, he put it very simply: 'The within, consciousness, spontaneity—three expressions for the same thing'" (Wilber, 1995, p. 111).

## ENTELECHY: THE PULSE OF PURPOSE IN LIFE

Of all the terms cast off by modern science as "unscientific," perhaps the ancient Greek-derived word entelechy (pronounced "en-tel-eky") will turn out to be of central importance for future science. In the search for a new paradigm beyond mechanism and blind matter, and embracing life and consciousness, postmodern science may rediscover the power and profound meaning encapsulated in this ancient concept.

The word combines the meanings for "complete"—i.e., "in perfection"—(en-teles) and "having" (ekein). It means something like having or fulfilling an essential, dynamic purpose. The entelechy is what propels us to actualize our essence—the "form" or organizing principle of the body. The term originates with Aristotle, who used it to mean the essence of a thing being fully realized. Leibniz called it the active principle in all created substances that makes them complete, or self-sufficient. Entelechy is innate and inherent in all substances, or processes—as a soul—and acts from within to bring about change and development.

The idea of entelechy was revived earlier this century by philosophers and scientists, such as Hans Dreisch, to indicate a nonmechanistic vital force that urges an organism to self-fulfillment. Henri Bergson proposed a similar notion with *élan vital,* which he saw as a creative force pulsing through evolution, and responsible for the purposeful drives in all evolving organisms. Teilhard de Chardin, also, spoke of the "within" of things, a sort of psychic, subjective complement to the external forms and energy of atoms, cells, plants, and animals.

These later thinkers recognized that the conventional Darwinian view of evolution as the result of blind matter in motion (the mechanism of chance mutations in the DNA of an organism's genes) and external natural selection was inadequate to the task of explaining how evolution produces its multitude of species' forms, or how an individual organism develops its particular unique form from its single fertilized seed cell.

The mechanistic models fail to account for biological phenomena such as morphogenesis (how an organism develops its particular overall form and the specific forms of its organs); speciation (how one species may so radically change its form so as to become a new species); teleological processes (how organisms develop purposeful goal-directed behaviors);

and self-organizing fields (how living things can ward off the chaos and decay of entropy for the life of the organism). Faced with such mysteries, philosophers, biologists, and psychologists have sought for alternative explanations to the exclusive dogmatism of mechanism and matter. It seems as if something else may be at work in evolution and in the unfolding of our personal lives. It is the entelechy of an acorn, for example, to be an oak tree; it is the entelechy of a baby to be a grown-up human being; it is every individual's entelechy to be uniquely who he or she is.

In his dream work with clients, Jungian analyst Edward Whitmont recognized the presence of entelechy shaping the forms that arise in a person's psyche (images and symbols) and soma (bodily illnesses and injuries).[13] For Whitmont, entelechy complements and augments the current preference in Western philosophy, science, and medicine for purely physical determinism. The conventional notion of "determinism" reduces all life processes—including the operations of our psyches—to mechanistic causes. Such a science reduces us to little more than complex thinking machines, automatons, with no free will, no power to exercise choice against the random winds of fate.

In contrast, entelechy combines the sense of a "given" purpose with the sense of a freedom to resist or accept the unfolding of our unique purpose. We are not blindly driven or determined. Yet it is as if we were each dealt a specific hand of cards, and our task in life—Whitmont calls it our life's "drama"—is to exercise our consciousness in how we "play" our hand. It invokes the image of sailing a ship: The movement of the ship is constrained by its particular bulk, by the turbulence of the waves, by the ocean currents, and by the caprice of the winds—yet as captain and crew of our own ships (our self-consciousness blending with our unique entelechy or essence) we do have choice and power in the unfolding of our destiny. We must blow with the winds of fate; nevertheless, we have the option for what Buckminster Fuller called "trim-tabbing": making slight adjustments to the rudder that can result in major shifts of direction.

Working with his clients, Whitmont acknowledged that the dynamics of illness and healing (both psychological and somatic) are expressions of our inherent entelechy, our individual pulse of purpose informing us that we may be off-course and calling our attention to the need for a course correction, some adjustment in the forms of our life's "drama."

Ontologically, soma and psyche are all one reality—body and mind invariably go together. They go together not as two separate modes of being that mysteriously interact; they go together in the sense that body is implicit in mind, and vice versa. Physicist David Bohm expressed a similar idea when he spoke of phenomenal, explicate reality enfolded or implicit in the universal "holomovement" of the implicate order.[14] As embodied beings, we experience both explicate body and implicate mind. And when we attempt to express (make explicit) this experience we invariably introduce a conceptual dualism: We speak of body and mind as if they were separate and distinct. The mind-body problem arises only when we conflate this conceptual and linguistic dualism with an ontological dualism of substance.

Another way to talk about the relationship between body and mind is as a coupling of matter and form, akin to Aristotle's hylomorphism and Bruno's *mater-materia*—where "form" is dynamic, the *in*-forming process giving shape to matter. Psychodynamic theorists such as Carl Jung (1953–1979, CW-9), Marie-Louise von Franz,[15] and Edward Whitmont[16] have expressed this psyche-soma relationship in terms of dynamic "archetypes" underlying and shaping the development of our emotional and somatic selves. Again, these archetypes are not external forces acting on separate substance; they are expressions of the intrinsic entelechy of matter itself.

## THE CHINESE CONCEPTS OF "LI" AND "CH'I"

We should be careful about how we interpret this way of talking about the mind-body relationship in case we create an impression that either mind or form has priority over matter or body. That would be a misunderstanding. Form and matter always go together, as both Aristotle and Bruno insisted. Medieval neo-Confucian Chinese expressed a similar idea in their concepts of *li* and *ch'i*.[17] *Li* is a universal organizing principle, an intrinsic patterning, while *ch'i* refers to what we might call "matter-energy." *Li* and *ch'i* always go together: Matter-energy could not exist without some form or patterning, and the patterning naturally expresses itself through some substance.

For the Chinese, a thing is always "becoming" itself and, at the same time, changing into something else. Hence, their emphasis on "relations" and organizing principles according to which parts unite in wholes. The key word in Chinese thought, as the great sinologist Joseph Needham pointed out, is "order" or "above all *pattern* and *organism*."[18] The Chinese word is *li,* and is perhaps best left untranslated, though it definitely has the meaning of "principle of organization,"[19] or a tendency toward order, associated with the "within" of matter, of *ch'i.*

The complementary concept to *li,* therefore, is *ch'i,* matter-energy, the "without," which if left to itself would tend to run down into chaos. In the Chinese worldview, the "within" and "without," *li* and *ch'i,* are mutually dependent. Matter-energy alone, without the organizing action of *li,* is unthinkable; it could achieve no form or order. And *li* alone, without the basis of *ch'i,* is likewise unthinkable. Organization has to be organization of something.

The Chinese worldview was essentially organic. According to Needham, they saw the universe as not only capable of self-organization, but of realizing the highest expressions of human consciousness:

> Composed of matter-energy (*chhi*) and ordered by the universal principle of organisation (*Li*), it was a universe which, though neither created nor governed by any personal deity, was entirely real, and possessed the property of manifesting the highest human values (love, righteousness, sacrifice, etc.) when beings of an integrative level sufficiently high to allow of their appearance, had come into existence. This was a world-outlook consonant with science indeed . . .[20]

As we have seen, from the time of Plato, Greek philosophy tended to split spirit and matter apart and conceive of them in some sort of opposition. The soul or spirit was seen to be struggling with material bodies, either trying to impose and maintain order and form, or spirit was understood to be longing to escape from the imprisoning restrictions of material form. Hence Western knowledge has been afflicted with what I have been calling a "pathology," and what Needham called "the typical schizophrenia of Europe"[21]—its inability to bridge the fissure between mechanistic materialism and theological spiritualism. This antagonism between matter and spirit, between atomistic materialism and theological idealism, has left consciousness or the psyche as victim, without satisfactory meaning or explanation. The Chinese never experienced this metaphysical conflict since they viewed the world as a continuum passing from the void at one end to the grossest and most complex matter at the other—the universal energy (*ch'i*)-organization (*li*) matrix.

In ancient Chinese cosmology, *ch'i* and *li* issue from the void (or the unmanifest and unknowable Tao). At its origin, *ch'i* is the rarest rarefied field of matter-energy, and *li* is the "within" of *ch'i*, organizing matter-energy into a growing, organic hierarchy of complexity thresholds. But the organization of *ch'i* is not a simple one-way process. It is also acted on by the waxing and waning oscillations of the primordial cosmic principles of *yin* and *yang*. *Ch'i*, therefore, is constantly in flux, undergoing endless condensations and dispersions, producing transitory vortices of complexity throughout the cosmos. These vortices may condense and disperse in a multitude of ways, but due to the organizing influence of *li*, there is a definite order in the formation of things.

The Sung philosopher Chang Tsai underlined the eternal "becomingness" of the world, and pointed out that only by the careful examination of the cyclical nature of *ch'i* could we achieve what we call scientific understanding. And Chuang Tzu emphasized the cyclical and organic development of *ch'i* to the complexity threshold of life, and its eventual decay into death and disorder. Yet there is always the one *ch'i* in the universe, concentrating here and spreading itself thin over there.

The Taoist and neo-Confucian use of the concept *ch'i*, applying it to mean matter *and* energy, predated by more than a thousand years their equivalence by Einstein in Europe. Today, we are inclined to accept this equivalence without much question; it almost seems obvious to us. But it is not at all obvious; it took perhaps the greatest genius of twentieth-century Europe to express it formally. Chu Hsi in the Middle Ages, and Chuang Tzu hundreds of years before that, had come near to the same idea in the concept of *ch'i*. Furthermore, the naturalistic outlook of ancient Chinese philosophers that fostered the concepts of complementary *ch'i* and *li* is very similar to the modern view of the universe as organic, and process philosophers see it. The Taoist and neo-Confucian sages developed a philosophy of nature far more aligned with modern thinking, for instance in the works of Whitehead and some quantum philosophers such as David

Bohm, than the European philosophies of the eighteenth and nineteenth centuries. Today orthodox science recognizes only *ch'i* or matter-energy as being real.* But the ideas of organicist philosophers have been filtering through into biology, physics, and cosmology, where *li,* or nonmaterial organizing fields, exists at all levels of the organic hierarchy.

Both *li* and *ch'i* are of equal ontological and cosmic significance; neither is more real than the other. They represent the "within" and the "without," the proto-psychic and the proto-physical nature of the primordial universe evident in the process philosophies of Whitehead, Bergson, and Teilhard de Chardin.

In Chinese philosophy, consciousness does not present the same sort of awkward problems that have befuddled Western thinkers struggling with mind-body relations. *Li* and *ch'i* are in everything, or rather everything is made of *ch'i* according to the organizing fields or patterns of *li.* As *li* produces more complex patters of *ch'i,* matter-energy ascends the organic hierarchy until the threshold of self-reflective consciousness is reached. Thus all human mentality is the result of an evolutionary process. In the twelfth century the neo-Confucian philosopher Chu Hsi had this to say about consciousness:

> Someone asked whether consciousness is an inward stirring of something spiritual or due to activity of *ch'i?* The philosopher answered, "it is not entirely a question of *ch'i* because the *li* of consciousness exists beforehand. *Li* alone is not conscious, but when *li* is combined with *ch'i,* then consciousness arises. Take, for example, the flame of this candle: It is because it receives so much good wax that we receive so much light."[22]

When Chu Hsi says, "the *li* of consciousness exists beforehand," he is referring to the *logically* prior necessity of *li;* he does not mean that *li* precedes *ch'i* in time—*chronologically.* The ontological complementarity of *li* and *ch'i* is apparent when he goes on to say, "*li* alone is not conscious, but

---

*Western scientific notions of matter-energy, in fact, are not nearly as comprehensive as the Chinese idea of *ch'i*—which includes forms of "subtle energy" yet to be detected by modern scientific instrumentation.

when combined with *ch'i,* then consciousness arises." Both are needed: Consciousness is always embodied.

When we recognize the essentially organicist thinking behind terms such as *li* and *ch'i,* we can see how the ancient Chinese managed to bridge the split—or rather avoided creating it—between the theological view of some celestial law-giver ordering things from above, and the materialist view that order arises by chance. In the Chinese view, the order and harmony in the universe are neither divinely inspired nor the serendipity of chance arrangements, but result from the spontaneous cooperation of all organisms that follow the *interior* necessities of their own natures. Echoing Anaximander's concept of the rotating *apeiron,* the neo-Confucian Chang Tsai wrote: "All rotating things have a spontaneous force, and thus their motion is not imposed upon them from outside."[23]

This spontaneous "force" or "law" is the combined effect of *li* and *ch'i,* the Tao of all beings, and is intrinsic to them (their entelechy), whatever their level of organization or complexity. It is a natural, organic *patterning* of nature, rather than an imposed law. According to Needham:

It is the law to which parts of wholes have to conform by virtue of their very existence as parts of wholes. And this is true whether they are material parts of material wholes, or nonmaterial parts of nonmaterial wholes. . . .

"Law" was understood in a Whiteheadean organismic sense by the Neo-Confucian School. One could almost say that "law" in the Newtonian sense was completely absent from the minds of Chu Hsi and the Neo-Confucians in their definition of *Li;* in any case it played a very minor part, for the main component was "pattern," including pattern living and dynamic to the highest extent, and therefore "organism."[24]

The terms *Tao* and *li* can have similar meanings, and are fundamental to the Chinese organismic concept of "pattern." Tao may be understood as the Great Pattern, a way or tendency within which the innumerable conglomerations of *ch'i* are ordered into subsidiary patterns according to *li.* The complementarity of *li* and *ch'i,* of the "within" and the "without," is fundamental to the organic nature of change in patterns anywhere in the cosmos. Organic change always arises from within.

Without any transcendental supreme deity consciously directing the changes in the universe, and without leaving it all to chance or external natural laws, the Chinese Taoists and neo-Confucianists could apprehend how there could yet be complexity and multiplicity without chaos and confusion. Everything moves, acts and reacts, and changes according to the Tao, to its own *te* (virtue), or *li,* according to the intrinsic nature of its existence— its entelechy. *Li,* then, can be understood to refer to an active principle in nature, "within" all things, the process that gives form to matter.

## EMBODIED CONSCIOUSNESS

Combined, the concepts of process and form suggest a dynamism, a patterning we may call, for simplicity, "in-formation"—the process of forming from within. Given the fundamental existential coupling between in-formation and matter, we can see how this has practical application in our real-world lives, in our "being-in-the-world" to use Heidegger's evocative phrase. We know from direct experience that we cannot uncouple our mind from our body (except conceptually). As day-to-day lived experience, our body and our consciousness always go together. Whenever we attempt to divorce them, we create a psychological or physiological pathology (or both). We can know our body only through the process we call "mind," through the action of consciousness. This is almost so obvious it may seem redundant. Of course, we can gain knowledge about the body only if we use our mental faculties: Knowing cannot take place without consciousness. But such "obviousness" is actually a hangover from our Cartesian inheritance. For we cannot know the body through our mind without at the same time knowing consciousness through our body. In a very literal sense: The body knows itself—it *feels.*

As human beings, we are grounded in our bodies; they are our vehicles for the practical business of getting on with living. We are embodied beings. But our bodies are not separate from our consciousness; they are the media through which we experience our being-in-the-world, through which we experience our selves and the world. Of course, this in no way implies that our bodies or brains generate consciousness, as various forms of materialism claim. On the contrary, our bodies are particular expressions of the in-formation, entelechy, or *li*—the intrinsic organizing principle—that we happen to be.

This was Descartes's blind spot. In formulating his famous *cogito*— "I think, therefore I am"—he dismissed the empirical groundedness of his being in his body. Without a brain, without a body, his consciousness would not have even come up with the idea of doubting anything, never mind everything—the starting point of his revolutionary philosophy.

The empirical fact is that whatever the true, ultimate nature of matter, we, as living human beings, have no consciousness separate from embodied form. Like *hyle* and *morph*, and *ch'i* and *li*, they go together—*always*.

This is not to deny the possibility of "disembodied consciousness" or of some form of survival beyond biological death.* For when we speak of "disembodied" consciousness, we usually mean, "not embodied in our biological body." It remains possible that our being may have (or be capable of having) more than one form of body. Many of the traditions that express the core wisdom of the perennial philosophy—Vedanta, Tibetan Buddhism, Theosophy, or Rudolf Steiner's Anthroposophy, for example—speak of different "subtle" bodies. It may be that such bodies are, as claimed, finer, subtler, less dense manifestations or organizations of some deep universal field of energy. Or, such bodies may be expressions of "energy fields" at different dimensional levels, distinct from our familiar space-time field of energy. Whatever the nature of such energies or fields (or whatever we choose to call them) they would still be "bodies," occupying some kind of dimensionality (even if these putative dimensions were wholly different from our notion of three-dimensional space). It is quite conceivable that such bodies could exist independently of our biological bodies—like Rupert Sheldrake's morphic fields.[25] But any consciousness

---

*Reports of out-of-body experiences (OBEs) are so numerous and widespread throughout geography and history that it would be nothing short of dogmatic scientism to dismiss them. However, if the mind-body model proposed here is correct, then so-called OBEs would be more accurately described as "out of *this* (familiar biological) body" but would still involve the subject's consciousness being associated with some subtler form of body (for instance, possibly a *ch'i* body). Perhaps we should rename such events "UBEs"—ultra-body experiences?

or intelligence associated with them would still be the expression of ent-elechy in-forming or processing *that* substance, whatever its nature hap-pened to be.

Given this radical view of the relationship between mind and body, between consciousness and matter, the implications for philosophy and science are far reaching. I began this book calling for a new cosmology story, and I have attempted to trace the lineage of the idea that the cos-mos itself is the unfolding of a great story. The evolution of galaxies, stars, and planets, and everything that populates them is nothing less than the intrinsic narrative and great adventure of matter—of matter that feels. Matter really is adventurous and evolution is its unfolding epic drama. And, as the bard said, we too must play our part.

I will conclude with a brief account of some of the elements of the new cosmology story suggested by this worldview of radical naturalism.

## Elements of the New Story

Evidence from the new sciences—such as quantum nonlocality and self-organization from chaos—supports many of the new ideas in postmod-ern philosophy and cosmology.[26] With this new perspective we can now embrace the actuality of consciousness and meaning in a self-organizing cosmos. Elements of the new story will include: (1) complementarity rather than dualism, (2) organicism rather than mechanism, (3) holism complementing reductionism, (4) interconnectedness rather than separate-ness, (5) process rather than things, (6) synchronicity as well as causal-ity, (7) creativity rather than certainty, (8) participation and engagement rather than objectivity. But most of all, the new cosmology will empha-size (9) that matter is inherently sentient *all the way down,* and (10) that, therefore, nature, the cosmos—*matter itself*—is inherently and thoroughly meaningful, purposeful, and valuable in and for itself. Nature, we must see, is sacred.

Within this "new" cosmology story, the foundations for a new par-adigm are in place: A sense of the cosmos where all bodies, including human bodies, resonate and participate in the web of cosmic matter, mat-ter that is intrinsically sentient and capable of nonlocal communication of *feelings,* where one body's being literally *incorporates* the being of other bodies both local and nonlocal.

## "DISEMBODIED BODIES"

The central problem with the "old story" is that it presents us with not only "disembodied" souls (à la Descartes), or even with "disensouled" bodies (Newtonian mechanics, positivism, materialism), but it also presents us with *disembodied bodies.* A "disembodied body" is an individual clump of matter (a body) existing independently and isolated from other clumps of matter (except where living organisms need to ingest other organisms or parts of them for nourishment, or to exchange genetic material for propagation of the species). This is the worldview that regards the "environment" (the rest of nature) as incidental, only contingently relevant, or as a source of nourishment. According to this view, the ontological relevance—the being of the body—is self-subsistent. This, in other words, is the *substance* view of bodies—bodies as isolated, independent clumps of self-subsisting matter.

## EMBEDDED BODIES

In contrast, the "new view" of the body sees it as a node in a creative matrix of material processes, *embedded* within an ecology of other interdependent bodies. It is a view of the body as "embedded and embodied," where the being of each body is interdependent with the flux and procession of relationships within the matrix of other bodies.

## RADICAL "MATERIALISM"

But the "body as a node in a creative matrix of material bodies" also involves a view of *matter* radically different from the dominant story's interpretation of it. In this new view, *matter is inherently sentient* all the way down. Matter itself has the intrinsic capacity for *feeling;* it is intrinsically experiential and subjective. Matter, in other words, is itself the bearer of consciousness. Thus, *bodies embedded in the creative matrix of matter are equally embodiments of the creative matrix of mind.*

Besides being a radical ontology, this also implies a radical epistemology—a way of knowing the presence of consciousness in other beings. If we accept radical naturalism, where all matter-energy is subjective and sentient, and where the being of other bodies is literally incorporated into one's own being, then we can know the *presence* of others directly. Such an epistemology would complement first- and third-person perspectives with a second-person perspective that accounts for shared knowing between subjects. Otherwise, the presence of consciousness in all matter remains speculation or, at best, a logical deduction. Empirical knowledge of sentience in other creatures requires direct experience of presence in others—that is, *intersubjectivity*. Radical naturalism implies an epistemology of shared feeling. An epistemology of intersubjectivity, therefore, is a way around the otherwise impenetrable "problem of other minds" discussed in chapter 5, "Problems of Consciousness."

## NATURE IS SACRED

In this view, then, nature, composed of experiential matter, is inherently and thoroughly sentient. It is intrinsically meaningful and purposeful. Nature is valuable in and for itself. It is sacred.

## COSMIC FEELING

Nature, of course, does not end at the boundaries of the biosphere, or even at the atmosphere. Terrestrial nature is itself an embodied node in the larger ecology of cosmic processes. With this new story comes a new ontology, where the basic ingredients of the world are not substantial things, but *experiential events or processes*. This is a "process ontology," where all parts of the cosmos feel (Whitehead used the word "prehend") the being and presence of other "organisms."

And since, as Whitehead showed, all beings are organisms—including cells, molecules, atoms, and "elementary" particles—it is clear that this cosmic feeling operates without the medium of the five senses and their sensory organs and nervous systems. Cosmic feeling, in other words, is *extra-sensory* or nonsensory communication. Without the constraints of the physical (including electromagnetic) contiguity required of the physiological sensory organs, cosmic feeling may operate via action-at-a-distance.[27]

## COSMIC ORGANISM

Therefore, all of nature, the cosmic organism, is, at least potentially, in mutual communication with all of its constituents. All the multitude of "moments of experience" that constitute each body can *feel* the presence of every other body in the universe. Meaning, not mere mechanism, becomes the connection between beings; synchronicity, not causality, patterns these meanings and connections—and the cosmos as a whole resonates to the creative meaning of its own never-ending story, a narrative of ensouled matter and embodied experience, embracing the sublime paradox of "subjective objects," of multiplicity-in-unity.

# Conclusion

The solution of the mind-body problem, then, begins by recognizing that mind and matter are not distinct substances. The Cartesian error was to identify consciousness as a kind of substance, and not to recognize it as a process or as dynamic form inherent in matter itself. Mind is the self-becoming, the self-organization—the *self-creation*—of matter. Without this, matter could never produce consciousness. Throughout this book, my central thesis has been: It is inconceivable that sentience, subjectivity, or consciousness could ever evolve or emerge from wholly insentient, objective, nonconscious matter-energy. Consciousness and matter, mind and body, *li* and *ch'i* always go together. They are a unity, a nondual duality.

The paradox is that we must speak of this unified reality of "body-mind," of "form-process," in dualistic terms. The singular nature of the ground of being is, ultimately, unrepresentable and ungraspable. We may hint at it with words such as "psychoid," "archetypes," "entelechy," "essence," "Self," "Spirit," or "Tao"—but once conceived or uttered such words block out the light of being itself. Our languages can only point like fingers at the moon. The "what is" does not stand still—any more than the "now" has any meaning beyond the momentary flow of experience. Yet it is all we have and are.

# CONCEIVING THE "INCONCEIVABLE"?*

Having spent the last three hundred or so pages developing the thesis of radical naturalism, calling on the long lineage of supporting arguments for panpsychism and panexperientialism, I will now risk undoing the whole thing. Not only is this thesis at stake, but my whole intellectual orientation, years of dedicated research into the issue of the mind-body problem, is now on the line.

The issue is this: The underlying premise of radical naturalism (and therefore of panpsychism and panexperientialism) is the notion—no, the *assertion*—that mind cannot emerge from wholly insentient matter. More specifically, and more emphatically, it is *inconceivable* that subjectivity could emerge from pure objectivity. If the world began as wholly objective matter-energy, without even a minimal trace of subjectivity, then there is no conceivable way that first-person experience could ever emerge in the cosmos. The universe would always and forever be unexperienced and unknown. It would never contain a point of view, not even a "view from nowhere," to use Thomas Nagel's famous and evocative phrase.[1] There would be no point of view, period. You simply can't get "here" from "there."

Yet very clearly and definitely the world does contain a point of

---

*An earlier version of this chapter previously appeared in the *Journal of Consciousness Studies* 7, no. 4 (2000), as "Conceiving the Inconceivable? Fishing for Consciousness with a Net of Miracles."

view—there is a view from "here." Following the lead of Campanella and Descartes, I can be certain of one thing: I am thinking, I am conscious, I am experiencing, I know what it feels like to be me. In short, I have a subjective point of view. That is certain. And, since I am not inclined to solipsism, I am willing to bet that you, too, have a point of view. In fact, I am willing to bet that the universe is populated with countless billions of viewpoints. Subjectivity is an indisputable fact.

Given this fact, and the premise of the inconceivability of subjectivity arising from pure objectivity, I am compelled to conclude that the universe could not *ever* have been *purely* objective. There must have been, *always,* something of the nature of subjectivity inherent in the universe. This is the lynch-pin of my thesis of "radical naturalism"—that the raw "stuff" of the universe, its primordial "matter," must have always possessed an "interiority" (Wilber), a "within" (de Chardin), an "occasion of experience" (Whitehead), a quantum of consciousness (Young), a capacity for a subjective viewpoint (Nagel), a self-organizing "intelligence" (Bruno). Matter, in other words, as I have argued here, is, and was always, intrinsically intentional, significant, and meaningful.

Thus, the inconceivability of objective matter giving rise to subjective experience is the foundational premise of radical naturalism, panexperientialism, and panpsychism (and, as a matter of fact, it is also an argument that supports idealism). If this foundation were to be removed, the entire edifice of radical naturalism and panexperientialism would come tumbling down.

In his essay on "Panpsychism" in the *Encyclopedia of Philosophy,* Paul Edwards asked a penetrating and challenging question: "What would the universe have to be like so that there would be no evidence for panpsychism?"[2] His point was that the ontological issue of the presence (or absence) of mind in matter could not be resolved by empirical evidence alone. Panpsychism, he concluded, could therefore not be a scientific position (and, presumably, by implication must be "mere" metaphysics).

The argument is this: Given that scientific methodology involves observation and measurement, and (based on such data) the possibility of prediction (leading to confirmation or refutation), how would it be possible to refute (or confirm) the attribution of consciousness or subjectivity to some entity? Since we cannot observe or measure subjectivity, its inference remains untestable and unempirical. Even if we had empirical evidence (which we don't) that the elements that constitute conscious, subjectively experiencing organisms, such as ourselves, were utterly different from the elements in some nonhuman creature (say, an extraterrestrial alien), a panpsychist could always say that would just indicate how *very different* that creature's consciousness would be from ours. There is no empirical* difference (that is, a detectable difference in physical composition or behavior) that could confirm or refute the presence of consciousness.

The fact that we would be saddled with an enormous, perhaps even insurmountable, epistemological problem of knowing "What is it like to be an alien?" would not necessarily deter a panpsychist nor invalidate his or her claim. It would always be possible for a panpsychist to come up with an ad hoc postulate of "different" consciousness. Just because alien material composition may be utterly different from ours would not entitle us to assume that such a creature did not enjoy subjective experience. This same line of argument may be applied even more forcefully to creatures and entities that *do* share our elemental make up, such as bats, dogs, cats, worms, brain cells, amoebae, viruses, DNA molecules, atoms, electrons, quanta, and quarks. Just because their consciousness may be *very* different from ours, does not mean that they have *no* consciousness. The argument for consciousness all the way down, therefore, is not an empirical issue; it *is* metaphysical. It is based on an ontological assumption guided by an epistemological preference (the "Ep-On" loop) for a cosmological story that is coherent, consistent, and sufficiently adequate to account for all the data.

This is the argument I have been defending in this book. Among the data that exist in the universe, and that need to be taken into account, are the experiences of meaning, of purpose, of values—and, of course, of the mere fact of experience itself. Any complete cosmology must have a

---

*Remember that I'm here using "empirical" in the materialist tradition of Bacon, Hobbes, Locke, Hume, and Kant, meaning *sensory* experience—that is, data gained through some combination of our five human senses (or some physical extension of them). We do, of course, have "radical empirical" evidence for consciousness in the sense that William James advocated radical empiricism: accepting as valid data only and *all* phenomena that show up in our experience.

foundational ontology that is adequate to the full range of data, and that includes consciousness.

But now, to turn Edward's question on its head, what if we ask: "What would the universe look like if insentient, objective matter *could* give rise to sentience and subjectivity, and to the whole domain of intentionality, meaning, purpose, and value?" What if the "inconceivable" were, after all, conceivable? Well, if this apparent impossibility were possible, the universe might not look any different at all. In short, absolute materialism—rooted in the Cartesian assumption of wholly insentient matter—would be able to account for all the phenomena for which the panexperientialist cosmology of radical naturalism has been invoked.* We would then be left with a choice of ontologies: either absolute materialism (as in most modern science and philosophy) or radical naturalism (as proposed by panexperientialists and panpsychists). Would there be a criterion upon which to base our choice, or would we be tangled in an eternal "Ep-On" loop?

Given the fundamental premise of radical naturalism and panexperientialism, there is a very clear choice: namely, if absolute materialism *could* provide an explanation for subjectivity emerging from objectivity, then there would be no reason for supporting the panexperientialist position. In fact, as already suggested, the entire structure would collapse once we removed the lynch-pin keeping it all in place. If the inconceivable were conceivable, there would be no need for radical naturalism or panexperientialism.

Is there such an explanation? I have argued here that none of the major variations of materialism—from behaviorism to functionalism to eliminativism—can adequately account for subjectivity (for the intentionality and qualia of consciousness). They fail to meet the criterion of providing a comprehensive cosmology.

---

*However, ostensible psi phenomena such as telepathy, clairvoyance, psychokinesis—*any* phenomena involving extrasensory perception or action-at-a-distance—would, of course, remain anomalous and problematical within an absolute materialist worldview. A plausible explanation for the evolution of consciousness from the matter of brains could account for psi phenomena only if we assume that in producing consciousness, the brain is actually generating some form of highly subtle physical energy that *appears* to involve action-through-a-void.

In the interests of intellectual integrity, however, I must now disclose that after I had completed the first draft of this book I came across a theory that, if true, would be potentially fatal to my thesis, and could undo decades of research committed to elucidating an argument in support of radical naturalism and panexperientialism. Nevertheless, since my underlying motivation is to get at the truth behind the mind-body problem, rather than be hostage to any particular metaphysical position, I feel compelled to acknowledge what I think is the most coherent, consistent, and adequate explanation that I have yet encountered for the emergence of consciousness from insentient matter.

## Fishing for Consciousness

*A History of the Mind: Evolution and the Birth of Consciousness,* by experimental psychologist Nicholas Humphrey, had been buried in my pile of books for months. While I was putting together the final draft of this book, Humphrey's came to the top of my pile, and I began reading. Not only was I struck by the literacy of his style, and the easy accessibility of his ideas, I found that as he led me through the step-by-step logic of his theory, I could see no obvious point where his reasoning was flawed. When I finished the book I realized that even if his theory were incomplete or wrong—even if his particular model of how mind emerged from matter turns out to be factually in error—I was still left with the uncomfortable realization that the mere existence of such a theory meant that the previously inconceivable was now, at the very least, conceivable (even if it wasn't true). My thesis was in real trouble.

I will now outline Humphrey's theory of the "extended present" or of the "thickened moment," as he variously calls it.[3, 4] The following summary will condense the main steps in his argument. Here, I am interested only in the salient links in his chain of logic. Necessarily, I will not be able to fill in all the details, and I urge anyone interested in exploring Humphrey's theory to read his book. It is short, easygoing, and rewarding for anyone interested in the perennial issue of the mind-body relation.

Humphrey calls his book *A History of the Mind* because he explains consciousness as the result of evolution, which is *the* major part of history. He is interested in the grand sweep, which means going back to the creation of Earth (and even earlier), because, as he says, he wishes "to make no preliminary assumptions about when mind and consciousness emerged," and also "to make no assumptions about objective reality." On the first point, he says:

> I take it for granted that the human mind does indeed have an evolutionary history, extending through nonhuman prototypes—monkeys, reptiles, worms—all the way back to the first glimmerings of life on Earth.

And on the second point:

> Before life emerged, let's say four billion years ago, when the planet Earth was formed, there were presumably no minds at all. It follows that four billion years ago the world was totally unexperienced and unknown.[5]

So, on point one, he is with the panexperientialists in assuming that consciousness goes back a long way, even to the first flourishings of life. In other words, like panexperientialists (and unlike many biologists), he does not assume that consciousness *per se* is an emergent property of higher brains and nervous systems. Something of the quality of human consciousness is to be found way back, even in single-celled creatures. And this "quality," of course, is nothing like introspective thought, or self-reflective feelings. It is something much more primitive, what he calls "consciousness as raw sensation," and "what it is like to experience consciousness from the inside."[6, 7]

With this definition, then, we know from the start that he is talking about consciousness as subjectivity, not merely the psychoanalyst's "conscious" (as contrasted with the "unconscious"), or the neuroscientist's neural correlates of mind, or the functionalist's or AI theorist's computer-simulated algorithms of mental operations such as computational thinking or symbol generation and syntax. That's what piqued my interest in the first chapter of his book: He was out to catch and to fry the very same "fish"* that I have been after all these years. He was after "subjective feeling," and he wanted to account for intentionality, meaning, and qualia, too.

But on point two, he broke rank with the panexperientialists when he assumed (as any self-respecting materialist would) that before life appeared on Earth, there was no such thing even resembling mind at all. When the planet formed "the world was totally unexperienced and unknown," and had been that way for the eleven or so billion years since the big bang. (So, despite what he says, he *does* make an assumption about "objective reality.") Taking the original meaning of "phenomenon" (from the Greek *phainein*, "to appear")—that is, "an event as it appears to an observer, as distinguished from what it might consist of in itself"[8]—he says of the big bang, that whatever it was like, "there was no phenomenal bang at the time it occurred."[9] At the big bang, there was no observer, no subjective point of view, therefore there was no phenomenon. There was only the raw physical event (which, of course, we can only infer because we now exist as experiencing subjects, to whom the residual three-degree background radiation—the faint "echo" of the big bang—is *now* a phenomenon). Back then, there only was the raw "is."

## GETTING WINE FROM WATER?

But between then and now, we know that consciousness did appear. The big question is how? Humphrey lays out the central problem of the mind-matter mystery in terms of the human mind-brain puzzle. He lists three facts:

1. We experience subjective feelings, which are beyond description in purely physical terms. Phenomena such as "pain" are not a part of the objective world. They belong to a *first-person point of view*.
2. Subjective phenomena, such as the pain felt when we bite our tongue, are related to processes going on in our brains. These processes are

---

*Humphrey employs the metaphor of catching a fish to indicate his approach to coaxing consciousness out of its hidden lair in evolution: "I believe the way to catch consciousness will be to tickle it. That is to say we should discover where it is lying, approach it slowly, and then charm it into our hands" (1992, p. 37).

describable in the objective language of physics and chemistry. They are accessible from a *third-person point of view.*

3. So far as we know, "Fact 1 wholly depends on Fact 2. In other words the subjective feeling is brought about by the brain processes."[10] And it is this third fact—the mind-body relation—that has been inexplicable for science and philosophy ever since the problem was noticed.

Faced with this mystery, the great nineteenth-century British evolutionist T. H. Huxley said:

> How it is that anything so remarkable as a state of consciousness comes about as a result of irritating nerve tissue is just as unaccountable as the appearance of the Djin, where Aladdin rubbed his lamp.[11]

And Colin McGinn expressed a similar sense of cognitive defeat:

> Somehow, we feel, the water of the physical brain is turned into the wine of consciousness, but we draw a total blank on the nature of this conversion. . . . The mind-body problem is the problem of understanding how the miracle is wrought.[12]

Invoking or materializing the *Djin* and turning water into wine require magic if not miracle. Getting consciousness from "the dark foam of insensate matter," as Humphrey poetically calls it, has seemed to many philosophers and scientists to require no less of a miracle.[13] It is what I have been calling "the inconceivable." But having rejected the panexperientialist position by assuming that in the beginning the universe consisted only of insensate matter, and given his "Fact 1," Humphrey is convinced that such a "miracle" *must* have, in fact, occurred. Of course, he is intent on arguing that it was not at all a miraculous event, but something wholly natural, wholly explicable by normal materialist science.

He declares his physicalist bias later: "The first task of a theory of consciousness has to be to . . . describe a physical process in the brain whose properties, at the appropriate level of description, correspond to the properties of felt sensations."[14] Precisely such a description is what Humphrey claims to deliver.

Here's my interpretation of how he structures the components of his theory. I'll identify four major elements, each of which involves its own chain of argument. The major elements are

1. The importance of boundaries;
2. The distinction between sensation and perception;
3. Sensations are "instructions"; and
4. The thick moment of the extended present.

## THE IMPORTANCE OF BOUNDARIES

Humphrey begins his opening chapter by declaring "Everything that is interesting in nature happens at the boundaries: the surface of the Earth, the membrane of a cell, the moment of catastrophe, the start and finish of a life."[15] He builds his theory as follows:

First—*no boundaries.* In the beginning, the big bang was a wholly physical event, wholly nonsubjective. (He wouldn't use "wholly objective" because, as he rightly notes, something can only be objective if there exists a subjective point of view to contrast it with. Since there was no subjectivity, strictly speaking there was no objectivity either. There just was "is.") In the initial moments after the big bang the emerging universe was completely chaotic, an amorphous plasma of interfused "particles" and radiation. There was no distinctiveness or separateness to speak of. No individuality. No distinction between "here" and "there," no "inside" or "outside," and certainly no "self" or "other." Although a buzzing chaos of light-speed activity and interacting forces, the universe was "dead," intrinsically inert and meaningless.

Second—*physical boundaries emerge.* After billions of years of cosmic expansion and progressive cooling of the universe, individual particles, atoms, and molecules had formed. As a result of chemical evolution in the hearts of stars, matter began to settle down, stabilizing as chemical elements. Planets, rich with complex chemical ingredients, formed, and from these ingredients, a primeval soup brewed under intense solar and cosmic radiation.

Third—*chemical boundaries and self-replication emerge.* Through the action of chance collisions of molecules in the primordial soup, the first molecules capable of making copies of themselves happened to form. The first raw materials of life, "packets of worldstuff,"[16] emerged with an increasing capacity for maintaining the integrity of their boundaries, and improving their capacity for reproduction.

Fourth—*biological boundaries emerge.* Simple "packets" of self-replicating molecules, wrapped up in the protective sheath of a semipermeable membrane form the first primitive cells. These "creatures" are able to actively control the passage of information and energy across their membrane—the boundary separating what is "inside" from what is "outside." The evolution of membranes, primitive "skin," was crucial for the maintenance of life, and would be the deciding factor in the emergence of mind.

Fifth—*Discriminating boundaries/selective membranes.* The appearance of semipermeable biological boundaries gave rise to the first distinction between "inside" and "outside" and between "self" and "other."* These membranes, capable of allowing some external material in while keeping other stuff out, and also capable of maintaining an optimal internal state of cooperation among its self-replicating chemicals and between these and the membrane, gave rise to the first distinction between what was "good" or "bad" for the organism. Anything that enhanced survival and reproductive ability was "good," anything that threatened these was "bad."

Sixth—*Natural selection kicks in and favors **sensitivity***. Through chance variations in the replicating mechanism, some copies of the original organisms would have developed membranes with greater selectivity or

---

*This is an interesting aspect of Humphrey's theory. The distinction between "inside" and "outside," based on a *physical* boundary, is the source of the distinction between "self" and "other." Now, as critics of materialist ontologies (such as Ken Wilber, in *Sex, Ecology, Spirituality: The Spirit of Evolution*) point out, there is a world of difference between "inside" (meaning a physical location) and "interior" (meaning a nonspatial experiential dimension). To equate the two is to collapse a fundamental ontological distinction. However, since it is precisely Humphrey's stated aim that the flat-level ontology of materialism is sufficient to account for subjectivity and consciousness, one of his first tasks is to show how "inside" (within a physical boundary) is, in fact, the origin of the sensation or experience of "interiority" and "self." If he succeeds in this, his theory poses a serious challenge to panexperientialism/radical naturalism and idealism.

sensitivity to discriminate between "good" and "bad" stimuli impacting on the organism's surface. Evolution would, therefore, favor those organisms that developed a greater sensitivity for discrimination because they would have improved survival and reproductive "fitness."

Seventh—*Natural selection favors flexibility of* **response**. Again through the processes of chance variations and natural selection, some organisms would improve their "sensitivity," that is, their ability to react selectively at the location where the stimulus occurred. A greater repertoire of reactive responses, such as retraction of the surface away from "bad" stimuli, or expanding the surface to engulf "good" stimuli, would further enhance differential survival and reproductive fitness.

Eighth—*Natural selection favors* **nonlocal reactivity**. Organisms that developed the ability to *delay* and *displace* their responses, so that they didn't always immediately react at the spot on the surface where the stimuli impinged, would lead to increased flexibility of responses and improved adaptive fitness. With the evolution of nervous systems, organisms could relay information from one part of the surface to other parts. Such displaced reactivity would amount to a *delay* in the organism's response.

Ninth—*Natural selection favors* **affective reactions**. Discrimination between "good" and "bad" stimuli, coupled with an ability to move toward or away from the stimuli (with variations of these responses) amounts to "liking" what is good for "me" (the bounded individual) and "disliking" what is bad for "me." Using words "like" and "dislike" indicates the presence of "affect" or discriminatory sensitivity or "feelings" and, therefore, the appearance of protomentality.

The introduction of "like" and "dislike" is justified because the surface discrimination/sensitivity implies a *preference* for good over bad stimuli. Further, "like" also implies a preference for *self-similar* stimuli or objects because they can be assimilated through the membrane and more easily incorporated in the internal activities of the cell. The organism likes (selects/prefers) what is like itself (self-similar). And, from another perspective, to like (prefer) what is like (self-similar) implies that there is something it is *like* to be the *subject* within the self-boundary (subjectivity).

Thus at stage nine, we already have the basic ingredients for mind or consciousness: We have *subjectivity* within the bounded individual; we have *feeling* at the surface where the selectivity between incoming stimuli amounts to sensitivity; we have *affect* also at the surface where the variations in response patterns (moving toward or away) amounts to *preference* or unconscious choice between "like" and "dislike"; we have *meaning* and *intentionality* where events at the surface are discriminated as either "good" or "bad" for *"me"* (that is, the internal structure and dynamics of the membrane-encapsulated individual). Discriminatory sensitivity (sensory affect) based on distinctions or "preferences" for "good" or "bad" stimuli is, therefore, the basis of what later comes to be called "consciousness" or "experience."*

Tenth—*Delayed reaction patterns require stored representations, and that means* **mind.** With the evolution of displaced or nonlocal reactions to local stimuli, responses are *delayed,* and to some extent decoupled, from sensitivity. This means, in effect, that a "central site evolved, where representations—in the form of action patterns—were held in abeyance before they were put into effect. . . . The place where they were held in store could be said to be the place where they were held in mind."[17] Humphrey goes on to say:

> In short, animals first had "minds" when they first became capable of storing— and possibly recalling and reworking—action-based representations of the effects of environmental stimulation on their own bodies. The material substrate of the mind was nervous tissue. . . . The neural tube which forms the brain during embryological development derives from an infolding of the skin.[18]

This is a "first-pass" summary of Humphrey's theory of mind emerging from wholly insensate matter, and of subjectivity emerging from "objectivity." If, so far, this is a plausible story, then, already the radical materialist thesis of panexperientialism based on the "inconceivability" of such emergence is seriously weakened. But this is only the start. Humphrey

---

*Humphrey emphasizes that unless and until psychology reinstates the central role of "sensory affect," the sense of enjoyment, of pleasure and pain—which William Drummond in 1623 called "the organs of delight"—psychology will go on "fishing for consciousness in an empty pool" (1992, p. 51).

goes on to lay out in clear detail many more elements of his theory.

Thus far, his theory accounts only for the phenomenon of subjectivity, for how an animal can answer the question "What is happening to me?" or "What something is like for me." But the theory does not yet explain how the animal could account for "what is happening out there?"—for the external location or source of the incoming stimuli. And such an ability is of paramount importance. When an animal doesn't have to wait until a stimulus makes physical contact with its skin—for example, the feeling of a hawk's talons gripping the skin of a rabbit—the animal's survival will be significantly enhanced. If, instead, the animal can sense and interpret a distant stimulus, such as the hawk's shadow, as a "sign" for a hawk, then the animal can take timely evasive action. But this requires an ability to associate a (delayed) internal representation of the "sign" (the shadow) with an abstracted or stored memory of a representation of the "signified" (the hawk). And now we're really talking mind.

## SENSATION AND PERCEPTION

According to Humphrey, the evolution of consciousness involved the emergence of two distinct but complementary modes of representation: (1) internal representations of "what is happening to me," that is the "qualia of subjective feelings and first-person knowledge of the self," and (2) representations of "what is happening out there," of third-person "intentional objects of cognition and objective knowledge of the external physical world."[19]

We now come to the second major element of Humphrey's theory. Having established that the evolution of sensation may be explained as a natural consequence of increasing selectivity and sensitivity of the membrane encapsulating the individual organism, Humphrey's next step is to explain perception, and to emphasize how sensation and perception are different phenomena. His theory depends on interpreting sensation as oriented toward subjective events ("what is happening to me"), whereas perception is directed outward toward objective events ("what is happening out there"). In other words, evolution has given organisms two distinct but complementary modes of experiencing the world, two "alternative and essentially nonoverlapping ways of interpreting the meaning of an environmental stimulus arriving at the body."[20]

He finds that this portion of his theory has antecedents among psychologists such as Freud and an "obscure" psychologist of religion Edwin D. Starbuck, as well as in the writings of the eighteenth-century Scottish philosopher Thomas Reid (1710–1796). He quotes Reid from his *Essays on the Intellectual Powers of Man:*[21]

> The external senses have a double province—to make us feel, and to make us perceive. They furnish us with a variety of sensations, some pleasant, others painful, and others indifferent; at the same time they give us a conception of and an invincible belief in the existence of external objects. . . . This conception and belief which nature produces by means of the senses, we call *perception*. The feeling which goes along with perception, we call *sensation.*[22]

Humphrey defines sensation as a representation of "what is happening to me"; and perception is defined as a representation of "what is happening out there" (to "not me"). Sensation and perception may be related in either of two general ways, in parallel or serially:

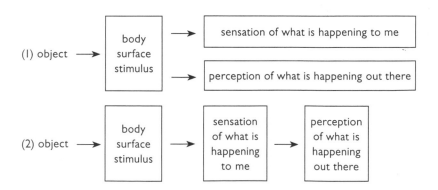

Since it is crucial for Humphrey's theory that perception can occur in the total absence of sensation, he goes with option (1). And as evidence in support of the "parallel" option, he devotes chapters to the psychological phenomena known as "skin-vision," "blindsight," and "visual agnosia." He says: "Sensation lends a here-ness and a now-ness and a me-ness to the experience of the world, of which pure perception in the absence of sensation is bereft."[23] Sensation is a mode of processing information that is focused on the subjective present, on immediate responsiveness, while perception is focused more on external object permanence, on future possibilities.

Later he points out that "Sensations prepare the subject to take immediate action to extend or escape or ameliorate his present situation *vis-à-vis* the stimulation arriving at his body surface."[24] And "The process of sensory representation need not involve much more than making an internal *copy* of the physical stimulus as it is occurring at the body surface; but the process of perceptual representation has to involve something more like making up a *story* about what this stimulus signifies to be occurring in the outside world."[25] The making of an internal copy is also another term for "imagery"—and imagery involves sending a signal back to the sensory center in the brain.

The distinction between sensation and perception, according to Humphrey, is this: *sensation* is "what is happening to me" at *my* boundary. It involves an internal representation, or "copy," of the stimulus as it concerns *this* membrane-encapsulated individual, this "self" or "ego." The sensation carries with it an affect-quality: the stimulus is either "good" or "bad" (or neutral) for the "self." Sensation is immediately *felt* in the present; it is oriented toward subjective experience, related to "I" or ego.

*Perception,* on the other hand, is about "what is happening out there" beyond my boundary. It is about the external, objective world of events. Perception involves representations of "signs" that signify something nonlocal; it is an *interpretation* about what the stimulus signifies about the state of the outside world. Since it is externally focused, perception is not about any specific "ego/self"—that is, anyone can perceive the same object (whereas only *"I"* have the sensation of what is happening to me).

In a nutshell, then: *sensation* is an internal (subjective) *copy* of the stimulus; *perception* is an interpretation, a *story,* about (objective) significance in the outside world. For example, sensation is *feeling* the hawk's claws in my skin *now;* perception is seeing the shadow (or hearing the squawk) and inferring that there is a hawk close by—and if I don't do something in the very near *future* I will feel those razor-sharp talons.

## The Basis of Consciousness

About halfway through the book, Humphrey begins to home in on his quarry. He has the silvery outline of the fish clearly in view, just below the surface. His hand is cupped underneath its belly, the tips of his fingers gently soothing its scales. He just needs to make a few more careful, charming moves before he scoops it out and lands it at his feet. One of the most important—and slippery—moves is to firmly establish sensation (as he has defined it) as the basis of consciousness. In chapter 15, he lists eight assertions that he believes he has already established. These include:

- To be conscious is essentially to have sensations: that is, to have affect-laden mental representations of something happening here and now to me.
- The subject of consciousness, "I," is an embodied self. In the absence of bodily sensations "I" would cease. *Sentio, ergo sum*—I feel, therefore I am.
- All sensations are implicitly located at the spatial boundary between me and not-me, and at the temporal boundary between past and future: that is, the "present."
- Mental activities other than those involving direct sensations enter consciousness only insofar as they are accompanied by 'reminders' of sensation, such as happens in the case of mental imagery and dreams.
- If and when we claim that another living organism is conscious we are implying that it too is the subject of sensations (although not necessarily of a kind we are familiar with).
- If we were to claim that a nonliving organism [such as a robot] was conscious, the same would have to apply.[26]

A few pages later he offers a more succinct definition of consciousness: "'to be conscious' is indeed essentially 'to have sensations'—or more generally 'to have affect-laden mental representations of something happening here and now to me.'"[27] And "any theory of consciousness that is not a theory of the having of sensations has failed to address the *real problem"*—which is that consciousness "has to involve the raw feel of 'what it is like to be me.'"[28]

Having committed himself to the virtual identity of sensation and consciousness, he goes on to reveal an apparent contradiction: "namely that certain states of mind can also enter consciousness that do not arise directly from stimulation of the sense organs."[29] In order to resolve the "contradiction," he says we have to answer the question "What is it to have sensations?" And he reemphasizes that "the function of sensations is to provide the subject with representations of 'what is happening to me'—originally to serve as a mediator of affect, but later with important secondary uses in connection with perception and imagery."[30]

But he does more than merely repeat himself. Given the central importance of sensation in his argument, he devotes an entire chapter to the "five characteristics" of sensation: "sensations *characteristically* (i) belong to the subject, (ii) are tied to a particular site in the body, (iii) are modality-specific, (iv) are present tense, (v) are self-characterizing in all these respects." We can take a look at these individually.

1. *"Sensations characteristically belong to the subject."* That is, "what is happening to me" means what is happening to "my *embodied* self," to that being inside the physical boundary between "me" and "not-me." Only "I" have my sensations—I *own* them, they are exclusively *mine*. No other bounded being has this relationship or point of view with regard to the sensations at this "me/not-me" boundary. My first-person point of view is, thus, wholly dependent on the location of my own bounded body. I can, of course, have a third-person view of my own body, too; a view that can be shared by many other observers. In other words, I can also *perceive* my body, just as other people can. But only I can both perceive and sense what is happening to my body.

2. *"Sensations are characteristically tied to a location in bodily space."* This point has already been touched on above: namely that sensations always occur at some particular location, a location defined by the coordinates of the target body. Quite simply, I *always* feel a sensation at a *particular location* in or on my body (for example, if I taste something, it is associated with my mouth; if I feel something with

my fingers, it is associated with my hand; and so on with the other senses). By contrast, my perceptions don't have to refer to any particular region of my body. I can perceive an object outside my body with any one or combination of my senses.

3. *"Sensations are characteristically modality-specific."* All sensations belong to a distinctive sensory modality—vision, touch, hearing, smell, taste. "Their absolute distinctiveness—the gulf between one modality and another—is one of the most mysterious facts about sensations. . . . There is no imaginable bridge."[31]* Perceptions, however, are never concerned with the nature of the stimulus as such, but with what it signifies about some condition in the external world.

4. *"Sensations are characteristically present-tense."* Whatever I sense is happening to me *always* happens in the present. "That is to say every sensation persists for roughly so long as the surface stimulation continues."[32] Perceptions can refer both to the past and future, as well as to the present. "Perceptions unlike sensations do not *exist* for any length of time. . . . Perception itself is not an enduring entity with a life of its own. . . . [it is] already complete—whereas sensations are generally . . . continuing and unfinished."[33]

5. *"Sensations are self-characterizing."* "Sensations tell their own story."[34] Unlike perceptions that require interpretation, sensations are known directly and immediately; they do not need to be inferred. They are "self-disclosing"; that is, they directly reveal the above four qualities or characteristics about themselves.

## SENSATIONS ARE "INSTRUCTIONS"

The next move, following elucidation of the five characteristics of sensations, is to explore more closely what is meant by the notion that "I own my sensations," that they belong exclusively to me. This is important because it is this sense of exclusive ownership that gives rise to the distinction between subjectivity and objectivity. Another term for "exclusive" ownership is

---

*This seems to ignore the well-documented phenomenon of synesthesia, where the usually clear distinction between the senses is bypassed or transcended. Some people can "taste shapes," "see sounds," or "hear colors." See, for instance, Richard Cytowic's *The Man Who Tasted Shapes*.

"private" ownership. No one else has access to my sensations. No one else *ever* has access to *my* pain. By contrast, my perceptions are not exclusive or private: They belong in the public domain. They are objective. Any number of people can perceive the nail sticking into my toe—but only I *feel* it.

I own my sensations, therefore, in a way that I don't "own" my perceptions. And it is this quality of ownership that is a major clue to Humphrey in his search for consciousness. He spends a chapter or two investigating the concept of ownership and its relationship to "volition." He shows us how the notion of ownership is ultimately derived from our awareness of voluntary control over our own bodies. I know that this is *my* body ultimately by the test of whether or not it or its parts move when I will them to. That's the basic criterion for deciding between my body and what is not my body. From this, he goes on to ask whether ownership of sensations, likewise, is because—"in some peculiar way"—they, too, are under executive orders? Answering this question affirmatively—that sensations are volitional or *intentional*—Humphrey wriggles his index finger and tickles the fish a little bit more. He's pointing at a line of argument that concludes:

> [any] mental state will be self-indicating if and only if it both refers to a particular site in the body and produces a physical disturbance at the very site referred to. . . . In fact any mental state that unites these two elements of referring to a site in the body and reaching out to create a disturbance at this site would belong to the class of bodily activities by definition. . . . We can conclude that sensations themselves are indeed a form of bodily activity.[35]

Sensations, in other words, are *instructions*. They are issued by the bounded self (in the form of nerve signals), directed to a particular site on its body to *create a physical disturbance at that particular bodily location.* Contrary to what people usually believe: Sensations don't just *happen to* us; they happen because we *create* them in response to a stimulus.

> Being "sensitive" need have meant, to begin with, nothing more complicated than being locally reactive: in other words, responding selectively at the place where the surface stimulus occurred.[36]

Later on in evolution, when organisms developed nervous systems they began relaying information from one part of the skin to other parts and caused reactions there; and those *self-initiated* reactions were felt as sensations at those other locations. The relayed and delayed reactions resulted in flexible patterns of action that *represented* the original stimulus. These "action patterns" were *affective,* in that they discriminated between welcome and unwelcome stimuli. Humphrey moves in closer now: "sensitivity evolved primarily as a means of *doing something about the stimulus at the point of stimulation.*"[37]

> The activity of sensing, even in human beings, is a direct descendent of the primitive affective response. The "sensory loop" has gradually lengthened. Nevertheless an unbroken tradition links the sensations of modern human beings to those original amoeboid wriggles of acceptance or rejection.[38]

Humphrey is moving, deliberately and carefully, toward the conclusion that what began in evolution as a local surface response to an external stimulus later became a centralized representation of a flexible action pattern (or set of instructions). In other words, what began as a real *bodily* activity, evolved into some sort of *brain* activity: "Sensations involve a sensory response, with a signal being sent from a central site back out to a peripheral location (originally to the body surface itself but later to a surrogate location at the cortex of the brain)."[39]

## THE "THICK MOMENT" OF THE EXTENDED PRESENT

The physicalist core of Humphrey's theory of consciousness—and where it differs ontologically from panexperientialist and idealist theories—is the derivation of sensation from mechanical reactivity at the boundary or surface of a membrane-encapsulated "packet of worldstuff"—wholly insensate worldstuff, at that. Sensation, then, is ultimately nothing more than highly refined loops of mechanical reactions of otherwise inert matter. And since, as we have seen, he defines consciousness in terms of sensation, he effectively presents a mechanical, materialist explanation of consciousness.

His challenge is to make his explanation account for the peculiar characteristics of consciousness, such as its "raw feel," its subjectivity, its qualia, its first-person perspective, its in-the-present quality, its intentionality and meaningfulness. And he claims to have done just this by describing the evolution of sensation from primitive acceptance-rejection responses to sophisticated representations of flexible action patterns centrally located in the brain. A key element in the development of this theory is the argument that *sensations are intentional*—that sensations are created by the host organism in the form of "instructions" relayed from the central nervous system to the periphery where they *create a physical disturbance.* This "physical disturbance" is what the organism experiences as the sensation.

However, there is a problem: If all the organism has to work with is "insensate raw stuff," purely physical matter, how could it produce *instructions?* It could certainly send "signals" down the nerve fibers (computers do something similar all the time), but signals differ from instructions in one critical respect. Whereas signals convey information from one location to another, "instructions" also involve intentionality and *anticipation.* Instructions convey an intended effect yet to be realized. In other words, instructions are oriented toward the future. This is a real problem for a physicalist theory of brain-mind relations. And it's a problem that Humphrey recognized: "No signal, no matter what its *effects* are, can be an instruction unless its sender *already has these effects in mind.*"[40]

One reason this is a major problem is that it threatens to send the theory off into an infinite regress. For the whole point of the theory is to provide an *explanation* of consciousness, yet here we seem to be compelled to assume that key elements of the theory themselves *already* possess mind or consciousness—namely, the brain cells involved in sending the instructions down the nerve fibers. And if the brain cells are conscious experiencing entities, how do we explain *that?* If their molecules are conscious. . . . The "infinite regress," of course, is panexperientialism— consciousness all the way down.

Since Humphrey is decidedly not out to present a panexperientialist theory, he is committed to avoiding the infinite regress of mind at all costs. And, consistent with the ingenuity of his theory so far, he comes up with a novel solution: the hypothesis of the "extended present." And it may be just at this point where we discover his theory's Achilles' heel. I will come back to this shortly, but for now it's interesting to note that his theory is potentially vulnerable at just the point where panexperientialism threatens to come back into the story.

Admitting that "a signal, just on its own, *cannot* amount to an instruction" and that a "pattern of nerve impulses traveling either to the body surface or the cortex cannot just on its own constitute an instruction,"[41] Humphrey's creative leap is to stretch time and insert a feedback loop. A "signal" can become an "instruction," he proposes, if a return signal from the body's surface informs the brain of the fate of the original signal. Thus, once in possession of the "end-state" information, the brain would "know" what the effect would be and therefore could anticipate the result. Such a scenario would, of course, involve "backward causation in time," where a future event informs or changes the state of a prior event. And *this* blatantly contradicts one of the foundation principles of physicalist science: the law of causality. This law states that a cause must necessarily (and therefore *always*) precede its effect. In fact, this is how "cause" and "effect" are defined, in terms of their sequential, temporal relations.

So Humphrey, in his efforts to provide a logical, coherent, and comprehensive explanation for the evolution of consciousness from wholly insensate matter, now finds himself on shaky ground. He is in real danger of slipping into the stream and scaring off the fish once and for all. His physicalist theory has come to this: In order to take the next step he is compelled to violate the very foundation of the system of physics he draws on to support his theory. He is about to fall into a fatal *reductio ad absurdum*.

But he recovers his equilibrium enough to make his decisive move: Admitting that "What becomes of something in the *future* . . . cannot change its *present* meaning," he counters that

> it all depends on what is meant by "present meaning": in particular, on when the "present" happens and on how long the "present" lasts. Suppose the present were to be stretched out a bit. Suppose it were to last long enough for the present and the past to overlap.[42]

In other words, what if the present moment was stretched sufficiently for the outgoing and return signals to overlap or interleaf their information. In such a situation, the outgoing signal could "know" what happened at the "end" of the line *before the outgoing signal completed its journey.* Now in possession of the "end-state" information, the original signal could anticipate its own effect and thereby qualify as an "instruction." *Et voila!* Humphrey weaves in the problematic anticipatory and intentional qualities of instructions into a purely physical system of feedback loops. He has turned water into wine, and landed the fish in the frying pan in one fell swoop.

> Conscious feeling, it has emerged, is a remarkable kind of intentional doing. Feelings enter consciousness, not as events that happen *to us* but as *activities* that we ourselves engender and participate in—activities that loop back on themselves to create the thick moment of the subjective present. . . . All we seem to have ended up with is a string of nerve impulses, or information, flowing around a physical circuit in the brain.[43]

But not so fast. Let's run that story by one more time. As Humphrey says, it all depends on what we mean by the "present," and "how long the present lasts." It all depends, in other words, on stretching time, by replacing the notion of instantaneous present with the notion of "extended present" or the "thickened moment." But how, exactly, does this feat come about? Is it any easier, or more meaningful, to "stretch the present" than to turn water into wine? In physics, the present has even less duration than a quantum has space. In fact, the present has no duration, or at best an infinitely short duration (which amounts to the same thing). Humphrey's solution is to bifurcate time into what he calls "physical present" and "subjective present."

> The "physical present," strictly speaking, is a mathematical abstraction of infinitely short duration, and nothing happens in it. By contrast the "subjective present" is arguably the carrier and *container* of our conscious life, and everything that ever happens to us happens *in it.*[44]

But where did the "subjective present" come from? It can't have come from the feedback loop of brain-sensation signals, since that is precisely what was *required* to allow the feedback loop to turn signals into instructions in the first place. It showed up in the theory as an ad hoc insertion by Humphrey *because his own theory compelled him to do so.* The theory contains *no explanation* for the appearance of "subjective time."

In order to avoid the infinite regress of panexperientialism, Humphrey had to bifurcate time, and invoke the ghost of subjectivity out of thin air (you can't have "subjective time" without subjectivity). Or, rather, he invoked subjectivity out of the raw material of his feedback loops. Either he created subjectivity out of nothing, or it was there *all the time* in the "packets of worldstuff" from which the feedback loops evolved. Since it makes no sense to say he created subjectivity out of nothing, we must conclude that it was there all along, intrinsic to the raw material of evolution.

The problem with Humphrey's theory is not so much the idea of "subjective time" as contrasted with "physical time." After all, as he said, the physicist's time is merely a mathematical abstraction of infinitesimal duration; or else the physicist's time is reduced to a dimension of space, completely devoid of any durational or experiential qualities. Rather than being problematical, then, subjective time may well be the only meaningful way of understanding durational time. Panexperientialists, such as David Ray Griffin, would be sympathetic to Humphrey's need to introduce the "subjective present," and would agree with his statement that the "'subjective present' is arguably the carrier and *container* of our conscious life, and everything that ever happens to us happens *in it*"—because, they would say, that's the only kind of present there is.[45]

Ironically, then, Humphrey's theory stands or falls on the notion of "subjective present," and if it stands, it does so because it must accept the panexperientialist ontology that subjectivity was present in matter all down the line. It was there in the first wiggles of the first amoebae, in the molecules that filtered through its boundary wall, and in the molecules of the membrane itself; it was there in the first self-replicating molecules, and in the atoms that constituted their helical spines; it was there in the primeval chemical soup, and in the photons radiating down on them from a sun more than ninety million miles away; it was there in the nuclear reactions in the hearts of the stars themselves; and it was there in the primordial plasma-radiation that filled the universe in the first few moments after the big bang. And it was there, too.

Despite Humphrey's clever and coherent analysis of the origins and evolution of sensations and consciousness, an analysis rich in subtleties and hues of logic and experimental data, he still ends up with colored water, thinking he has produced the "wine of consciousness." His colored water is a very good facsimile of the best vintage—but it is still only "fools' wine." Despite the almost imperceptible sleight of hand by which he introduced the "dye" of the subjective present, his physical facsimile of consciousness cannot produce the miracle. The fish is off the hook—and the inconceivable remains inconceivable.

# GLOSSARY

**Causal:** Causality is the view that every effect has a cause. If so, and if all causes are exclusively physical then materialism, mechanism, and determinism would be true. If consciousness is not *epiphenomenal* (q.v.) then some causes would be nonphysical—and though causality may still be true, materialism, mechanism, and determinism would not be true.

**Consciousness:** Two fundamental meanings: *Philosophical,* where "consciousness" refers to a *state of reality* characterized by interiority, subjectivity, sentience, feeling, experience, self-agency, meaning, and purpose. Anything that has any of these has consciousness. Anything that does not would be non-conscious—blank, void, vacuous, wholly objective. In short, it is contrasted with wholly *non*-conscious things (whatever they might be!).

*Psychological* consciousness, on the other hand, refers to *a state of consciousness* (e.g., awake, dreaming, joyful, fearful, mystical) above threshold awareness. It presupposes the existence of philosophical consciousness. Psychological consciousness is typically contrasted with the *un*-conscious, which is below threshold awareness (e.g., asleep, trance, coma, habit, instincts). Unconscious is not the same as *non*-conscious—the former still has some psychic or subjective activity present, the latter is *wholly* objective.

A third meaning of consciousness refers to higher mystical or spiritual states of consciousness typified by experiences of oneness, interrelatedness, compassion, and love. However, because *spiritual* consciousness is a *state* of consciousness (albeit higher or highest), it too qualifies as a form of psychological consciousness. It is typically contrasted with "unenlightened" or "unevolved" ordinary states of consciousness.

**Determinism:** The view that everything that ever happens is strictly determined by prior causes. It is contrasted with ideas such as randomness, free will, creativity, and choice.

**Emergence:** Any new property that comes into being from a combination of pre-existing objects that did not themselves possess that property is said to be emergent. Thus, in materialism, combinations of pre-existing matter (such as brain cells), which themselves are supposed to be wholly insentient (without any subjectivity or consciousness), are said to be responsible for the emergence of consciousness from the brain. If what emerges is without any power to cause anything to happen in the world, it is said to be not only emergent but also *epiphenomenal* (q.v.).

**Epiphenomenon:** An epiphenomenon is purely an effect of some cause without having any causal power of its own. Consciousness is said to be epiphenomenal if it hovers "above" (*epi*) the brain without having any causal influence on it. Epiphenomena are characterized by one-way "upward causation."

**Epistemology:** The branch of philosophy that studies the nature of knowledge. It asks questions such as "What ways of knowing are available to us?" "How can we know anything?" "How can what we know match what is real?" and "What constitutes *evidence* for what is real?"

**Insentient:** Any entity that is wholly devoid of *sentience* (q.v.)—of experience, subjectivity, consciousness, mind—is said to be insentient. It is "vacuous."

**Local:** When two or more events are connected through space-time via exchange of forces or signals, they are said to be local. A "local" event, then, may in fact cover vast regions of space-time as long as there is an unbroken chain of signals or forces at work.

**Materialism:** The worldview that claims everything that exists consists of material or physical objects, events, or forces and that the fundamental matter or physical stuff is "dead" or insentient.

**Matter:** Some of the great minds of history could not agree on what matter is:

Democritus: Atoms in the void.

Plato: Imperfect reflection of perfect Forms.

Aristotle: Pure potentiality. That which changes.

Plotinus: Nearest to non-being, furthest from spirit.

Augustine: Formless substrate. No existence by itself.

Aquinas: Prime substrate. Unknowable by sense or reason.

Bruno: *matter-materia.* The intelligent womb of nature.

Descartes: Extension in space.

Locke: Mysterious source of sensory qualities. ("We know not what.")

Berkeley: Something that doesn't exist.

Hume: Don't know.

Kant: Can't know.

Whitehead: Expired moments of experience.

Einstein: A form of energy.

Bohr, de Broglie, Heisenberg, Schrödinger: Uncertain quantum waves.

Eddington: Mostly ghostly empty space.

Bohm: Forms of explicate order.

**Mechanistic:** Mechanism goes hand-in-hand with most versions of materialism. It claims that all relationships in the universe involve pushes or pulls between bits of matter; everything operates like a machine. It is closely related to *"determinism"* and *"causal"* (q.v.).

**Noncausal:** If an event occurs spontaneously, i.e., without any prior cause, it is said to be "noncausal" or "acausal." It would be an effect without a cause. Examples would be pure randomness, pure choice, pure creativity. In Jungian psychology, the term "synchronicity" is used to refer to events that involve meaningful connections between mind and matter that are acausal.

**Nonlocal:** An event in one region of space-time that is connected (causally or acausally) with another region of space-time without any force or signal passing between them is nonlocal. Its effects are not confined to any particular local region of space-time. A nonlocal effect is radically opposite to a mechanistic effect.

**Objectivity:** Any event or object that exists independently of, or uninfluenced by, any perceiving mind is said to be objective. Its existence is wholly external. Objectivity, in this sense, means knowledge of such objects, where the act of knowing does not change the object in any way.

**Ontology:** The branch of metaphysics that studies the nature of being. It is the study of the "furniture of reality"—what kinds of entities actually exist? Fundamental ontology studies the basic-level kinds of entities. Following Descartes, the big question in Western philosophy is whether mind and matter are ontologically different kinds, or whether they share the same fundamental nature.

**Paradigm:** The dictionary definition of "paradigm" is "1. a pattern, example, or model." Etymologically it derives from the Greek *paradeigma,* composed of *para* meaning "alongside of," "beside," or "beyond" and *deigma* meaning "example," "a showing." So "para-digm" means "beside or beyond example"; we could say it is that which is alongside or "fits" an example—hence a "model." We could also say it is that which is "beyond showing," implying it is something that is somehow invisible or unnoticed. So "paradigm" catches a double sense: meaning both a model of something (for instance the world) and an invisible structure (for instance the system of thinking within which we view the world). A paradigm is a set of assumptions, beliefs, opinions, "facts," theories, injunctions, and "laws" according to which we understand the world. It is like a superstructure of ideas, a scaffolding upon which we hang our understanding, our "knowledge" of reality.

**Sentience:** Any organism, any entity, that has an ability to *feel* is sentient. Such an entity has *subjectivity* (q.v.) because it has a point of view—it feels like something to be that entity. Sentience, thus, is virtually interchangeable with other terms such as experience, consciousness, and mind.

**Story:** Stories reveal how things came to be the way they are. They tell of beginnings, and of middles, and, if they don't always have endings, they point, and leave the way open. Stories are suggestive, rather than certain. They are lures or invitations to action. Stories enact the process of creation, whereby actualities emerge from a pool of potential. They make explicit, through becoming, the implicit fecundity of being.

Stories are the unfolding of meaning: They represent changes of states where the later states require reference back to their antecedents to complete their own being. More simply, stories require *memory* of what has happened, *experience* of what is happening, and *anticipation* of what is to come. All this requires consciousness.

**Synchronicity:** Carl Jung defined synchronicity as "a coincidence in time of two or more causally unrelated events which have the same or similar meaning." The feeling accompanying synchronicity is typically a sense of hidden order or pattern, accompanied by a tone of eerieness, a wondrousness, a mysteriousness, an inexplicable sense of *meaningful connection* linking otherwise disparate events at a moment in time—instead of being linked by causality or chance. The sense of inexplicable meaningful connection and coincidence, combined with a knowledge that this could not be due to any *thinkable* causal connection, is often accompanied by an unmistakable sense of numinosity: *Some deeper, higher, or wider pattern enfolds these otherwise apparently unconnected events.*

Synchronicities are often numinous because they come with a sense that the perceived meaning is *more than personal*—more than subjective projection. The meaning somehow transcends any individual psyche (or psyches) involved, and is as much a part of the *objective* situation. The meaning is sensed to be inherent in the *material world* as much as in a human mind. Both matter and mind seem to cooperate, even conspire, in the unfolding of events—as if "persuaded" or coaxed by some deeper, larger pattern that gives order and arrangement to the ways of the world (including our individual parts in it).

**Subjectivity:** Any object or event that possesses a point of view, that has an interiority, a "what-it-is-like to be that entity from within" is said to possess subjectivity. Any such entity is a subject rather than an object.

# NOTES

## Introduction

1. Chalmers, *The Conscious Mind.*
2. Rosen, *Science, Paradox, and the Moebius Principle.*
3. Koch, *American Psychologist,* 257.
4. Harman, *A Re-Examination of the Metaphysical Foundations of Modern Science.*
5. Schrödinger, *What is Life?,* 121.

## Chapter 1. Openings: A Place for Meaning

1. Griffin, *Unsnarling the World-Knot.*

## Chapter 2. Breakthrough: A New Cosmology Story

1. Ryle, *The Concept of Mind;* Koestler, *The Ghost in the Machine.*
2. Dawkins, *The Blind Watchmaker.*
3. Monod, *Chance and Necessity.*
4. Young, *The Reflexive Universe.*
5. Hooker, "The Nature of Quantum Mechanical Reality: Einstein versus Bohr," in *Paradigms and Paradoxes.*
6. Aspect, Dalibard, and Roger, *Physical Review Letters,* 49.
7. Bohm, *Wholeness and the Implicate Order.*
8. Prigogine and Stengers, *Order Out of Chaos.*
9. Searle, *The Rediscovery of the Mind.*
10. Griffin, "Introduction: The Reenchantment of Science" in *The Reenchantment of Science.*
11. Dawkins, *Blind Watchmaker.*
12. Dennett, *Consciousness Explained.*
13. Nagel, *The View from Nowhere.*
14. McGinn, *The Problem of Consciousness.*

15. Strawson, *Mental Reality.*
16. Griffin, *Unsnarling the World-Knot.*
17. De Quincey, "Consciousness All the Way Down?" in *Journal of Consciousness Studies,* 217–29.
18. McGinn, "Can We Solve the Mind-Body Problem?" in *Mind,* 349–66, and in *The Mind-Body Problem,* 99–120.
19. Jahn and Dunne, *Margins of Reality;* Radin, *The Conscious Universe.*
20. Schrödinger, *What Is Life?*
21. Churchland and Churchland, *On the Contrary.*
22. Griffin, "Introduction: The Reenchantment of Science"; Spretnak, *States of Grace;* Tuana, *Woman and the History of Philosophy;* Jagger and Bordo, *Gender/ Body/Knowledge;* Bigwood, *Earth Muse;* Abram, *The Spell of the Sensuous.*
23. Spretnak, *States of Grace.*
24. Daly, *Pure Lust;* Jagger and Bordo, *Gender/Body/Knowledge.*

## Chapter 3. Narratives: Rediscovering the Soul of Matter

1. Harman and de Quincey, *The Scientific Exploration of Consciousness.*

## Chapter 4. Meanings: Language, Energy, and Consciousness

1. Dossey, "Energy Talk" in *Network,* 3–7.
2. De Chardin, *The Phenomenon of Man.*
3. Whitehead, *Science and the Modern World.*
4. Rao, *Cultivating Consciousness.*
5. Young, *The Nature of Information.*
6. Shannon and Weaver, *The Mathematical Theory of Communication.*

## Chapter 5. Knots: The Problems of Consciousness

1. Rosen, *Science, Paradox, and the Moebius Principle.*
2. Cytowic, *The Man Who Tasted Shapes.*
3. Nagel, *What Does It All Mean?,* 24.
4. Ibid., 27.
5. Ibid.
6. Ibid., 29.
7. Ibid., 30.
8. Ibid., 33.
9. Ibid., 33–34.
10. Ibid., 34–35.

## Chapter 6. Panpsychism: A Long Lineage of Mind-in-Matter

1. Abram, *The Spell of the Sensuous.*
2. Bamford, *Homage to Pythagoras.*
3. Heisenberg, *Physics and Philosophy,* and in *Physics and Beyond.*
4. Bohm, *Wholeness and the Implicate Order.*
5. Wigner, *Symmetries and Reflections.*
6. Jung, *Memories, Dreams, Reflections.*
7. Thompson, *On Growth and Form.*
8. Waddington, *The Human Evolutionary System* in Banton, *Darwinism and the Study of Society.*
9. Sheldrake, *A New Science of Life.*
10. Eigen, "Self-Organization of Matter and the Evolution of Biological Macromolecules" in *Naturwissenschaften,* 456–523.
11. Bateson, *Mind in Nature.*
12. Heidegger, *Poetry, Language, Thought.*
13. Spencer-Brown, *Laws of Form.*
14. Gleick, *Chaos;* Briggs and Peat, *Turbulent Mirror;* Lewin, *Complexity.*
15. Taylor, "Our Roots: The American Visionary Tradition" in *Noetic Science Review,* 6–17.
16. Bamford, *Homage to Pythagoras,* 16.
17. Ibid., 157.
18. Ibid., 20.
19. Ibid., 19.
20. Ibid., 20.
21. Barfield, *What Coleridge Thought.*
22. Bamford, *Homage to Pythagoras,* 29.
23. Edwards, *Encyclopedia of Philosophy.*
24. Whitehead, *Science and the Modern World,* 41–42.
25. Reese, *Dictionary of Philosophy and Religion.*
26. Mendoza, *The Acentric Labyrinth,* 243.
27. Burnet, *Early Greek Philosophy* in *Treasury of Philosophy,* 55.
28. Bamford, *Homage to Pythagoras.*
29. Runes, *Treasury of Philosophy,* 495.
30. Ibid., 496–97.
31. Ibid., 48.
32. Ibid., 48–49.
33. Mendoza, *The Acentric Labyrinth,* 124.
34. Runes, *Treasury of Philosophy,* 48–49.
35. Mendoza, *The Acentric Labyrinth,* 124.

36. Ibid.

37. Runes, *Treasury of Philosophy,* 1257.

38. Armstrong, "Plotinus" in *The Concise Encyclopedia of Western Philosophy and Philosophers;* Wilber, *Sex, Ecology, Spirituality.*

39. Reese, *Dictionary of Philosophy and Religion,* 445.

40. Urmson and Rée, *The Concise Encyclopedia of Western Philosophy and Philosophers,* 249.

41. Reese, *Dictionary of Philosophy and Religion,* 445.

42. Armstrong, "Plotinus" in *The Concise Encyclopedia of Western Philosophy,* 249.

43. Ibid., 248.

44. Reese, *Dictionary of Philosophy and Religion,* 398.

45. Lovejoy, The *Great Chain of Being,* 338.

46. Reese, *Dictionary of Philosophy and Religion,* 78.

47. Leibniz, "The Monadology" in *The Rationalists.*

48. Reese, *Dictionary of Philosophy and Religion,* 299.

49. Ibid.

50. Ibid.

51. Koestler, *The Ghost in the Machine,* and in *Janus;* Toulmin, *The Return to Cosmology.*

52. Wilber, *Sex, Ecology, Spirituality.*

53. Spinoza, "The Ethics" in *The Rationalists;* Munitz, *Theories of the Universe.*

54. Graham, *Disputers of the Tao.*

55. Bohm, *Wholeness and the Implicate Order.*

56. Blackburn, *The Oxford Dictionary of Philosophy.*

57. Bortoft, *The Wholeness of Nature.*

58. Von Goethe in Bamford, *Homage to Pythagoras,* 30.

59. Bamford, *Homage to Pythagoras.*

60. Perkins, *Coleridge's Philosophy.*

61. Barfield in Bamford, *Homage to Pythagoras,* 21.

62. Bamford, *Homage to Pythagoras,* 21.

63. Nagel, "Panpsychism," in *Mortal Questions,* 181–95.

64. McGinn, *The Character of Mind.*

## Chapter 7. Resolution: Whitehead's Postmodern Cosmology

1. Griffin, *Unsnarling the World-Knot;* Griffin, et al., *Founders of Contructive Postmodern Philosophy.*

2. Lucas, *The Rehabilitation of Whitehead.*

3. Descartes, *Descartes' Philosophical Writings.*

4. Whitehead, *Science and the Modern World,* 144.

5. Ibid., 174.

6. Ibid., 71.

7. Ibid., 58.

8. Ibid., 51.

9. Ibid., 69.

10. Ibid.

11. Ibid.

12. Ibid., 119.

13. Ibid., 72.

14. Ibid., 91.

15. Ibid., 103.

16. Elliot, *Japanese Buddhism.*

17. Humphrey, *Buddhism.*

18. Whitehead, *Process and Reality,* 24.

19. Leclerc, *Whitehead's Metaphysics.*

20. Whitehead, *Process and Reality,* 18.

21. Ibid., 41.

22. Ibid., 24.

23. Whitehead, *Science and the Modern World,* 103.

24. Ibid., 174.

25. Ibid., 123.

26. Ibid., 104.

27. Ibid.

28. Ibid.

29. Ibid., 127.

30. Ibid., 79.

31. Ibid.

32. Ibid., 80.

33. Lucas, *The Rehabilitation of Whitehead,* 148.

34. Whitehead, *Process and Reality,* 176.

35. Griffin, *Parapsychology, Philosophy, and Spirituality.*

36. Targ and Katra, *Miracles of Mind;* Radin, *The Conscious Universe;* Schmidt and Stapp, "Study of PK with Pre-recorded Random Events and the Effects of Pre-observation" (Unpublished); Stapp, "Theoretical Model of a Purported Empirical Violation of the Predictions of Quantum Theory" in *Physical Review,* 18–22.; Jahn and Dunne, *Margins of Reality;* Schmidt, "Mental Influence on Random Events," in *New Scientist;* Schmidt, "PK Effects on Pre-Recorded Targets," in *The Journal of the American Society for Psychical Research,* 267–91.

37. Whitehead, *Science and the Modern World,* 176; Cobb, "Alfred North Whitehead," in *Founders of Constructive Postmodern Philosophy.*

38. Hume, "An Inquiry Concerning Human Understanding," in *Philosophical Classics*, 318–414.

39. Kant, *Critique of Pure Reason*.

40. Cobb, "Alfred North Whitehead," in *Founders of Constructive Postmodern Philosophy*.

41. Ibid., 176.

## Chapter 8. Panexperientialism: Consciousness All the Way Down?

1. McGinn, *The Problem of Consciousness*.

2. Whitehead, *Process and Reality*, and in *Process and Reality* (Corrected edition).

3. Hartshorne, *The Philosophy of Charles Hartshorne*.

4. Griffin, "Pantemporalism and Panexperientialism" (Unpublished manuscript).

5. Polanyi, *Personal Knowledge*.

6. Harman and de Quincey, *The Scientific Exploration of Consciousness*.

7. Grof, *The Adventure of Self-Discovery*; Spretnak, *States of Grace*.

8. Roll, "A New Look at the Survival Problem," in *New Directions in Parapsychology*.

9. Young, *The Reflexive Universe*; and *Which Way Out?*

10. Young, *The Geometry of Meaning*.

11. Young, *The Reflexive Universe*.

12. Sperry, "Structure and Significance of the Consciousness Revolution," in *The Journal of Mind and Behavior*.

13. Schlitz, "Direct Mental Influences on Living Systems."

14. Waddington, *The Human Evolution System*, p. 22; and Waddington in Edwards, *Encyclopedia of Philosophy*, 31.

15. Lovejoy, *The Great Chain of Being*.

16. Paulsen, *Introduction to Philosophy*, 99–100.

17. Edwards, *Encyclopedia of Philosophy*.

18. Ibid., 26.

## Chapter 9. Integrating Worldviews: Past Matter, Present Mind

1. Chalmers, *The Conscious Mind*.

2. Griffin, *Unsnarling the World-Knot*.

3. Whitehead, *Process and Reality*.

4. Charles Hartshorne, *The Philosophy of Charles Hartshorne*.

5. McGinn, *The Problem of Consciousness*.

6. De Quincey, "Consciousness All the Way Down?" in *Journal of Consciousness Studies*, 217–29.

7. Strawson, *Mental Reality.*

8. Dennett, *Consciousness Explained.*

9. Churchland and Churchland, *On the Contrary.*

10. Nagel, *The View from Nowhere.*

11. Griffin, *Unsnarling the World-Knot,* 184.

12. Ibid., 213.

13. Whitehead, *Process and Reality.*

14. James, *A Pluralistic Universe,* 207–8.

15. Bohm and Edwards, *Creating Consciousness.*

16. Rorty, *Philosophy and the Mirror of Nature.*

## Chapter 10. Conclusion: Stories Matter, Matter Stories

1. Jaynes, *The Origins of Consciousness in the Breakdown of the Bicameral Mind.*

2. Mendoza, *The Acentric Labyrinth.*

3. Ibid.

4. Ibid.

5. Ibid.

6. Ibid., 111.

7. Ibid., 115.

8. Ibid., 114.

9. Lotze, *Microcosmus.*

10. Mendoza, *The Acentric Labyrinth,* 114.

11. Ibid., 119.

12. James, *The Writings of William James.*

13. Whitmont, *The Alchemy of Healing.*

14. Bohm, *Wholeness and the Implicate Order.*

15. Von Franz, *Psyche and Matter.*

16. Whitmont, *Psyche and Substance.*

17. Needham, *Science and Civilization in China (vol. II);* Chan, *Chu Hsi and Neo-Confucianism;* Tillman, *Confucian Discourse and Chu Hsi's Ascendancy.*

18. Needham, *Science and Civilization in China,* 281.

19. Ibid.

20. Ibid., 412.

21. Ibid., 154.

22. Chu Hsi, trans., *The Philosophy of Human Nature,* chapter 42; quoted in Needham, *Science and Civilization in China,* 488.

23. Needham, *Science and Civilization in China,* 562.

24. Ibid., 567–68.

25. Sheldrake, *A New Science of Life* and *The Presence of the Past.*
26. Young, *The Reflexive Universe;* Capra, *The Turning Point;* Spretnak, *States of Grace.*
27. Needleman, *A Sense of the Cosmos.*

## Epilogue. Conceiving the "Inconceivable"?

1. Nagel, *The View from Nowhere.*
2. Edwards, *Encyclopedia of Philosophy,* 28.
3. Humphrey, *A History of the Mind.*
4. Humphrey, "The Thick Moment," in *The Third Culture,* 198–208.
5. Humphrey, *A History of the Mind,* 38.
6. Ibid., 18.
7. Ibid., 25.
8. Ibid., 38.
9. Ibid., 39.
10. Ibid., 25.
11. McGinn, "Consciousness and Space," in *Explaining Consciousness,* 99.
12. Ibid., 99–100.
13. Humphrey, *A History of the Mind,* 23.
14. Ibid., 202.
15. Ibid., 23.
16. Ibid., 39.
17. Ibid., 42.
18. Ibid., 42.
19. Ibid., 44.
20. Ibid., 47.
21. Reid, *Essays on the Intellectual Powers of Man,* 17.
22. Humphrey, *A History of the Mind,* 46.
23. Ibid., 93.
24. Ibid., 98.
25. Ibid., 101.
26. Ibid., 115–16.
27. Ibid., 120.
28. Ibid., 128.
29. Ibid., 128.
30. Ibid., 129–30.
31. Ibid., 136.
32. Ibid., 137.
33. Ibid., 138.

34. Ibid.
35. Ibid., 155–56.
36. Ibid., 157.
37. Ibid., 158.
38. Ibid., 159.
39. Ibid., 179.
40. Ibid., 181.
41. Ibid.
42. Ibid., 183.
43. Ibid., 217.
44. Ibid., 183.
45. Griffin, "Summary: Unsnarling the World-Knot."

# BIBLIOGRAPHY

Abram, D. *The Spell of the Sensuous: Perception and Language in a More-than-Human World*. New York: Pantheon, 1996.

Aristotle. *De Anima*. Hugh Lawson-Tancred, trans. London: Penguin Books, 1986.

Armstrong, A. H. *Plotinus*. In J. O. Urmson and J. Rée, eds. *The Concise Encyclopedia of Western Philosophy and Philosophers*. London: Unwin Hyman, 1991.

Aspect, A., J. Dalibard, and G. Roger. *Physical Review Letters* 1804, no. 49 (1982).

Aurobindo, Sri. *The Life Divine*. New York: Sri Aurobindo Library, 1951.

Bacon, F. *Novum Organum*. In W. Kaufmann, ed. *Philosophical Classics: Bacon to Kant*. Englewood Cliffs, N.J.: Prentice-Hall, 1964.

Bamford, C., ed. *Homage to Pythagoras: Rediscovering Sacred Science*. New York: Lindisfarne Press, 1994.

Barfield, O. *What Coleridge Thought*. Middletown, Conn.: Wesleyan University Press, 1971.

Bateson, G. *Mind in Nature: A Necessary Unity*. New York: Dutton, 1979.

———. *Steps to an Ecology of Mind: A Revolutionary Approach to Man's Understanding of Himself.* New York: Ballantine Books, 1972.

Bergson, H. *Creative Evolution*. A. Mitchell, trans. New York: Henry Holt, 1911.

———. *Duration and Simultaneity*. Leon Jacobson, trans. Indianapolis, Ind.: Bobbs-Merrill, 1966.

———.*Matter and Memory*. N. M. Paul and W. S. Palmer, trans. New York: Zone Books, 1994.

Berkeley, G. *Essay Towards a New Theory of Vision*. London: J. M. Dent, 1709.

Berman, M. *The Reenchantment of the World*. New York: Cornell University Press, 1991.

Berry, T. *Dream of the Earth*. San Francisco: Sierra Club, 1988.

Bigwood, C. *Earth Muse*. Philadelphia, Pa.: Temple University Press, 1993.

Blackburn, S. *The Oxford Dictionary of Philosophy*. Oxford, U.K.: Oxford University Press, 1994.

Bohm, D. *Wholeness and the Implicate Order*. London: Routledge and Kegan Paul, 1980.

Bohm, D., and M. Edwards. *Creating Consciousness: Exploring the Hidden Source of the Social, Political and Environmental Crises Facing our World*. New York: HarperCollins, 1991.

Bohr, N. *Atomic Theory and the Description of Nature*. Cambridge, Mass.: Cambridge University Press, 1961.

Bortoft, H. *The Wholeness of Nature: Goethe's Way Toward a Science of Conscious Participation in Nature*. New York: Lindisfarne Press, 1996.

Briggs J., and D. Peat. *Turbulent Mirror: An Illustrated Guide to Chaos Theory and the Science of Wholeness*. New York: Harper and Row, 1989.

Burnet, J., ed. and trans. *Early Greek Philosophy*. London: A. and C. Black, 1930. Cited in Dagobert D. Runes, ed. *Treasury of Philosophy*. New York: Philosophical Library, 1995.

Capra, F. *The Turning Point: Science, Society and the Rising Culture*. New York: Simon and Schuster, 1982.

Chalmers, D. *The Conscious Mind: In Search of a Fundamental Theory*. Oxford, U.K.: Oxford University Press, 1996.

———. "Facing up to the Problem of Consciousness." *Journal of Consciousness Studies* 2, no. 3 (1995): 200–219.

Chan, W. T., ed. *Chu Hsi and Neo-Confucianism*. Honolulu: University of Hawaii Press, 1986.

———. *A Source Book in Chinese Philosophy*. Princeton, N.J.: Princeton University Press, 1973.

Chu Hsi. *The Philosophy of Human Nature*. J. P. Bruce, trans. London: Probsthain, 1922.

Churchland, P. *Matter and Consciousness: A Contemporary Introduction to the Philosophy of Mind*. Cambridge, Mass.: MIT Press, 1993.

Churchland, P., and P. Churchland. *On the Contrary: Critical Essays 1987–1997*. Cambridge, Mass.: MIT Press, 1998.

Cobb, J. B. "Alfred North Whitehead." In D. R. Griffin, J. B. Cobb, Jr., M. P. Ford, P. A. Y. Gunter, and P. Ochs, eds., *Founders of Constructive Postmodern Philosophy: Peirce, James, Bergson, Whitehead, and Hartshorne*. Albany, N.Y.: State University of New York Press, 1993.

Crick, F. *The Astonishing Hypothesis: The Scientific Search for the Soul*. New York: Simon and Schuster, 1994.

Cytowic, R. E. *The Man who Tasted Shapes: A Bizarre Medical Mystery Offers*

*Revolutionary Insights into Emotions, Reasoning, and Consciousness.* New York: Tarcher/Putnam, 1998.

Daly, M. *Pure Lust: Elemental Feminist Philosophy.* Boston: Beacon Press, 1984.

Dawkins, R. *The Blind Watchmaker: Why the Evidence of Evolution Reveals a Universe Without Design.* New York: W. W. Norton and Co., 1987.

De Chardin, T. *The Phenomenon of Man.* New York: Harper and Row, 1965.

De Quincey, C. "Conceiving the Inconceivable? Fishing for Consciousness with a Net of Miracles." *Journal of Consciousness Studies* 4 (2000). Essex, England: Imprint Academic.

——. "Consciousness All the Way Down? An Analysis of McGinn's Critique of Panexperientialism." *Journal of Consciousness Studies* 1, no. 2 (1994): 217–29. Essex, England: Imprint Academic.

——. "Consciousness: The Final Frontier?" *Noetic Sciences Review* 42 (Summer, 1997): 30–33.

——. "Embodied Meaning and Health: Messages from Nature Experienced in the Body." *Somatics* X, no. 1 (Fall–Winter, 1994): 4–6.

——. "Past Matter, Present Mind: A Convergence of Worldviews." *Journal of Consciousness Studies* 6, no. 1 (1999): 91–106. Essex, England: Imprint Academic.

——."Philosophy of Consciousness." Class notes, John F. Kennedy University. Orinda, Calif.: 1997.

——. "The Promise of Integralism: A Critical Appreciation of Ken Wilber's Integral Psychology." *Journal of Consciousness Studies* 7, no. 1 (2000): 177–208. Essex, England: Imprint Academic.

——. "A Theory of Everything?" *IONS Review*, 55 (Spring, 2001): 8–15 and 38–39.

Dennett, D. *Consciousness Explained.* Boston: Little Brown, 1991.

Descartes, R. *Descartes' Philosophical Writings.* Norman Kemp Smith, trans. London: Macmillan and Co., 1952.

Dossey, L. "Energy Talk." *Network* 63 (1997): 3–7.

——. *Healing Words: The Power of Prayer and the Practice of Medicine.* New York: HarperCollins, 1993.

——. *Space, Time and Medicine: Beyond Illness.* New York: Shambhala, 1982.

Edwards, P., ed. *Encyclopedia of Philosophy,* vol. 6. New York: Macmillan, 1967.

Eigen, M. "Self-Organization of Matter and the Evolution of Biological Macromolecules." *Naturwissenschaften* 58 (1971): 456–523.

Eliot, Charles. *Japanese Buddhism.* New York: Barnes & Noble, 1959.

Gleick, J. *Chaos: Making a New Science.* New York: Penguin Books, 1988.

Goethe, J. W. *Goethe's Botanical Writings.* Bertha Mueller, trans. Honolulu: University of Hawaii Press, 1952.

Goodwin, B. "A Science of Qualities." In B. T. Hilary and F. D. Peat, eds. *Quantum Implications: Festschrift for David Bohm*. London: Routledge and Kegan Paul, 1987.

Goswami, A. *The Self-Aware Universe: How Consciousness Creates the Material World*. New York: Tarcher/Putnam, 1993.

————. *Science within Consciousness: Developing a Science Based on the Primacy of Consciousness*. Sausalito, Calif.: Institute of Noetic Sciences, 1994.

Grayling, A. C., ed. *Philosophy: A Guide through the Subject*. Oxford, U.K.: Oxford University Press, 1995.

Graham, A. C. *Disputers of the Tao: Philosophical Arguments in Ancient China*. Chicago: Open Court, 1989.

Griffin, D. R., ed. *Physics and the Ultimate Significance of Time*. Albany, N.Y.: State University of New York Press, 1986.

Griffin, D. R. "Introduction: The Reenchantment of Science." In D. R. Griffin, ed. *The Reenchantment of Science: Postmodern Proposals*. Albany, N.Y.: State University of New York Press, 1988.

————. *Parapsychology, Philosophy, and Spirituality: A Postmodern Exploration*. Albany, N.Y.: State University of New York Press, 1997.

————. "Summary: Unsnarling the World-Knot." Paper presented at the Consciousness Conference, Claremont Theological School, Calif., October 6–9, 1994.

————. *Unsnarling the World-Knot: Consciousness, Freedom, and the Mind-Body Problem*. Berkeley: University of California Press, 1998.

Griffin, D. R., et al., eds. *Founders of Constructive Postmodern Philosophy: Peirce, James, Bergson, Whitehead, and Hartshorne*. Albany, N.Y.: State University of New York Press, 1993.

Grof, S. *The Adventure of Self-Discovery: Dimensions of Consciousness and New Perspectives in Psychotherapy and Inner Exploration*. New York: State University of New York Press, 1988.

Guralnik, D. B., ed. *Webster's New World Dictionary of the American Language*. New York: Simon and Schuster, 1984.

Guttenplan, S., ed. *A Companion to the Philosophy of Mind*. London: Blackwell, 1994.

Hameroff, S. R., A. W. Kas26niak, and A. C. Scott. *Toward a Science of Consciousness: The First Tucson Debates*. Cambridge, Mass.: MIT Press, 1996.

Hamilton, E., and H. Cairns, ed. *Plato: The Collected Dialogues*. Princeton, N.J.: Princeton University Press, 1989.

Hansen, C. *A Daoist Theory of Chinese Thought*. New York: Oxford University Press, 1992.

Harman, W. *A Re-Examination of the Metaphysical Foundations of Modern Science*. Sausalito, Calif.: Institute of Noetic Sciences, 1991.

Harman, W., and C. de Quincey. *The Scientific Exploration of Consciousness: Toward an Adequate Epistemology.* Sausalito, Calif.: Institute of Noetic Sciences, 1994.

Hartshorne, C. *The Philosophy of Charles Hartshorne: Library of Living Philosophers XX.* Lewis Edwin Hahn, ed. La Salle, Ill.: Open Court, 1991.

Heidegger, M. *Poetry, Language, Thought.* Albert Hofstadter, trans. New York: Harper and Row, 1971.

Heisenberg, W. *Physics and Beyond.* London: Allen and Unwin, 1971.

———. *Physics and Philosophy.* New York: Harper and Row, 1958.

Honderich, T., ed. *The Oxford Companion to Philosophy.* Oxford, U.K.: Oxford University Press, 1995.

Hooker, C. A. "The Nature of Quantum Mechanical Reality: Einstein versus Bohr." In R. G. Colodny, ed. *Paradigms and Paradoxes: The Philosophical Challenge of the Quantum Domain.* Pittsburgh, Pa.: University of Pittsburgh Press, 1972.

Hume, D. *An Enquiry Concerning Human Understanding.* In W. Kauffmann, ed. *Philosophical Classics: From Bacon to Kant.* New Jersey: Prentice-Hall, 1977.

———. *A Treatise of Human Nature.* L. A. Selby-Bigge, ed. second edition, rev. P. H. Nidditch, ed. Oxford, U.K.: Clarendon Press, 1978.

Humphrey, N. *Buddhism: An Introduction and Guide.* London: Penguin Group, 1990.

———. *A History of the Mind: Evolution and the Birth of Consciousness.* New York: Simon and Schuster, 1992.

———. "The Thick Moment." In J. Brockman, ed. *The Third Culture: Beyond the Scientific Revolution.* New York: Simon and Schuster, 1995.

Huxley, A. *The Perennial Philosophy.* New York: Harper and Row, 1945.

Jacobi, J. *Complex, Archetype, Symbol in the Psychology of C. G. Jung.* R. Manheim, trans. Princeton, N.J.: Princeton University Press, 1959.

Jagger A., and S. Bordo, eds. *Gender/Body/Knowledge: Feminist Reconstructions of Being and Knowing.* New Brunswick, N.J.: Rutgers University Press, 1989.

Jahn, R. G., and B. J. Dunne. *Margins of Reality: The Role of Consciousness in the Physical World.* New York: Harcourt, Brace, Jovanovich, 1987.

James, W. *Essays in Radical Empiricism.* London: Longmans, Green and Co., 1912.

———. *A Pluralistic Universe.* New York: Longmans, Green and Co., 1909.

———. *The Varieties of Religious Experience.* New York: Collier Books, 1900/1961.

———. *The Writings of William James: A Comprehensive Edition.* J. J. McDermott, ed. Chicago: Chicago University Press, 1977.

Jaynes, J. *The Origins of Consciousness in the Breakdown of the Bicameral Mind.* Boston: Houghton Mifflin, 1990.

Jonas, H. *The Gnostic Religions.* Boston: Beacon Press, 1963.

Jung, C. G. *The Collected Works of C. G. Jung,* vols. 1–20, Bollingen Series XX. R. F. C. Hull, trans. H. Read, M. Fordham, G. Adler, and W. McGuire, eds. Princeton, N.J.: Princeton University Press, 1953–1979.

———. *Memories, Dreams, Reflections.* Aniela Jaffé, ed. New York: Vintage Books, 1989.

Kafatos, M., and R. Nadeau. *The Conscious Universe: Part and Whole in Modern Physical Theory.* New York: Springer-Verlag, 1990.

Kant, I. *Critique of Pure Reason.* N. K. Smith, trans. New York: St. Martin's Press, 1977.

———. *The Philosophy of Kant.* Carl J. Friedrich, ed. New York: Modern Library, 1977.

Kauffman, S. *The Origins of Order: Self-Organization and Selection in Evolution.* New York: Oxford University Press, 1993.

Kaufmann, W., ed. *Philosophic Classics: Bacon to Kant.* Englewood Cliffs, N.J.: Prentice-Hall, 1964.

Kim, J. *Supervenience and the Mind.* Cambridge, U.K.: Cambridge University Press, 1993.

Kirk, G. S. "Pythagoreans." In Urmson, J. O., and J. Rée, eds. *The Concise Encyclopedia of Western Philosophy and Philosophers.* London: Unwin Hyman, 1989.

Koch, S. *American Psychologist* 36 (1981): 257. Cited in Rosen, 1994.

Koestler, A. *The Ghost in the Machine.* London: Hutchinson, 1967.

———. *Janus: A Summing Up.* New York: Vintage Books, 1979.

Koestler, A., and J. R. Smythies, eds. *Beyond Reductionism: New Perspectives in the Life Sciences. The Alpabach Symposium 1968.* London: Hutchinson, 1969.

Korzybski, A. *Science and Sanity.* New York: Science Press, 1941.

Kuhn, T. *The Structure of Scientific Revolutions.* Cambridge, Mass.: MIT Press, 1962.

Langer, S. *Philosophy in a New Key.* Cambridge, Mass.: Harvard University Press, 1952.

Laszlo, E. *Introduction to Systems Philosophy: Toward a New Paradigm of Contemporary Thought.* New York: Harper Torchbooks, 1972.

Lawson-Tancred, H. *Aristotle: De Anima (On the soul).* London: Penguin Books, 1986.

Leclerc, I. *Whitehead's Metaphysics.* New Jersey: Humanities Press, 1965.

Leibniz, G. "The Monadology." In *The Rationalists.* New York: Doubleday, 1960.

Levine, J. "Materialism and Qualia: The Explanatory Gap." *Pacific Philosophical Quarterly* 63 (1983): 354–61.

Lewin, R. *Complexity: Life at the Edge of Chaos.* New York: Collier Books, 1992.

Locke, J. *Essay Concerning Human Understanding.* P. H. Nidditch, ed. Oxford, U.K.: Oxford University Press, 1975.

Lotze, R. H. *Microcosmus.* E. Hamilton and E. E. C. Jones, trans. New York: Ayer, 1890.

Lovejoy, A. O. *The Great Chain of Being.* Cambridge, Mass.: Harvard University Press, 1964.

Lucas, G. *The Rehabilitation of Whitehead: An Analytic and Historical Assessment of Process Philosophy.* Albany, N.Y.: State University of New York Press, 1989.

McGinn, C. "Can We Solve the Mind-Body Problem?" *Mind* 98 (1989): 349–66. And in *The Mind-Body Problem: A Guide to the Current Debate.* R. Warner and T. Szubka. Oxford, U.K.: Blackwell, 1989.

———. *The Character of Mind.* Oxford, U.K.: Oxford University Press, 1982.

———. "Consciousness and Space." Paper Presented at the Consciousness Conference, Claremont Theological School, Calif., October 6–9, 1994. Subsequently published in J. Shear, ed. *Explaining Consciousness: The 'Hard Problem.'* Cambridge, Mass.: MIT Press, 1994.

———. *The Mysterious Flame: Consciousness Minds in a Material World.* New York: Basic Books, 2000.

———. *The Problem of Consciousness: Toward a Solution.* Oxford, U.K.: Blackwell, 1991.

Mendoza, R. G. *The Acentric Labyrinth: Giordano Bruno's Prelude to Contemporary Cosmology.* Shaftesbury, U.K.: Element, 1995.

Michalson, G. E. *Fallen Freedom: Kant on Radical Evil and Moral Regeneration.* Cambridge, U.K.: Cambridge University Press, 1990.

Mitchell, S. *The Tao Te Ching.* New York: Harper and Row, 1988.

Monod, J. *Chance and Necessity: An Essay on the Natural Philosophy of Modern Biology.* New York: Vintage Books, 1971.

Munitz, M. K. Theories of the Universe. New York: Free Press, 1965.

Nagel, E. *The Structure of Science: Problems in the Logic of Scientific Explanation.* New York: Harcourt, Brace, and World, 1961.

Nagel, T. "Consciousness and Objective Reality." In R. Warner and T. Szubka, eds. *The Mind-Body Problem: A Guide to the Current Debate.* Oxford, U.K.: Blackwell, 1994.

———. "Panpsychism." In *Mortal Questions.* New York: Cambridge University Press, 1992.

———. *The View from Nowhere.* Oxford, U.K.: Oxford University Press, 1986.

———. *What Does It All Mean? A Very Short Introduction to Philosophy.* Oxford, U.K.: Oxford University Press, 1987.

———. "What Is It Like to be a Bat?" *Philosophical Review*, LXXXIII. Reprinted 1992 in *Mortal Questions*. New York: Cambridge University Press, October, 1974.

Needham, J. *Science and Civilization in China (vol. II): History of Scientific Thought*. London: Cambridge University Press, 1977.

Needleman, J. *A Sense of the Cosmos: The Encounter of Modern Science and Ancient Truth*. London: Penguin/Arkana, 1975.

Needleman, J. and C. de Quincey. "Questions of the Heart: Inner Empiricism as a Way to a Science of Consciousness." *Noetic Sciences Review* 26 (1993): 4–9.

Onians, R. B. *The Origins of European Thought: About the Body, the Mind, the Soul, the World, Time, and Fate*. Cambridge, U.K.: Cambridge University Press, 1994.

Paulsen, F. *Introduction to Philosophy*. Second American edition. F. Thilly, trans. (1906). Cited in P. Edwards, ed., *Encyclopedia of Philosophy*, vol. 6. New York: Macmillan, 1967.

Pearce, J. C. *The Crack in the Cosmic Egg: Challenging Constructs of Mind and Reality*. New York: Julian Press, 1971.

Perkins, M. A. *Coleridge's Philosophy: The Logos as Unifying Principle*. Oxford, U.K.: Oxford University Press, 1994.

Petersen, A. "The Philosophy of Niels Bohr." *Bulletin of the Atomic Scientists* (September, 1963): 8–14.

Plato. *Collected Dialogues*. Edith Hamilton and Huntington Cairns, eds. Princeton, N.J.: Princeton University Press, 1989.

Polanyi, M. *Personal Knowledge*. London: Routledge and Kegan Paul, 1958.

Prigogine, I., and I. Stengers. *Order out of Chaos: Man's New Dialogue with Nature*. New York: Bantam, 1988.

Radin, D. *The Conscious Universe: The Scientific Truth of Psychic Phenomena*. San Francisco: HarperEdge, 1997.

Rao, K. R., ed. *Cultivating Consciousness: Enhancing Human Potential, Wellness, and Healing*. Westport, Conn.: Praeger, 1993.

Reese, W. L. *Dictionary of Philosophy and Religion: Eastern and Western Thought*. Atlantic Highlands, N.J.: Humanities Press, 1991.

Reid, T. *Essays on the Intellectual Powers of Man*, Essay 2, (17). Cambridge, Mass.: MIT Press, 1969.

Roll, W. "A New Look at the Survival Problem." In J. Beloff, ed. *New Directions in Parapsychology*. Metuchen, N.J.: Scarecrow Press, 1974.

Rorty, R. *Philosophy and the Mirror of Nature*. Princeton, N.J.: Princeton University Press, 1980.

Rosen, S. M. *Science, Paradox, and the Moebius Principle: The Evolution of a*

*'Transcultural' Approach to Wholeness.* Albany, N.Y.: State University of New York Press, 1994.

Runes, D. D., ed. *Treasury of Philosophy.* New York: Philosophical Library, 1955.

Russell, B. "A Free Man's Worship." In R. E. Egner and L. D. Dennon, eds. *The Basic Writings of Bertrand Russell 1903–1959.* New York: Simon and Schuster, 1961.

Ryle, G. *The Concept of Mind.* London: Hutchinson, 1949.

Schlitz, M. "Direct Mental Influences on Living Systems: A Review of Data and Implications for Consciousness Studies." Paper presented at the Consciousness Conference, Claremont Theological School, Calif. (October 6–9, 1994).

Schmidt, H. "Mental Influence on Random Events." *New Scientist* (June 24, 1971).

———. "PK Effects on Pre-Recorded Targets." *The Journal of the American Society for Psychical Research* 70 (1976): 267–91.

Schmidt, H., and H. Stapp. "Study of PK with Pre-recorded Random Events and the Effects of Pre-observation." (1995, unpublished.)

Schopenhauer, A. *Philosophy of Arthur Schopenhauer.* Belfort Bax and Bailey Saunders, trans. New York: Tudor Publishing Co., 1936.

Schrödinger, E. *What is Life? With Mind and Matter and Autobiographical Sketches.* Cambridge, U.K.: Cambridge University Press, 1989.

Searle, J. R. *The Rediscovery of the Mind.* Cambridge, Mass.: MIT Press, 1992.

Shannon, C., and W. Weaver. *The Mathematical Theory of Communication.* Chicago: University of Chicago Press, 1949. Cited in P. Young, *The Nature of Information,* New York: Praeger, 1987.

Shear, J., ed. *Explaining Consciousness—The "Hard Problem."* Cambridge, Mass.: MIT Press, 1995–1997.

Sheldrake, R. *A New Science of Life: The Hypothesis of Formative Causation.* Los Angeles: J. P. Tarcher, 1981.

———. *The Presence of the Past: Morphic Resonance and the Habits of Nature.* New York: Vintage Books, 1988.

Smythies, J. R., and J. Beloff, eds. *The Case for Dualism.* Charlottesville, Va.: University Press of Virginia, 1989.

Spencer-Brown, G. *Laws of Form.* New York: The Julian Press, 1972.

Sperry, R. "Holding Course amid Shifting Paradigms." In W. Harman and J. Clark, eds. *New Metaphysical Foundations of Modern Science.* Sausalito, Calif.: Institute of Noetic Sciences, 1994.

———. "Mental Phenomena as Causal Determinants in Brain Functions." *Process Studies* 5, no. 4 (1975): 247–56.

———. "Structure and Significance of the Consciousness Revolution." *The Journal of Mind and Behavior* 8, no. 1 (1987).

Spinoza, B. "The Ethics." In *The Rationalists*. New York: Doubleday, 1960.

Spretnak, C. *States of Grace: The Recovery of Meaning in the Postmodern Age*. San Francisco: HarperSanFrancisco, 1991.

Stapp, H. P. "Theoretical Model of a Purported Empirical Violation of the Predictions of Quantum Theory." *Physical Review A* 50, no. 1 (1994): 18–22.

Strawson, G. "The Experiential and the Non-Experiential." In R. Warner and T. Szubka, eds. *The Mind-Body Problem: A Guide to the Current Debate*. Oxford, U.K.: Blackwell, 1994.

———. *Mental Reality*. Cambridge, Mass.: MIT Press, 1994.

Stumpf, S. E. *Socrates to Sartre: A History of Philosophy*. New York: McGraw-Hill, 1966.

Suppe, F., ed. *The Structure of Scientific Theories*. Chicago: University of Illinois Press, 1977.

Swimme, B., and T. Berry. *The Universe Story: From the Primordial Flaring Forth to the Ecozoic Era—A Celebration of the Unfolding of the Cosmos*. San Francisco: HarperSanFrancisco, 1992.

Targ, R., and J. Katra. *Miracles of Mind: Exploring Nonlocal Consciousness and Spiritual Healing*. Novato, Calif.: New World Library, 1998.

Tarnas, R. *The Passion of the Western Mind: Understanding the Ideas that Have Shaped Our World View*. New York: Harmony Books, 1991.

Taylor, E. "Our Roots: The American Visionary Tradition." In *Noetic Science Review* 27 (1993): 6–17. Sausalito, Calif.: Institute of Noetic Sciences.

———. "Radical Empiricism and the Conduct of Research." In W. Harman and J. Clark, eds. *New Metaphysical Foundations of Modern Science*. Sausalito, Calif.: Institute of Noetic Sciences, 1993.

Thandeka. *The Embodied Self: Friedrich Schleiermacher's Solution to Kant's Problem of the Empirical Self*. Albany, N.Y.: State University of New York Press, 1995.

Thompson, D. *On Growth and Form*. J. T. Bonner, ed. London: Cambridge University Press, 1961.

Tillman, H. C. *Confucian Discourse and Chu Hsi's Ascendancy*. Honolulu: University of Hawaii Press, 1992.

Toulmin, S. *The Return to Cosmology: Postmodern Science and the Theology of Nature*. Berkeley: University of California Press, 1985.

Tuana, N. *Woman and the History of Philosophy*. St. Paul, Minn.: Paragon House, 1992.

Urmson, J. O., and J. Rée, eds. *The Concise Encyclopedia of Western Philosophy and Philosophers*. London: Unwin Hyman, 1991.

Varela, Francisco. "The Origin of Perception: A Cartography of Current Approaches." In F. Varela and J. P. Dupuy, eds. *Understanding Origins*. Norwell, Mass.: Kluwer Associates, 1991.

Velmans, M. "Consciousness, Brain and the Physical World." *Philosophical Psychology* 3, no. 1 (1990): 77–99.

———. "A Reflexive Science of Consciousness." In G. R. Bock and J. Marsh, eds. *Experimental and Theoretical Studies of Consciousness*. New York: John Wiley and Sons, 1993.

———. "Symposium: Consciousness and the Physical World." *Philosophical Psychology* 5, no. 2 (1992): 155.

Von Franz, M. L. *Psyche and Matter*. Boston: Shambhala, 1992.

Waddington, C. H. *The Human Evolutionary System*. In Michael Banton, ed., *Darwinism and the Study of Society*. London: Tavistock, 1961.

Warner, R., and T. Szubka, eds. *The Mind-Body Problem: A Guide to the Current Debate*. Oxford, U.K.: Blackwell, 1994.

Whitehead, A. N. *Adventures of Ideas*. New York: Macmillan, 1933.

———. *Process and Reality: An Essay in Cosmology*. New York: Macmillan, 1969.

———. *Process and Reality: An Essay in Cosmology*. D. R. Griffin and D. W. Sherburne, eds. New York: The Free Press, 1978.

———. *Science and the Modern World*. Glasgow, U.K.: Fontana, 1975.

Whitmont, E. C. *The Alchemy of Healing: Psyche and Soma*. Berkeley: North Atlantic Books, 1994.

———. *Psyche and Substance: Essays on Homeopathy in the Light of Jungian Psychology*. Berkeley: North Atlantic Books, 1991.

Whorf, B. L. *Language, Thought, and Reality*. New York: John Wiley and Sons, 1956.

Wigner, E. *Symmetries and Reflections*. Cambridge, Mass.: MIT Press, 1970.

Wilber, K. *Sex, Ecology, Spirituality: The Spirit of Evolution*. Boston: Shambhala, 1995.

Young, A. M. *The Geometry of Meaning*. Mill Valley, Calif.: Robert Briggs Associates, 1976.

———. *The Reflexive Universe: Evolution of Consciousness*. Mill Valley, Calif.: Robert Briggs Associates, 1976.

———. *Which Way Out? And Other Essays*. Berkeley: Robert Briggs, 1980.

Young, P. *The Nature of Information*. New York: Praeger, 1987.

# INDEX

# Books of Related Interest

**Consciousness from Zombies to Angels**
The Shadow and the Light of Knowing Who You Are
*by Christian de Quincey*

**Radical Knowing**
Understanding Consciousness through Relationship
*by Christian de Quincey*

**The Biology of Transcendence**
A Blueprint of the Human Spirit
*by Joseph Chilton Pearce*

**The Crack in the Cosmic Egg**
New Constructs of Mind and Reality
*by Joseph Chilton Pearce*

**A Brief Tour of Higher Consciousness**
A Cosmic Book on the Mechanics of Creation
*by Itzhak Bentov*

**Transcending the Speed of Light**
Consciousness, Quantum Physics, and the Fifth Dimension
*by Marc Seifer, Ph.D.*

**Quantum Shift in the Global Brain**
How the New Scientific Reality Is Changing Us and Our World
*by Ervin Laszlo*

**Science and the Akashic Field**
An Integral Theory of Everything
*by Ervin Laszlo*

INNER TRADITIONS • BEAR & COMPANY
P.O. Box 388
Rochester, VT 05767
1-800-246-8648
www.InnerTraditions.com

Or contact your local bookseller